# WRITING THE PAST

How do archaeologists make knowledge? Debates in the latter half of the twentieth century revolved around broad, abstract philosophies and theories such as positivism and hermeneutics which have all but vanished today. By contrast, in recent years there has been a great deal of attention given to more concrete, practice-based study, such as fieldwork. But where one was too abstract, the other has become too descriptive and commonly evades issues of epistemic judgement.

*Writing the Past* attempts to reintroduce a normative dimension to knowledge practices in archaeology, especially in relation to archaeological practice further down the 'assembly line' in the production of published texts, where archaeological knowledge becomes most stabilized and is widely disseminated. By exploring the composition of texts in archaeology and the relation between their structural, performative characteristics and key epistemic virtues, this book aims to move debate in both knowledge and writing practices in a new direction.

Although this book will be of particular interest to archaeologists, the argument offered has relevance for all academic disciplines concerned with how knowledge production and textual composition intertwine.

**Gavin Lucas** is Professor of Archaeology at the University of Iceland, where he has been teaching since 2002. His main interests lie in archaeological method and theory as well as the archaeology of the modern world, with a special focus on the North Atlantic.

# WRITING THE PAST

Knowledge and Literary Production
in Archaeology

*Gavin Lucas*

Routledge
Taylor & Francis Group

LONDON AND NEW YORK

First published 2019
by Routledge
2 Park Square, Milton Park, Abingdon, Oxon OX14 4RN

and by Routledge
52 Vanderbilt Avenue, New York, NY 10017

*Routledge is an imprint of the Taylor & Francis Group, an informa business*

*British Library Cataloguing-in-Publication Data*
A catalogue record for this book is available from the British Library

*Library of Congress Cataloging-in-Publication Data*
Names: Lucas, Gavin, 1965- author.
Title: Writing the past : knowledge and literary
production in archaeology / Gavin Lucas.
Description: Abingdon, Oxon ; New York, NY : Routledge, 2019. |
Includes bibliographical references and index.
Identifiers: LCCN 2018035067| ISBN 9780367001049 (hardback : alk. paper) |
ISBN 9780367001056 (pbk. : alk. paper) | ISBN 9780429444487 (ebk.) |
ISBN 9780429815218 (epub) | ISBN 9780429815225 (web pdf) |
ISBN 9780429815201 (mobi/kindle)
Subjects: LCSH: Communication in archaeology. |
Archaeology--Documentation. | Archaeological literature. |
Archaeology--Philosophy.
Classification: LCC CC82 .L83 2019 | DDC 930.1--dc23
LC record available at https://lccn.loc.gov/2018035067

ISBN: 978-0-367-00104-9 (hbk)
ISBN: 978-0-367-00105-6 (pbk)
ISBN: 978-0-429-44448-7 (ebk)

Typeset in Bembo
by Taylor & Francis Books

For Elín, Marteinn, Benjamín and Elísabet June

# CONTENTS

# ILLUSTRATIONS

## Figure

## Tables

# ACKNOWLEDGEMENTS

By circumstance rather than design, the ideas in this book have not had much prior airing, which makes it novel but also risky. It was written fairly quickly over a period of 18 months while also working on other projects, although the intention to write a book of this nature extends back several years. I would like to thank two anonymous referees for their comments on a synopsis and sample chapters from this book, both of which improved its scope. I would, however, especially like to thank Alison Wylie who provided important feedback and links to recent literature, particularly in relation to the final chapter on the mobility of theory. I am deeply grateful for the support she has given to this project. I would also like to thank Gísli Pálsson for his comments relating to cyberinfrastructures discussed in Chapter 3 and to Þóra Petursdóttir for kindly allowing me to use one of her photographs for the cover image on this book. Finally, I would like to thank Matt Gibbons of Routledge for his swift and steadfast endorsement of the book, ensuring its publication, to Molly Marler and Ruth Berry, the editors who oversaw its production, and to Katherine Laidler, my copy editor.

# 1

# THE PRODUCTION OF ARCHAEOLOGICAL KNOWLEDGE

## The literary archaeologist

What do archaeologists do? The general perception of our profession is doubtless one involving fieldwork, especially excavation, and even among ourselves we tend to elevate the practices that engage with material remains as the most characteristic of – even unique to – our discipline. And this includes not just excavation, of course, but field survey as well as sorting and analysing all kinds of stuff from potsherds to pollen. And yet how much of your working day do you actually spend engaged in these practices? I am sure it varies; for students and academics much less than for those involved in development-led archaeology, for example, and even then it depends what role you play in these contexts. But whatever your position in the archaeological profession, you probably spend as much if not more time reading and writing than you do digging or looking down a microscope, not to mention talking about archaeology in meetings, seminars or the coffee room. Whether it is essay projects, fieldwork reports, preparing lectures or writing articles, our engagement with words and texts – usually via a computer screen – is a major part of what we do. Writing in particular is also inflected by a politics of authorship, which is nowhere more obvious than in the stark difference between the numbers of people involved in fieldwork and those select few acknowledged as authors. Some archaeologists have explicitly tried to tackle such imbalance by adopting collective pen names, although multi-authored articles and books are becoming more common. Such changes emphasize the important link between writing and other practices of knowledge production.

I suppose one reason we do not tend to think of writing as especially archaeological is because we are not the only ones who do it; this practice we share with all other academic disciplines. This is not to say we do not acknowledge writing and reading as an important part of constructing disciplinary knowledge and discourse; during the 1990s and even continuing up to today, there was and still is a great deal of attention paid to archaeology as a textual practice, something I review in detail in Chapter 3 (e.g. see Joyce 2002; Van Dyke & Bernbeck 2015). The importance of writing is also recognized as an important skill for archaeologists to develop in order to communicate their findings (Fagan 2006; Connah 2010). But the question I want to ask in this book is what the connections are between writing and knowledge production. In many ways I realize this might make this ambition seem doubly unfashionable: not only is it dealing with issues of textuality and narrative at a time when 'things are back', it is also resurrecting epistemological questions when ontology is the new watchword. But even those of us who follow this return to things still end up having to write about it – even if some also critically reflect upon this dependence on text and seek other forms of expression. Also, haven't we already been there? While the 'how-to-write' literature for archaeologists may not address the epistemological implications of writing, the same cannot be said for all that work on narrative.

It is certainly the case that questions about knowledge are central to a lot of studies on archaeological narrative and text, but, as I will argue, I think they only scratched the surface. Part of the problem lies in the self-imposed constraints established by adopting models of text from literary theory and especially the dominant focus on narrative itself as a mode of discourse. Part of it, though, also relates to the way such discussions create an image of a self-enclosed world of text, cut off from those material practices and all that dirt and dust. Although this book is, in many ways, also somewhat removed from that world, underwriting it is a deep sense of the connections and continuities between our practices of writing and our practices of digging, sorting, classifying and measuring. Continuities framed by notions of translation and mobilization derived from work in science studies (e.g. Latour 1987). It is also informed by a concern to connect the practice of writing with more traditional views of knowledge construction revolving around issues of evaluation and significance. The link between language and epistemology is not the preserve of postmodern literary theory; the logical positivists in their search for neutral observation languages and non-realist or instrumentalist accounts of knowledge also saw the critical importance of theorizing the relation of words to things (Carnap 1967). But I have no intention of resurrecting a positivist archaeology in these pages. I take a very different path, one informed both by the literature on narrative and texts and that of science studies and other post-positivist philosophies of science. These might seem like unlikely bedfellows, yet I think there is a lot to be gained from the juxtaposition. Some work in the science studies tradition has already explored this connection (see Lenoir 1998), although it does not seem to have had much influence and is certainly different from the approach I take in this book. So where to start in all this? Since I began by discussing the role of writing in archaeology, it seems only appropriate to pick up the other thread running through this book: knowledge.

## Epistemology on the move

Archaeologists arguably know a lot about the past. About human evolution and the spread of people around the globe, about the development of agriculture and settled life, of technological innovations such as metallurgy or glass-making, about the lifeways of other cultures and societies which existed hundreds and even thousands of years ago for which no written or oral memories may exist. Of course, a lot of detail is disputed, but our knowledge of our own species and its diverse forms of life is astounding really, especially when you compare it with the situation two hundred years ago. This might sound self-congratulatory, even promoting a view of our knowledge and the history of archaeology as progressive, but that is not where this is going. I actually do think our knowledge of who we are as a species has progressed and, in no small part, because of the work archaeology has done. But 'progress' is a tricky term which would require another book. Let's just stick with one problem at a time, which in this book happens to be about knowledge, specifically archaeological knowledge. What does it mean to say archaeologists know things?

In the wake of debates in archaeology during the 1980s and 1990s one can no longer entertain any naivety about archaeological knowledge as an untroubled road to the truth about what happened in the past. The acceptance of theoretical pluralism within the discipline and the intersection of archaeological and indigenous approaches to the material remains of the past seem to point to knowledge as a discontinuous, fragmented domain. There is not just one knowledge but multiple knowledges where multivocality is a virtue, not an obstacle. At the same time it is probably fair to say that most archaeologists nonetheless still hold some conviction about the verisimilitude or truthlikeness of their accounts: one can never be sure it was like this, but here is a plausible possibility at least. And just because we may have renounced any faith in absolutes or certainty and disavowed the notion of a single version of 'the way things were', this is not to say we are exempt from any responsibility of justifying our accounts or even adjudicating between them. The problem is: how do we square the idea of epistemic discontinuity implicit in pluralism with the need for some basis upon which to evaluate the plausibility of our accounts of the past?

Questions like this are not very topical right now; indeed, if anything the new millennium has thus far been characterized by an epistemic silence in archaeological discourse, where the issue of knowledge has very much been brushed to the side (e.g. see Hegmon 2003: 230–231; Lucas 2015a). It is a silence that is, though, now being breached especially in relation to the issue of evaluation. While the problem of evaluating multiple narratives has remained on our radar (e.g. see Habu et al. 2008), a more conscious reappraisal of these older issues is surfacing, as evident in the recent volumes of Bob Chapman and Alison Wylie (2015, 2016) that interlinks with a more general reconsideration of evidential reasoning within the humanities and social sciences (Bell et al. 2008; Twining et al. 2012). But it is also indicated by a resurgence of interest in critical thinking in academia which has manifested itself in archaeology in the recent books by Chuck Orser and Guy Gibbon (Gibbon

2014; Orser 2015). In an era of fake news, the issue of epistemic vigilance would seem to be ever more relevant (Sperber et al. 2010); at a time when access to massive online information systems such as Wikipedia makes finding things out as easy as a few clicks on a mouse, the problem of what to trust and not has never been more pertinent. And this is not just a problem that goes away by tracing the source of knowledge to an authoritative locus – that is, science. Some of the places where epistemic vigilance is needed most these days is actually among scientific studies, especially given the way archaeological science is having a massive resurgence in our discipline (e.g. Kristiansen 2014).

A recent review of literature drew out some shocking examples of archaeological science where the archaeological contextualization of scientific data was woefully simplistic (Lidén & Eriksson 2013). The issue here is not that archaeological science is bad; rather that to interpret scientific data such as aDNA really needs a deep sensitivity to archaeological theory (also see Ion 2017; Chapman & Wylie 2016). This is essentially the same problem but inverted, behind the politicized discourse of climate change where 'merchants of doubt' (i.e. one group of scientists) criticized the interpretations and data of another group of scientists. The problem here, though, is that those making the critique were not climate scientists, but a couple of retired physicists who had also been central to the tobacco industry's attempt to discredit scientific research suggesting a link between smoking and cancer (Oreskes & Conway 2010). Political interests are surely involved in all these cases and on all sides of the debate, so what is at stake here is something else; rather we are dealing with the question of expertise and the basis of claims to knowledge which, though entangled with the political, cannot be entirely reduced to the political either.

And so, inevitably perhaps, archaeologists seem to be returning to the becalmed waters of how we go about making and justifying our interpretations after the stormy seas of the processual–postprocessual debates. It is almost as if we needed some time for the storm to pass or the dust to settle before returning to the scene to see what is left to recover. I discuss this story in more detail in Chapter 2, so I will not dwell on it further here; rather I want to focus more on the other issue, that of epistemic discontinuity or multiple knowledges, as it is really this aspect that has been the most lasting legacy of the debates from the 1980s and 1990s.

The idea of epistemic discontinuity incorporates many different issues and really needs unpacking if we wish to avoid slipping back into the polarized positions of the late twentieth century. To begin, one might wish to distinguish between a theoretical pluralism internal to the discipline of archaeology and a broader perspective which articulates archaeological and non-archaeological ways of knowing. This is a somewhat false and indeed pernicious distinction, as we shall see, but making it actually helps to illustrate my argument. Let us start with the issue of theoretical pluralism internal to archaeology and map out its basic features. In many ways, this pluralism was already acknowledged in the 1970s when the paradigm concept diffused through archaeology. While some archaeologists considered the paradigm term as a general overarching category to characterize wholesale disciplinary development (typified in simplified historiographies which saw culture history replaced by processualism, which in turn was replaced by postprocessualism), others always saw it more as a lower-level concept to capture different ways of studying human societies (e.g. cultural ecology, structuralism; see Lucas 2017). It would be fair to say that the acceptance of pluralism over polarization became the new consensus toward the end of the 1990s (Hegmon 2003; VanPool & VanPool 2003), with archaeologists no longer seeing the need to assert any theoretical hegemony for their discipline.

Moreover, what has been interesting in the wake of this pluralism is not just an acceptance of differing ways of interpreting the archaeological record, but also an actual dialogue and cross-fertilization between quite different theoretical approaches. In other words, few people seem to regard this pluralism as a grid of theories each locked into their own worlds – what is often characterized as incommensurability. Evolutionary ecologists can talk to new materialists, and just because they don't agree on everything, it does not mean there are no points of contact either. No theory is so tightly woven that it does not have lacunae, gaps where there is room for connections to be explored. One thinks of the conversations between agency and evolutionary theory (Cochrane & Gardner 2011), or behavioural archaeology and operational chains (Skibo & Schiffer 2008). One could also suggest that this marks a shift from pluralism to eclecticism – that is, from a situation of multiple theoretical perspectives each going about their own business to one where archaeologists pick and mix from different theories to blend their own unique framework (e.g. Bintliff 2011). However, I find eclecticism a rather problematic notion as it seems to imply that theories are simply composed of 'trait lists' of ideas from which you can select what you like and leave what you don't. Ideas are not natural atoms; they come attached to other ideas because they have been forged together and to pull them apart and join them with other ideas is not an easy task.

At the same time, this does highlight a key feature of knowledge which I address in some detail in Chapter 5: the mobility of theory. Rather than discuss the dialogue between theoretical positions as eclecticism, I find it more promising to reflect on what actually is involved in migrating ideas, concepts and theories – what Wylie and Chapman designate as trading zones, after the philosopher of science Peter Galison (Chapman & Wylie 2016; Galison 1997). In other words, although archaeology today is defined by a theoretical pluralism and there will be epistemic fractures or discontinuities between different positions, these positions are still permeable and connections can be made. However, it is one thing to accept that theoretical pluralism within archaeology does not rule out any common ground and points of contact, but the case might appear to be harder to argue when one is leaving a broadly shared intellectual tradition to engage with other 'epistemic cultures'. Harder, yes, but I do not think we are dealing with a fundamentally different issue here. In fact, the debates are almost identical and can be resolved in almost identical ways.

If one thinks of archaeology as an epistemic culture producing its own type of knowledge (see Knorr-Cetina 1999), then traditionally it has had two main targets whose knowledge practices archaeology sought to distance itself from and devalue: pseudo-archaeology and indigenous views of the past. The former generally includes lay people (though sometimes scholars – especially natural scientists for some reason) who essentially share the same cultural and historical background as archaeologists but who develop their own interpretations of archaeological remains which often run quite counter to archaeological explanations (for quite different perspectives on this issue, see Cole 1980; G. Fagan 2006; Holtorf 2005; Moshenka 2008). This is a mixed bag and includes creationists, ufologists, layliners and white supremacists or simply the next-door neighbour (who may in fact be any of the above); yet lumping them all together is deeply problematic. But therein lies the core of the issue: the separation of archaeology from pseudo-archaeology as two distinct claims to knowledge, with a very clear message about which claim has the most authority and right to be believed.

Such sharp separations are a legacy of early twentieth-century positivism, epitomized in Popper's ambition to demarcate science from non-science through his method of falsification. It constitutes what Joseph Rouse called the legitimation project common to most Anglo-American philosophies of science of the twentieth century (Rouse 1996). One can also see it manifested in French philosophy of science of the same period, through the dominating influence of Bachelard and his notion of the epistemological break between scientific and pre-scientific thought (Bachelard 1984, 2002; Lecourt 1975), a concept which influenced both Althusser and Foucault, even if in different ways. Bachelard's historical epistemology was certainly quite different from Popper's falsificationism, yet the common thread cannot be ignored. More recently, Isabelle Stengers has offered a more novel interpretation of this demarcation, basing it on a political gesture where the very existence of science is predicated on its resistance to fiction (Stengers 2000: 82). For Stengers, what matters is not the various ways in which the demarcation has been defined (by Popper, Kuhn etc.) but the very necessity of the act insofar as it positions science as the arbiter of truth (*ibid.*: 133).

But we have to question whether such sharp separations can really be maintained, and indeed why we should want to; abandoning such a legitimation project is not to say that an archaeologist still cannot contest a theory of the pyramids which claims they were built by aliens from outer space. What it does say is that there is no simple rule by which we can cut knowledge claims apart into two halves: real and pseudo-archaeology. The epistemic continuities and discontinuities are more subtle than such polarizing rhetoric portrays. Part of this links up to the more recent recognition of the disunity of sciences (e.g. Galison & Stump 1996). Although the early to mid-twentieth century – especially under the influence of positivism – was an era which saw programmes calling for the unity of all sciences and the idea of a single scientific method, by the end of the century it was more than apparent that disunity was a more realistic portrayal of the diverse practices we call science. It is not just that biology was irreducible to chemistry, or chemistry irreducible to physics; even different physicists or biologists working on different models or traditions were using different languages. By the 1990s, the irreducible pluralism of the sciences became the new orthodoxy. With such pluralism came a new starting point for philosophies of science: local knowledge. And with a new starting point came new issues: how knowledge moves between localities; how, despite irreducible pluralism, communication and dialogue between sciences was still possible.

Very similar issues emerge with the case of indigenous archaeology. Again, much of the discourse has tended to polarize the debate as one of scientific versus indigenous knowledge, yet, as several scholars have argued, this opposition is overplayed and is actually deleterious to both sides (Agrawal 1995; Sillitoe 1998, 2002; Colwell-Chanthaphonh et al. 2010; Wylie 2014). Not only does it lump quite different epistemic cultures together as 'an indigenous other' to western science (why is an Apache epistemology any closer to Nuer ways of knowing than either are to 'western science'?; we saw the same lumping in the case of pseudo-archaeology), in doing so it perpetuates the message of a forced choice: the archaeological way or the highway (e.g. McGhee 2008). To counter such polarizations, Sillitoe in particular has argued for a multidimensional approach: "We are not talking about two tenuously connected knowledge traditions separated by a cultural–epistemological gulf, but rather a spectrum of relations"(Sillitoe 2002: 111). Sillitoe suggests that rather than stress different epistemologies or epistemic cultures, we focus more on specific epistemic practices, on concrete problems and issues, and in this way not only are the epistemic continuities and discontinuities more visible, there is also greater chance of dialogue and collaboration. Instead of informants, indigenous people become collaborators.

This is something that many archaeologists have been striving to put into practice for some time now, of course, and although things have improved drastically, a recent survey suggests that indigenous voices are still under-represented (Watkins 2005). But even if practice falls short of intent, the issue of epistemic discontinuity can still be explored and exposed as a relative or contingent property of the relation between archaeological and indigenous knowledge, not an absolute caesura. An interesting study by Kristensen and Davis compared the impact of indigenous knowledge on archaeological narratives in two situations – one where an indigenous presence was still active and one where it was not, on the west and east coasts of Canada respectively (Kristensen & Davis 2015). They found that the archaeological accounts in the two regions differed quite markedly, especially in relation to their incorporation of social and ideological factors. What is especially interesting about this study is that these effects seemed to have occurred in fairly traditional contexts of archaeological knowledge production, at least in many instances (i.e. in the absence of any explicit, reflexive strategies of collaboration).

Now arguably there are degrees of interaction between archaeological and indigenous knowledge; in some ways this study largely demonstrated the long-standing ability of modern science to incorporate or assimilate other knowledges into its own template. The extent to which such interactions actually altered the epistemic foundations of archaeology is questionable and the same might be said for many collaborative projects (e.g. see Zimmerman 2005, 2008). Indeed archaeological–indigenous collaborations vary widely in their symmetry and success. But this does not alter the fact that communication – however unbalanced – is possible between different epistemic traditions. If this balance is to be developed and deepened, then it may be that archaeologists need to examine more carefully the epistemic basis of this communication and one obvious model is that of standpoint theory. This was a feminist initiative, derived from Marxism which became a way to mediate between the relativism implied in the social constitution of knowledge and the need to retain some form of objectivity from which to enact critique. I discuss standpoint theory in more detail in Chapter 4, but it is interesting to see some scholars adopting the model in the realm of indigenous knowledge (something actually already indicated in the original feminist programme; e.g. see Harding 1991). Indigenous standpoint theory has not generated the same level of discourse as the feminist version, but the potential is there (e.g. see Foley 2003).

This is effectively the project that Sonya Atalay has proposed which nonetheless draws on the same insight as standpoint theory, namely the ability of marginalized or disenfranchised voices to counter the (in)visible bias within archaeology, specifically that associated with its colonial history (Atalay 2006, 2008, 2012; also see Smith & Wobst 2005; Haber & Gnecco 2007). The project of a decolonizing archaeology, although not always explicitly linked to standpoint theory (but see Wylie 2008a, 2014), strongly argues that the importance of indigenous archaeology lies not solely with how it affects the content of our archaeological narratives but the very epistemic and ethical structures which govern our practices of knowledge production (also see Watkins 2000; Zimmerman 2008; Colwell-Chanthaphonh et al. 2010). In this sense, it joins hands with a wider body of work, which stresses the politicized nature of knowledge production (e.g. Atalay et al. 2014; McGuire 2008) and manifests what one might call a critical epistemology – that is, a reflection on knowledge production which seeks not only to be reflexive about the conditions under which knowledge is created and disseminated but also to *change* those conditions.

Of course, the intersection of knowledge and power is a familiar theme which has pervaded archaeological discourse since the 1980s, but with this politicized epistemology came a more equivocal partner: relativism. Most archaeologists have chosen to steer clear of relativism, while nonetheless embracing pluralism or multivocality (see Chapter 2 for the historical context of this issue). However, the epistemological issues involved in mediating between these two positions are not always drawn out or indeed easily resolved (e.g. see Habu et al. 2008 for a useful discussion). For a start, relativism can mean different things to different people; the vulgar attribution would characterize it as anything goes: one person's (or culture's) knowledge or views on the past is as good as another. If we leave it at that, it basically puts an embargo on any critique and relativism then becomes a covert form of maintaining the status quo: business as usual. If, however, relativism just means there can be different views of the past, that no single perspective has a monopoly on the truth, then this leaves open the question as to how one deals with the relation between these views. This is how I would understand the idea of multivocality and pluralism as opposed to relativism (also see Wylie 2008a).

In this latter conception, one might still be in a position of having to adjudicate between two positions, and this is where multivocality can slide into relativism if we are not careful. For we need to remember that adjudication is not the only epistemic action available to us. In fact, one might go so far as to say that adjudication is a measure of last resort and may not often have to occur at all. Most of the interesting epistemological operations actually occur in that space between the acknowledgement of difference and deciding which view is most 'truth-indicative' or 'truth-tropic', as the philosophers might put it (Wylie 2014). These operations include understanding the logical and semantic intricacies of the two views, their hidden or taken-for-granted assumptions, the deeper historical and political positions from which they emerge. Conducting such dialogues is as likely to reveal epistemic continuities as it is discontinuities, but most importantly it helps to define more precisely the matter of concern for each party: what is relevant and thus what the real grounds of difference are (e.g. see Habu et al. 2008; Colwell-Chanthaphonh and Ferguson 2008; also see Meskell 2009).

The point here is not that epistemic differences do not exist, nor that sometimes we have to take sides or make epistemic judgements; rather the grounds and basis for such judgements are not fixed. They are certainly not fixed in any holistic way which pitches scientific against indigenous knowledge. It is at this point that one can now appreciate, if one did not before, the falsity of separating a discussion of internal and external pluralism, as the very distinction itself would seem to perpetuate the problems just discussed. But nor are such judgements fixed in the sense of being immutable. I suppose what we are talking about here is the idea of an epistemology which is on the move – one constantly triangulating its position vis-à-vis other epistemologies and making relevant and necessary adjustments so that it can remain as faithful as possible to both its object and co-constituents. It is an epistemology that needs to be always brought down to earth, grounded in the specifics of situations, issues and practices. The focus on practice moreover has greater relevance in terms of how academic interest in knowledge production has shifted, away from a focus on abstract and idealized models or norms of how archaeological knowledge is built up and assured to a focus on the concrete forms and processes in which knowledge is embedded.

## Knowledge and literary production

The practice-based notion of knowledge production is what science studies has excelled at over the past 30–40 years. It has also had an important impact on archaeology, especially on studies which have investigated the production of knowledge in the field, an area I have also explored in some detail in previous publications (Lucas 2001a, 2001b, 2012). However, like mine, most other studies have tended to focus on the coalface of archaeology – that is, knowledge production in the field or lab, linked to the performance and practice of fieldwork (e.g. Cobb et al. 2012; Gero 1996; Edgeworth 2003, 2006; Olsen et al. 2012). Similar studies on knowledge production further down the assembly line such as the writing of published monographs or journal articles are much rarer. Yet it is in published texts that most archaeological knowledge is ultimately stabilized and disseminated. And so we come full circle, back to my opening remarks on the significance of writing (and reading) in archaeology. But more importantly, a connection has now been clearly established between writing and knowledge production, and it is those practices where writing and knowledge production intersect that form the primary focus of this book.

Now approaching this through the paradigm of science studies is at one level fairly straightforward. In earlier work I discussed the idea of archaeology as a form of literary production, by which I meant that one of the aims of fieldwork was to translate things into words (Lucas 2012). Archaeological facts are composed of words and/or other semiotic characters such as images and numbers. Archaeological knowledge deals with these characters, not with the stuff itself. Site reports, journal articles, text books do not deal with things but with these signs which partly relates to the philosophical problem of semantic ascent – the problems encountered when we switch from observing the world to talking about the world (Quine 1960; Latour 1987). In my earlier work I almost exclusively focused on this initial issue – how we go from things to words – and used science studies, especially the work of Latour, to describe this process via the concept of translation. Thus a section drawing, as a translation of the wall of an excavation trench, involves multiple elements including the cutting of a clean, vertical face of soil as a material way to prefigure the drawing, a section line and tape measure to guide the translation process from soil face to paper, and so on. It was all about making the site look *physically* like the archive as much as possible so the translation process would require the minimum leap from soil to paper (also see Lucas 2001b).

The same process can be observed with artefact typologies; when faced with a pile of pottery sherds, what is the first thing the archaeologist does? Physically separate them, piece by piece, and sort them into piles of fragments that most resemble each other in terms of colour, glaze, decoration and so on. This is how typologies begin. Artefact classifications, field notes and drawing – these are the very beginnings of a long process of knowledge production, but what I did not fully acknowledge – or at least explore – in my earlier work is that such knowledge is of a somewhat different kind to the knowledge expressed in long texts, whether site reports or theoretical essays. Calling this translation work literary production is somewhat of an overstatement; it does involve translating things into words (and other signs), but it is more like a process of simple coding than complex textual production. Converting pottery sherds into words (e.g. 'cooking pot', 'Grooved Ware') or numbers (e.g. MNV 3, 405g) is a critical process in the production of knowledge, but barely constitutes useful knowledge in itself. Even reconstituting and reassembling these sherds as codes or signs into a database is not enough. It is what you subsequently do with these coded archives that matters; how you turn them into complex texts which make the kind of knowledge claims we are more familiar with. This is not to suggest a major gap between the two; lab notes and field diaries, for example, act as important intermediaries in this process, being textual but in a more fragmented fashion (see Mickel 2015), while unpublished grey reports lie further up the chain.

I recently read Jean-Claude Gardin's book *Archaeological Constructs*, now nearly half a century old, and was quite struck by the very similar way he approached this issue (Gardin 1980). Although I had been aware of Gardin's work and his logicism since my doctoral studies (e.g. see Gallay 1989), it was never something that I devoted any time to exploring in depth. Reading Gardin today, in the wake of science studies, it is easy to characterize his work as constructivist – the very title is a giveaway. At the same time, Gardin himself never makes this connection and in fact the intellectual links here are not really the point (but see Dallas 2016 for a recent and important retrospective). Gardin's work will crop up again in my work. but for now I just want to draw a connection between his discussion of archae-ological constructs as texts and, furthermore, his distinction of two basic kinds of texts or constructs: what he calls compilations and explanations.

Gardin's criteria for distinguishing these two texts are not quite the same as those I would adopt, but in terms of what they are meant to cover they do broadly correspond with the distinction I alluded to above: that between field records, archives and databases on the one hand, and interpretive texts on the other. Much of what Gardin has to say on the differences between these texts is very insightful, but a more detailed discussion of these differences will be postponed until Chapter 3. I should also briefly mention the more recent work of Giorgio Buccellati whose book *A Critique of Archaeological Reason* is strikingly reminiscent of Gardin's work, albeit expressed in a very different prose and terminology (Buccellati 2017). Structurally, though, the homologies are multiple, especially in his broad division between archaeological grammar and hermeneutics, which can be partly mapped on to Gardin's distinction of compilations and explanations.

None of this is meant to imply that texts are the only form in which knowledge occurs; images are a key part of archaeological knowledge production, from site plans to photographs, from graphs to diagrams. Unfortunately, for reasons of space, I cannot go into this form of knowledge, but there has been a lot of attention devoted to the visual aspect of knowledge in archaeology (and science in general) and I refer the reader to these works (e.g. Llobera 2011; Lopes 2009; Moser 2014; Perry 2015; Shanks & Webmoor 2010; Wickstead 2013; Hacıgüzeller 2017). Fur-thermore, we might not even want to confine our definition of knowledge to texts and images; what about other forms of material expression – performative expres-sions, whether a formal lecture or a more experimental, art-inspired work? In order to put some kind of focus and constraint on this book, I have decided to keep as its central objective, the production of knowledge in a textual form – texts which usually offer an account of the human past through material remains. The reason is simply because this remains the dominant expression of archaeological knowledge, whether one agrees it should be or not (see Gardin 1980 on this point too). I shall also focus on end-of-the-line texts rather than field and lab notes and reports; that is, published journal articles or monographs etc., which tend to have the greater stabilizing effect in terms of knowledge practices.

Now having mapped out the rough terrain of study, this is where things also start to get more difficult. Looking at the relation between texts and knowledge produc-tion in the field all seems fairly straightforward if one just follows the example of Latour and others in mapping translations from object to sign and the creation of those 'immutable mobiles' (i.e. inscriptions). But it is one thing to follow an inscrip-tion along a chain from the field to the published article, quite another to look at how that published article itself 'acts'. Fundamentally, the issue here revolves around the performative nature of texts: *what is it that texts do?* Obviously, they can do a lot of things, but if our concern here is in relation to knowledge practices, then we can be a bit more precise in our question. Adopting the same basic duality embodied in the concept of 'immutable mobile', we should ask ourselves these two questions: how do texts stabilize knowledge while still mobilizing it? That is, how do they act to help a knowledge claim to 'stick' on the one hand and, on the other, to move it beyond the specific context in which it is made so it can act within a wider set of practices?

In attempting to answer these questions, however, I found myself turning not to science studies but to the literature on text linguistics, composition studies and rhetoric, and more recent work in the digital humanities (see Chapter 3). Not all this literature addresses texts in terms of its performativity and almost none of it explicitly links itself to these questions born of science studies. Yet I have found this juxtaposition incredibly fertile. My suggested answers to these two questions are offered in Chapters 4 and 5 respectively. But that is not quite the whole story … There is one more thing I want to add which will also connect the focus on writing practices to the problem of epistemic discontinuity discussed earlier.

## Doing the right thing: epistemic virtues in archaeology

One issue that has constantly worried me, even in my attempts to apply a science studies approach to archaeology, is what this means for the more traditional episte-mological concerns in the philosophy of science, most particularly the problem of how we evaluate claims of archaeological knowledge and mediate epistemic discontinuity. A practice-based approach to knowledge production seems to be especially good at describing what archaeologists do and even showing why some accounts turn out to be more successful than others in such a way that they still preserve what Bloor has called a symmetry of explanation (Bloor 1976). But I have always felt that such accounts are also wise outside/after the event: they offer brilliantly insightful analyses, but precisely *because* they are detached from the processes they describe. That is to say, the success or failure of any particular context of knowledge production is not a matter of concern for sociologists of science, whereas it is for the scientists they are studying. What is lacking, in short, is any prescriptive element: how do I judge whether what I or others are claiming has any value?

It is this prescriptive element that is so central to traditional epistemological concerns in the philosophy of science. It is ironic that while traditionalist accounts such as positivism were criticized for offering an ideal image of science, one which no scientist actually embodied in real practice (even if they openly adhered to the ideal model provided by philosophers), they nonetheless maintained an insider's view of science as a practice, one where the difference between success and failure does matter. The detached, ethnographic position of science studies seems to me to run the risk of being too detached in this regard. In reminding us that scientific knowledge is an achievement, they seem to forget that the achievement is, in part, also dependent on making choices or decisions. Science studies excels in showing the consequences of certain decisions, but is silent on advising us how to make them – this 'normative vacuum' of science studies is something which Steve Fuller has suggested has a deeper social and political context (Fuller 2000; also see Fuller 2003; also see Rouse 1996 on a similar 'normative anaemia').

To some extent, this portrayal of the normative anaemia of science studies is unfair, if not outdated. Latour's own partial recanting of his earlier work as being overly concerned with 'matters of fact' against 'matters of concern' addresses this issue (Latour 2004a). And yet even here it seems that Latour does not engage with the normative dimension in quite the same way a political or moral philosopher might; true to form, Latour remains a sociologist even when studying matters of concern, treating them (I would suggest) as if they were matters of fact. At least that is how I read him and indeed almost all work in science and technology studies (STS) which deal with questions of value or the morality of things (e.g. Winner 1980; Verbeek 2006). Not that such studies are not deeply insightful – but they stop short of filling Fuller's normative vacuum. The closest Latour comes to this is in his general support for Stengers and Despret's 'political epistemology' which suggests a cumulative set of criteria for promoting good science (Latour 2004b). Another approach to the normative is taken by Michael Lynch, also deeply embedded in the STS tradition, one which stresses the role of expertise – but expertise always qualified as local and specific to certain practices rather than wholesale scientific expertise (Lynch 2014). Lynch was responding to the 'merchants of doubt' issue I raised earlier, and so his solution is an obvious attempt to steer between the dangers of scientific authoritarianism and complete relativism. But, at the end of the day, Lynch's account offers no basis for the even localized and contingent authority of specific scientific practices.

So where does this leave us? Are we stuck between choosing an approach which would describe what archaeologists do with great veracity and fidelity, yet is ultimately useless in helping us to be better archaeologists, or an approach which tries to offer prescriptions about what constitutes good archaeological knowledge, but in doing so reduces such knowledge to a one-dimensional caricature, with all the trappings of old-fashioned positivism? Of course, this probably over-polarizes our options, but I think it nonetheless captures the core dilemma of science studies versus conventional philosophies of science and succinctly states a problem which is at the core of this book. In many ways, the studies I have found most productive in helping to resolve this have come from work influenced by both streams of this opposition. For if science studies made some initial steps in acknowledging the normative dimension, so traditional philosophy of science has made even stronger moves to incorporate the benefits of a practice-based approach to traditional problems.

The practice-turn which invaded the humanities and social sciences from the late 1970s and 1980s – archaeology included – also impacted the philosophy of science (Pickering 1992; Soler et al. 2014). Its strongest and earliest impact was within the Edinburgh- and Bath-based programmes on the sociology of scientific knowledge (SSK) and related work of continental scholars such as Bruno Latour and Karin Knorr-Cetina, all of which now broadly fall under the field of STS. But it also spurred a parallel stream of practice-based studies, one with closer connections to more traditional philosophy of science. The key impetus of the 'Stanford group', such as Ian Hacking, Peter Galison and Nancy Cartwright, was based on a reaction to the theory-centrism of post-positivism, epitomized in Kuhn's paradigm model of normal science. For them, the solution was to reassess the nature of data and observations – but not as abstract ideals or concepts as they existed in the positivist (and post-positivist) literature, but in relation to what scientists actually do, which resulted in an explosion of studies on the nature of scientific experiments. It was also closely connected to a recognition of the irreducible pluralism of the sciences, as mentioned earlier, and the need to start locally when it comes to exploring knowledge practices (Galison & Stump 1996).

In a sense, both streams ended up focusing on the same object: scientific practices, especially at the coalface; experiments, laboratories, instruments and fieldwork all became key subjects of investigation. There was also a lot of shared ground, conceptually such as an emphasis on the materiality of science and a shift in register from normative to descriptive accounts of scientific practice, grounded in concrete case studies of actual science (Soler et al. 2014). But within the more traditional stream, the issue of the normative was reopened in a more productive way, especially through the work of Lorraine Daston and Peter Galison on objectivity as an epistemic virtue (Daston & Galison 1992, 1997). This notion of epistemic virtue will be central to my discussion of texts in Chapter 4, and in fact I think many of the tensions between a normative versus descriptive approach to the philosophy of science can be resolved by thinking about knowledge practices in relation to epistemic virtues. It might also be helpful to rephrase the tension between traditional philosophy of science and a social constructivist one as rather one expressing two epistemic responsibilities: that toward our object (i.e. the archaeological remains) and that toward our colleagues and other people who share the archaeological as a matter of concern.

This Janus-faced nature of the archaeological project underlines the fact that knowledge production is both a social activity and yet one focused on things (see Nicholas Thomas 1997 for a similar view of anthropological epistemology though articulated in slightly different terms). Our epistemic fidelity is not only to those things but also to others who share those things as a matter of concern; sometimes these two obligations will clash but in reframing the debate about knowledge in terms of epistemic virtues, there is a sense in which we can create the space for a normative/prescriptive account of knowledge production to sit alongside a practice-based approach rather than in tension with it. The very notion of virtue invokes both something one does, a way of behaving, and something one strives to meet, an ideal or norm.

The dilemma I have just sketched in many ways intersects with my own personal academic development. I did my undergraduate studies at the Institute of Archaeology, University College London, in the mid-1980s. My time there was fortunate enough to coincide with Ann Stahl who taught archaeological theory – mostly North American processual, but it had a lasting impact on me. It was at a time when not many archaeology departments in the UK had theory at all on the syllabus. While there, I also took a couple of courses in the Philosophy of Science programme at UCL with Nicholas Maxwell which was largely taught along traditional lines – Popper, Kuhn, Feyerabend, Lakatos. Maxwell's own brand of philosophy of science, however, has maintained a constant goal of situating epistemology within the broader concept of wisdom (e.g. Maxwell 1984). Of course, this theoretical and philosophical training was also tied to its time; in the mid-1980s, both science studies and postprocessualism were still in their infancy and fields with which I became much more familiar when I moved into doctoral studies under Ian Hodder at Cambridge in the early 1990s. Yet more central to my intellectual environment there was the narrative turn in the humanities which was probably just at its peak; Derrida, Hayden White and, above all, Paul Ricoeur were some of the key scholars influential on my doctoral studies.

I have sometimes thought that writing this book has partly been an exercise in nostalgia and in some ways it started out like that. Now, though, I see it rather as a dialogue between various traditions, or parts of myself, which makes it still personal but much less nostalgic. As I outlined in the last section, the immediate impetus of this book has come off the back of my last work on the archaeological record which adopted a science studies approach to fieldwork (Lucas 2012, especially chapter 5). Yet in developing those ideas into the domain of texts and literary production, I was recursively brought back to my earlier intellectual influences, both in narrative theory and traditional philosophy of science. Rather than view this as some reactionary or nostalgic return to the past, I think it rather underlines the very issues this book addresses about how knowledge stabilizes or falls apart, how its sticks or moves on. And all these issues – both about how texts stabilize and mobilize knowledge, and about how to incorporate a normative dimension into our knowledge practices – in many ways came together as I morphed from being a student to a teacher of archaeological theory.

Ever since I started teaching archaeological theory, one thing above all has bothered me: I have never felt quite satisfied with how I have taught it. I constantly fiddle with the course structure and, to some extent, with pedagogical techniques, but the real problem seems to relate to the subject matter itself. The problem I am sure is familiar to many: how to make theory more concrete and relevant to students learning to be archaeologists. In other words, how to make it interesting. It is a common enough refrain that theory courses are not very popular, often seeming too far removed from what students learn in other courses (Smith & Burke 2005). I particularly like Adrian Praetzellis's admonishment that theory is like your vegetables – you might not like them, but they are good for you so just eat them (Praetzellis 2015)! He is right, of course, but I imagine Adrian is also very good at making theory more appetizing (e.g. Praetzellis 2000). But I also feel there is something about the 'culture of theory' which is inherently alienating to many people, especially its abstractness. Good theory, of course, is always applicable theory and students will get examples of case studies to make the theory more concrete – some sauce to go with those vegetables. But still, somehow that is not enough. I also started to think of theory in relation to the method courses I had taught and the difference was only too obvious. Method courses were full of techniques, practical guides of how-to, whether it was representing the stratigraphy of a site through a Harris matrix or constructing a typology. Students seemed to love that. If we can do that for methods, then why not for theory?

I imagine many archaeologists like to think of theory as more of an art than a method; it cannot be taught in the same way. All we can really do is equip our students with the tool kit (e.g. concepts, theories), show them some examples of what you can make with that tool kit (case studies) and then hope they work the rest out for themselves. I can understand this view to an extent; theories are generally more pliant and flexible, less easy to codify into set procedures than methods. But at the end of the day a theory has to work on data like a method and I think theory has to start acknowledging that it is as much about know-how as know-that. We need to be better at understanding how theory *works*.

Thinking about theory as practical knowledge, as know-how, is a challenge but it helped me to see the significance of writing – because theory is, more than anything, deeply textual (although I know some may disagree with this statement). The problem is partly about how to mobilize those abstract ideas, make them work in different contexts with different data. While theory textbooks outline the abstract ideas and case studies provide concrete exemplars, there was still that gap – how did we get from here to there? Part of the solution is choosing good case studies and unpacking the work behind them. But a large part came from recognizing that archaeological interpretation deploys a variety of strategies for mobilizing concepts which have not really been properly addressed. This is something I attempt to tackle in Chapter 5. It also deploys a variety of strategies for embedding these ideas in a convincing, textual form, which is the topic of Chapter 4.

Thinking about theory as know-how also provided a way to link up the concerns of conventional epistemologies of science with the practice-based approach of science studies. Any practice which we teach to students, whether it is how to excavate stratigraphically or how to interpret a burial, will carry, implicitly or explicitly, norms about how best to do this. Archaeology, like anything, can be done well or badly. This is not to suggest there is only one right way to do archaeology; far from it. But the existence of multiple values does not invalidate the necessity of normative judgement, any more than multiple views on the past relieve us from any responsibility of critique. Now theory classes are probably those courses where such normative judgements are most exposed, especially in relation to the political context of knowledge production. This is not an area that needs rehearsing. But at the same time it sometimes feels as if the sole point of a theory course is to introduce the student to diverse ways of interpreting the archaeological record without addressing what counts as a good or bad interpretation (or theory). It is as if epistemic diversity pre-empts any need to discuss epistemic virtues; diversity itself is the only virtue we need.

Diversity, of course, is a virtue – that should be clear from my earlier discussion on multivocality and pluralism. But it is not the only virtue we can or indeed should adhere to. Given my argument for linking theory to writing, it should be no surprise that a chief concern of this book is how one engages with the specific epistemic virtues connected to writing. What I will suggest is that the structural form of our texts invokes specific epistemic virtues determining the criteria for their evaluation; that in producing knowledge through writing, we simultaneously create the criteria by which such knowledge is to be assessed. Significantly, different forms of writing carry different epistemic – and indeed ontological – commitments. These issues form the core part of discussion in Chapter 4.

Although these two issues – how texts stabilize/mobilize knowledge and how texts constitute specific epistemic virtues – might seem unrelated, in exploring them I actually found they also came together in an unexpected way. Later in this book, I will explore how these two questions can, in fact, be seen as two sides of the same coin. Thinking about knowledge and textual practices in terms of stability and movement is ultimately about the degree to which knowledge operates between a tension of embedding itself in a particular context and its capacity to be uprooted and transplanted, to move between sites, across domains. These horticultural metaphors of embedding and deracination, I think, capture this tension quite well. But the same kind of processes are found in the epistemic virtues implicit in archaeological writing, which, I argue, revolve around the tension between detachment and engagement between both the archaeologist and their object and co-constituents. The imperative to be faithful to both things and to other people who share your concern with those things means negotiating a position which not only lets those things and people 'speak for themselves' but also requires you to be deeply engaged and connected to them.

But I cannot do justice to this argument here. It is time to get on with the story. Let me end by briefly summarizing the organization of this book. In Chapter 2, I offer a historical review of epistemological debates in Anglo-American archaeology since the nineteenth century. For many readers, this will be a familiar story, but I have framed this in such a way as to capture what I regard as two subtly different epistemic cultures: British and North American archaeology. The epistemic discontinuities that I discussed in this chapter can be traced even within the discourse about knowledge production within archaeology, and so it is only fitting that I tell such a story with this in mind. This is followed by Chapter 3 which moves closer to the ambition of this book and addresses how texts have been discussed in archaeology, suggesting a need to broaden previous work in light of research in textual linguistics and discourse analysis. This critique sets the stage for Chapter 4 which examines four key text types used in archaeology, and discusses them in terms of their epistemic and ontological registers. This is a core part of the book and my argument, and attempts to answer the question of how texts work to stabilize knowledge. A recurrent theme in all text types is that of detachment, which I then take up in the final chapter to address how knowledge moves across texts through different conceptual vehicles. The mobility of knowledge is an equally important idea here, as it also acts to bind knowledge produced in different texts and material conditions together. It prevents the complete fragmentation that multiple epistemic registers seem to imply. More importantly, though, it shows how knowledge is mobilized between texts. The book ends by drawing out the affinities between epistemic virtues of detachment and engagement and the textual practices involved in stabilizing and mobilizing knowledge.

# 2

# MODELS OF REASONING IN ANGLO-AMERICAN ARCHAEOLOGY

## The legacy of the nineteenth century

The late nineteenth century was a period when archaeology and other related disciplines such as history and ethnography were becoming 'professionalized' (Levine 1986). What this entailed was the establishment of university chairs, journals and societies, among other things, which constituted an institutionalization of knowledge. It is at this time that one also sees the first texts on methodologies, such as manuals of excavation (see Lucas 2012). In journal papers and society lectures, scholars frequently refer to archaeology as a new science, and as a science, there was frequent reference to the standard nineteenth-century epistemology of knowledge through induction: the collection of facts followed by reasoned interpretation from those facts. Colt Hoare's famous motto "We speak from facts, not theory", which acts as a subtitle to his introductory chapter from *The History of Ancient Wiltshire* (1812), is often used to illustrate a stereotypical view of a naïve inductivism held by the nineteenth-century antiquarians, where archaeology should restrict itself to fact gathering. But theory in this context referred specifically to reason based on detached speculation, as opposed to reasoning from facts. Here is the full quotation: "I shall describe to you what we have found; what we have seen; in short, I shall tell you a plain unvarnished tale, and draw from it such conclusions as shall appear not only reasonable, but even uncontradictable" (Colt Hoare 1812: 7). Colt Hoare was quite happy to 'theorize' – so long as his theories were based on fact.

Such a method of reasoning in Britain was typically attributed to the seventeenth-century philosopher Francis Bacon as outlined in his book *Novum Organum*, whereby general axioms were inferred from particular observations (Bacon 2000 [1620]). However, what is often sidelined in Bacon's method is the stress he laid on eliminative rather than enumerative induction. That is, while gathering observations is crucial, more is not necessarily better; rather one uses the observations to eliminate ideas that do not stand up to empirical scrutiny. Moreover, knowledge is built up not by mass accumulation of facts but by constructing ever greater levels of generalization from the foundation of more modest generalizations, tested by eliminative induction. How closely nineteenth-century archaeologists and antiquarians followed Bacon's specific method is debatable, since they tend mainly to cite its general significance, but at the same time we must be conscious of the fact that induction to a nineteenth-century archaeologist may have meant something quite different to our contemporary understanding. Thus, in 1849 in a lecture to the British Archaeological Association, the physician and antiquarian Thomas Pettigrew stated what was no doubt general knowledge at the time: "Lord Bacon rectified the mode of philosophising, and pointed out the method of induction as the true mode of increasing knowledge" (Pettigrew 1850: 174).

By the nineteenth century, the most popular and systematic attempt to follow a Baconian method was that of William Whewell, particularly in his book on the *Philosophy of the Inductive Sciences* (1847). For Whewell, knowledge was "obtained by a common process of collecting general truths from particular observed facts, which process is termed *Induction*" (Whewell 1984 [1847]: 124; italics in original). General truths or propositions, which he called *theories*, were thus inductive (rather than deductive) and based on the colligation of *facts*, which were particular, experiential observations (ibid.: 143–145). The process of induction was characterized as an initial collection of facts by observation or experiment, then developing hypotheses to account for the facts, which, when confirmed through testing, become theories (ibid.: 209–211). Whewell used the term 'colligation' to characterize the role of a hypothesis in joining facts together – and in fact his concept of colligation was effectively synonymous with induction. Whewell very much considered himself the heir to Bacon; like Bacon, he considered simple enumerative induction inadequate, arguing the critical role of hypothesis formation. However, Whewell became embroiled in a debate with another English empiricist, John Stuart Mill, who argued that induction was fundamentally enumerative, and therefore where hypotheses are used, this did not constitute induction (Forster 2009). At one level this was a terminological dispute over the proper use of the term 'induction'; at another, it reflected two deeply different epistemologies, one that accepted a post-Kantian view of all knowledge as in part subjectively created (Whewell) and another that held tight to a British empiricist tradition (Mill).

Now the extent to which such debates explicitly affected archaeologists is hard to say, but it does point to a potential schism between two views of induction: one that acknowledged the critical role of theory in mediating generalizations, and the other that saw generalizations emerging from facts without the intermediary of theory. Which view an archaeologist adopted may have been more tacit or unconscious than explicit, as both views espoused the need to reason from the facts. Churchill Babington, the second Disney Professor at Cambridge, underlined the point that the inductive method was not simply about collecting facts but equally about their proper interpretation. In his inaugural address he reminds his audience that "The true antiquary must not only be well acquainted with his facts, but he must also, when there are sufficient data, proceed to reason upon them" (Babington 1865: 64).

The problem, of course, was what constituted a reasonable interpretation – and how much data was sufficient data? These are two different issues and, in fact, the second was the minor problem – at least for a Baconian. Indeed, the 'collection of facts' seems to have been considered one of the major successes of the new science; in the second edition of *Pre-Historic Times*, Lubbock already felt compelled to condense and summarize the quantity of data through the use of 'statistical tables', a fact he partly laments insofar as the force of example becomes diminished (Lubbock 1872: xi). At the same time, the nineteenth century ushered in the use of statistics as evidence in the form we understand and employ it today. Mary Poovey has analysed in great detail the genealogy of the use of numbers and quantification in the sciences of human society between the seventeenth and nineteenth centuries, and convincingly shows that it was only at the start of the nineteenth century that they came to be used as unambiguous evidence (Poovey 1998; also see Hacking 1990). However, as abstractions, numbers and statistics also became the most idealized form of a fact – a fact in its purest form, ostensibly untainted by subjectivity. Lubbock's use of statistical tables in the 1870s is, then, not just an apology for saving space but also a tacit acknowledgement of the power of numbers. This is underlined in his concluding chapter where he discusses the role of archaeology in society, citing statistics on the relation between education and criminality to support the idea that the practice of science can lead to a virtuous society (Lubbock 1872: 599–601). And Lubbock was by no means exceptional; the use of numerical data (albeit usually in simple tabular form) was employed by many others, such at Pitt Rivers and his Relic Tables (Bowden 1991: 85), and reveals not only an ease with the way facts are presented but also an implicit admission that such facts are not necessarily or always in short supply.

So the problem was not with facts but with the inferences drawn from them – the relation between facts and theory. However, here is where things also get somewhat vague. Most archaeologists in the late nineteenth century seemed comfortable with talking about their discipline as an inductive science, but for some archaeologists, over-hasty interpretations were potentially damaging to the scientific status of the discipline. Thomas Wright, one of the most famous late nineteenth-century antiquarians in England, thus wrote in what was a very popular book *The Celt, the Roman, and the Saxon*:

> His science [i.e. of the antiquary], however, is yet imperfectly developed … The great obstacle with which the student has had to contend was, the want of example brought together for comparison, which led him continually to make assumptions that had no foundation, and to appropriate incorrectly, the consequences of which are visible in almost every work touching on the primeval antiquities of Britain that has appeared until the last few years. This obstacle is now rapidly giving way before the increasing facility of communicating knowledge, the formation of local museums, and the greater number of good books on the subject. But there is another danger against which the student in British archaeology is to be especially warned; the old scholars failed in not following a sufficiently strict course of comparison and selection; but some of the new ones

run into the opposite extreme of generalising too hastily, and they form systems specious and attractive in appearance, but without foundation in truth. Such I am convinced is the system of archaeological periods, which has been adopted by the antiquarians of the north, and which a vain attempt has been made to introduce into this country.

*(Wright 1861: vi–vii)*

It was a concern repeated by others, such as the Archbishop of York in his inaugural address to the Royal Archaeological Institute, who claimed the "greatest peril to science is to theorise overmuch" (Thomson 1867: 86). In short, sufficiency of data was generally not the issue by this time; rather it was incautious extrapolation, or, more specifically, inappropriate induction. This was nowhere better exemplified than in the disagreements over the status of the Three Age System as alluded to at the end of the quotation from Thomas Wright (see Rowley-Conwy 2007 for the wider context of this debate). Wright was a vociferous opponent of what he saw as a muddled and incorrect theory imported from Scandinavia to England and argued in some detail against what he saw as its flaws. His arguments marshalled a range of evidence, yet, today, seeing his images of Bronze Age swords captioned as Roman appears like a classic case of incorrect interpretation on his part. The irony of his position is epitomized in his concluding sentence in an address to the British Archaeological Association in 1866: "The truth of science must eventually prevail" (Wright 1866: 84).

The battle between Wright and proponents of the Three Age System was thus not about competing epistemologies; both sides adopted the language of induction – and probably of the Baconian/Whewellian sort. Lubbock, perhaps the leading spokesperson for the Three Age System in England, quoted approvingly the Bishop of London's words about the integrity of proper science involving the collection of observations and making sound reasoning to legitimate conclusions (Lubbock 1872: ix). So wherein should one look for potential epistemic fractures in the birth of scientific archaeology? In many ways, I think the answer relates to the kind of sciences that archaeologists looked to as their closest allies, and during the late nineteenth century there was no doubt what these were: history on the one hand and geology and Darwin's evolutionary theory on the other. For many archaeologists, the antiquarian roots which archaeology shared with history were paramount. Wright, who explicitly recognized the important contributions and valuable role geology has and can play in relation to archaeology, nonetheless makes it clear that it has overstepped its mark in the case of the Three Age System and the antiquity of human history (Wright 1866: 81). Wright defends archaeology as a humanist discipline against its 'invasion' by geology:

Above all, we never supposed that geology could turn what is Saxon or Roman into British (or make it older even than British), any more than archaeology could turn an elephant into an ichthyosaurus … To judge these is absolutely the province of archaeology …

*(Ibid.)*

The humanist tradition in archaeology, however, was (and conceivably still is) stronger among those archaeologists working in the ancient world of Rome, Greece and the Middle East than in prehistory. Here the paragon of this tradition in mid-nineteenth-century England was Charles Newton, keeper at the British Museum. In a seminal paper on the study of archaeology from 1851, Newton, who rarely if ever refers to archaeology as a science, draws very clear connections between the working methods of archaeology and history. His division of historical evidence into the Oral, Written and Monumental echoes those of later German historiography (Newton 1851; Droysen 1897), and his description of the working methods for analysing the Monumental, especially what he calls the Imitative Arts, is directly modelled on textual analysis. Understanding artistic artefacts involves understanding not only the context in which the art was made but also the inner motivations which produced it: "We must not only know the mere external characteristics of style, we must know the meaning or motive which pervades it; we must be able to read and to interpret it" (Newton 1851: 14). And in summing up the skills required of the archaeologist:

> [H]e must combine with the aesthetic culture of an Artist, and the trained judgement of the Historian, not a little of the learning of the Philologer: the plodding drudgery which gathers together his materials, must not blunt the critical acuteness required for their classification and interpretation, nor should that habitual suspicion which must ever attend the scrutiny and precede the warranty of archaeological evidence, give too sceptical a bias to his mind.
>
> *(Ibid.: 25–26)*

Thus, the method of the archaeologist, like a philologist or palaeographer, follows what later one would describe as the hermeneutic method. There is no Bacon or inductive science here, although there is a very similar concern with the relation between data and theory. Moreover, Newton clearly saw that being over-cautious in interpretation was just as problematic as the opposite. However, for Newton, who was working on material and in periods where written sources existed alongside archaeological remains, the affinity between archaeology and history must have seemed all too obvious. For others who worked in contexts of relatively impoverished or absent textual sources, such as Thomas Wright, the alliance with history was more substantive than methodological, and if he adopted the language of inductive science, it was nonetheless to ensure that archaeology "walked hand-in-hand with history", not geology (Wright 1861: viii). Wright even invoked Newton's division of historical sources or relics into the literary and monumental (Wright 1866: 64–65). For others, however, the association with geology was what could guarantee the success of archaeology as an inductive science. The antiquarian and poet Dillon Croker, talking to the British Archaeological Association in 1849, argued explicitly that archaeology should model itself on geology, not history; for him, it was archaeology that acts as the true arbiter of history – without it, history is:

but fable, or, what is worse than fable, theory as regards the past … Archaeology establishes or contradicts the existence of nations, and whether they
flourished or fell. History may record their rise and progress, but archaeology
must be the evidence of whether history be true or false.

(Croker 1849: 289)

Lubbock too, of course, clearly saw archaeology more through the lens of geology
than history, even if he described archaeology as "the link between geology and
history" (Lubbock 1872: 2). For someone like Pitt Rivers, though, the alignment
of archaeology with the physical sciences, especially Darwin's evolutionary theory,
was an issue that needed emphasizing. In his paper "On the Evolution of Culture"
(1875), he offers a very explicit view of science as 'organized common sense', but
one that developed (in evolutionary fashion, of course) through three stages:
empirical, classificatory and theoretical (Pitt Rivers 1906: 20–21). For Pitt Rivers, a
mature science is a theoretical science which was synonymous with evolutionary
theory. More significantly, he disputed scholars who drew a division between the
natural and historical (i.e. human) sciences, and argued that the separation is spurious:
evolutionary theory encompasses both (ibid.: 24). Pitt Rivers' position on archaeology
is thus one which not only puts archaeology closer to the natural sciences but one
which would even subsume history into its orbit too.

Thus, by the end of the nineteenth century archaeology had two very different
epistemic models: that of an inductive science like geology and that of a humanistic
endeavour like history and philology. The difference between the two, however, was
never really expressed as an epistemic issue but more of an ontological or substantive
one, and, moreover, it was a difference only really felt within prehistoric archaeology.
For those archaeologists like Wright who saw archaeology as part of history, the 'new
archaeology' as he called it (Wright 1866: 81) which allied itself to geology was a
wrong turn. For those working in classical archaeology, such tensions never became an
issue – at least not until much, much later. However, since then archaeology in Britain
has remained entangled in this difference between the humanities and the natural sciences, although it is a difference which it managed to more or less juggle without ill-
effect for the next century. The explosion of differences on epistemic issues between
the 1960s and 1980s is, in many ways, a short-lived blip in the history of the discipline,
but one which nonetheless brought to the surface discontinuities that were established
at the end of the nineteenth century. In the next section, I want to explore how these
differences were mediated and articulated in the first half of the twentieth century
before looking into the ferment of the 1960s.

## Diverging traditions in the early twentieth century

In the last section I focused exclusively on the epistemic discourse in Britain; here I
want to contrast the developments between Britain and the United States in the
first half of the twentieth century. Such a contrapuntal reading offers the scope of
sharpening the differences as well as similarities between the two, but also, in doing

so, brings to the fore more hidden aspects of each. I want to begin with the United States because, in many ways, one sees similarities and continuities with late nineteenth-century Britain, but where the tensions between data and theory become the focus of increased attention, especially through what Wylie has called a recurrent series of crises debates (Wylie 2007; Chapman & Wylie 2016). If in Britain disagreements revolved around the extent or nature of interpretation or generalization – in short, finding the right balance – in the Unites States there seemed to be a growing feeling that there was an overall lack of any interpretation at all. Moreover, where in Britain there was tension over the appropriate framework for making interpretations – traditional history or cultural evolution – in the States there was generally only one role model – ethnology. In an oft-cited paper reviewing the state of archaeology in North America, Roland Dixon ends with a plea for moving beyond data collection to interpretation on an ethnological footing:

> The time is past when our major interest was in the specimen, the collection, the site as a thing in itself; our museums are no longer cabinets of curiosities. We are today concerned with the relations of things, with the whens and the whys and the hows; in finding the explanation of the arts and customs of historic times in the remnants which have been left us from the prehistoric ...
>
> *(Dixon 1913: 565)*

The published responses to Dixon's paper are unanimous on the relation between archaeology and ethnology, and only one suggested that the real problem was not theoretical but still insufficient data (Laufer 1913:576–577). Indeed, for some the problem with any poverty of interpretation lay primarily with the data itself, especially how it was collected (Smith 1911; also see Strong 1936: 368). In some ways, one can view this as an early manifestation of a concern for methodological development over grand theorizing; that is, a focus on the theory of fact collection and processing rather than the theory of interpretation. Such methodological concerns have arguably formed one of the most characteristic features of North American theory over the twentieth century. However, the language of discourse at the time tended to oppose theory and fact, so my reading of the situation may be anachronistic.

That the situation changed very little over the next decades, however, is evident in a number of publications by Clyde Kluckhohn on the state of theory in archaeology and anthropology in the States (Kluckhohn 1939; 1940). Kluckhohn's texts are actually remarkable for their depth of discussion and treatment of these epistemic issues; whereas most other previous texts had devoted a few lines or paragraphs to such matters, Kluckhohn brings a whole new level of theoretical scrutiny that was to become increasingly characteristic of theoretical discussions from the 1950s onward. Kluckhohn remarks on the still persistent aversion to theory in archaeology in favour of data collection. But what is novel is his insistence that even those engaged in data collection are still drawing on theory in the form of conceptual schemes, background assumptions and common sense (Kluckhohn 1939: 333–334). For Kluckhohn:

[T]he alternative is not, I think, between theory and no theory or a minimum of theory, but between adequate and inadequate theories, and, even more important, between theories, the postulates and propositions of which are conscious and which hence lend themselves to systematic criticism, and theories, the premises of which have not been examined even by their formulators.

*(Ibid.: 330)*

Yet by the 1940s there were still only a handful of archaeologists attempting to draw interpretations from their data beyond basic issues of chronology (e.g. Steward & Setzler 1938; Colton 1942; Bennett 1943; Taylor 1948). John Bennett defined these as experimentalists in opposition to the majority of empiricists – that is, fact collectors (Bennett 1946). For Bennett, where empiricists dealt with facts, experimentalists dealt with problems; for empiricists, truth comes inevitably from the accumulation of facts, for experimentalists, from the assessment of probabilities. This latter was to become a key issue in the development of statistics in archaeology beyond simple enumeration or tabulation, and Albert Spalding was a key figure here (e.g. Spalding 1953). Walter Taylor's conjunctive approach also stressed the role of problems in defining fieldwork and initiating the archaeological process, as opposed to blind collection of data. He was especially vocal on the value of interpretively 'sticking one's neck out' as an epistemic virtue, not a vice – even if the data were limited. It was in this context that he even discussed the notion of testing hypotheses, albeit framed within a larger discussion on the provisional nature of all archaeological knowledge (Taylor 1948: 157–159). Exactly the same sentiments were expressed by Julian Steward in an important paper on laws of cultural development the following year:

Unless anthropology is to interest itself mainly in the unique, exotic, and non-recurrent particulars, it is necessary that formulations be attempted no matter how tentative they may be. It is formulations that will enable us to state new kinds of problems and to direct attention to new kinds of data which have been slighted in the past. Fact-collecting of itself is insufficient scientific procedure; facts exist only as they are related to theories, and theories are not destroyed by facts – they are replaced by new theories which better explain the facts.

*(Steward 1949: 25)*

Thus, by the 1950s the interpretive floodgates opened and major syntheses and explanatory models were being put forward, such as those by Leslie White and Julian Steward in anthropology (Steward 1949, 1955; White 1945, 1949, 1959), and Gordon Willey and Philip Phillips in archaeology (1958). What they had in common was a goal of making archaeology a generalizing science which involved the search for laws or general processes affecting human cultural development. In archaeology, Willey and Phillips in particular very much set the tone of the 1950s with a spate of publications (Willey 1953; Phillips & Willey 1953; Willey & Phillips 1955, 1958) outlining their conceptual framework for American prehistory. They critiqued what they saw as the intellectually moribund idea of archaeology as an inductive science where interpretation would inevitably emerge from the accumulation of data like pieces of a jigsaw filling out a picture:

> As time wore on, however, and the archeologist got his teeth into mountainous accumulations of facts, the expected miracle failed to take place. Something was apparently wrong with the "jigsaw" hypothesis. It became apparent that such order as could be discerned was not altogether inherent in the data but was in large part the product of the means employed to organize the data … It became, then, necessary to examine those means and the conceptual bases that underlay them.
>
> *(Phillips & Willey 1953: 615)*

What is important about this statement is the recognition not only that theory was necessary, but that perhaps theory needed to come first – or rather be present right from the start of data collection, rather than afterward as in the model of inductive science. It also reveals the critical difference between the British and the North American versions of inductivism. In North America, it seems as if archaeologists thought that theory would naturally emerge by itself from the data (hence the jigsaw metaphor), whereas in Britain it was assumed that theory still needed the input of the archaeologist – which perhaps also explains why there was never any equivalent debate about the lack of theory in British archaeology at this time. In short, whereas in Britain induction was conceived as eliminative (Bacon/Whewell), in the States it seems primarily to have been regarded as enumerative (Mill). Consequently, two different, albeit related, changes were afoot in the States: the acknowledgement on the one hand of the necessity of theory, and on the other that theory was entangled with data in such a way that neither was primary. Although not characterized in the same way as the later concept of the theory-ladenness or dependence of data (see below), the same basic idea is there. However, instead of adopting a Baconian version of induction, other models of reasoning linked to deduction and positivism were ultimately followed in the States.

This is perhaps most explicit in Raymond Thompson's short piece on 'The subjective element in archaeological inference' (1956) which came out partly in response to Willey and Phillips's papers. Although Thompson's main point seems to be to underline the inescapable subjective aspects of inference, he does nonetheless dispense with the traditional model of knowledge production as an inductive process in favour of a pragmatist position. He thus explicitly adopts a distinction (drawn from the pragmatist philosopher Dewey) between indicative and probative inferences as two phases in the general process of reasoning in archaeology. The indicative phase is mostly subjective and based on a 'feel' for the data – it is essentially a sense of what the data might be able to tell us, and this sense is largely based on the background knowledge and experience of the archaeologist. The probative phase is mostly objective (but still with a subjective element, as this is Thompson's key point) and based on the explicit mobilization of the data to test an inference. In the language of logical positivism, these two phases correspond to the two moments of hypothesis formation and testing, or, otherwise, as the logic of discovery and the logic of justification (also see Wylie 2002: 48). It is precisely this reconceptualization of the inferential process that broke with the century-old model of inductivism prevalent in archaeology and anticipated the epistemological restructuring of the discipline in the New Archaeology of the following decade.

To recap: in North America, the key debate over the first half of the twentieth century was primarily about the lack or poverty of any interpretation at all; critics from Dixon to Kluckhohn complained about the 'intellectual cowardice' of archaeologists refusing to engage in interpretation in favour of amassing more and more data under the naïve belief that the facts would eventually speak for themselves (Kluckhohn 1939: 334). As Kluckhohn pointed out, archaeology is always theoretical, at every stage of the process, and thus, for Willey and Phillips, theory was needed from the very beginning, not just at the end. Hints of hypothesis testing in Taylor's conjunctive approach and Thompson's pragmatist theory of inference provided the first articulation of how theory and data might work together in a new way. Seen in this light, the New Archaeology of the 1960s was almost inevitable and, in many ways, not so much a revolution as the culmination of this gradual shift. But before I discuss the epistemic issues raised in the 1960s and their aftermath, it is useful to compare this story with what was happening on the other side of the Atlantic, in Britain. Because, there, the older distinction between the humanities and natural sciences was starting to manifest itself in a new way.

The humanist tradition was exemplified in Flinders Petrie's discussion on the nature of archaeological evidence in the beginning of the twentieth century, where he draws explicitly on analogies with legal evidence (Petrie 1904, chapter X; 1906). Petrie discusses archaeological evidence under four headings: witnesses, material facts, exhaustion and probability. The first two clearly belong to what one might conventionally call facts –written texts and inscriptions on the one hand and artefacts on the other. But the second two allude to background knowledge or assumptions as well as general processes of inference, with exhaustion in particular evoking Bacon's model of eliminative induction. Although Petrie does not explicitly discuss induction (Baconian or otherwise), he does broadly appear to a follow a Baconian model, accepting the role of theories or hypotheses in reasoning. This is also why Petrie is more comfortable with the idea of fieldwork and data collection as selective, as opposed to the more obsessive quest for a total record promulgated by others (Carver 1989, 1990; also see Lucas 2012). But it is not Petrie's implied 'Baconism' that I want to highlight here, but his connections to another genealogy. Petrie's discussion is one of the first explicit and extended treatments on the nature of archaeological interpretation in Britain, and his alignment of archaeological with legal evidence can be seen as part of a general humanistic attitude where the links between historical scholarship and jurisprudence ran deep (Franklin 1977; also see Thomas 2015 for a contemporary discussion of the relation between archaeological and legal forms of inference). At the same time, Petrie, as an Egyptologist, was also clearly working in an area and material whose links to textual history and art history were very strong, so it is perhaps no surprise that he, like Newton half a century earlier, should make such close alliances to the humanities.

This alliance is less clear in the case of other archaeologists. Randall-MacIver, who began his career working under Petrie but later worked in East Africa, reviewed the nature of archaeology in the 1930s, describing it as a science and one generally closer to anthropology than history (Randall-MacIver 1933). Moreover, in stark contrast to Newton's idea of an archaeologist as art historian, for Randall-MacIver:

> In itself, archaeology has nothing to do with art … The immense majority of the objects with which he deals have very slight aesthetic worth; in so far as a man is purely archaeologist aesthetic values do not exist for him. The archaeologist works like a naturalist – it is his business to trace evolution, patterns, migration, and development.
>
> (Randall-MacIver 1933: 13–14)

However, of greater interest are Randall-MacIver's remarks on the process of archaeological reasoning; like any good scholar in the Baconian tradition, he saw it as imperative to "keep his fancies and his facts distinct" in order to remain scientific (ibid., 15). The problem lay rather in distinguishing valid from invalid forms of reasoning and he proceeds to give examples which largely hang on false assumptions. One of the most striking generalizations he makes about logical inference, however, relates to the archaeologist's ability to draw conclusions about people in the past in terms of how advanced (i.e. 'like us') they were: "In short, it is only possible to reason convincingly when manufactures or arts and crafts have reached a high point of intricacy" (ibid., 19). Christopher Hawkes was to use a more sophisticated version of this argument to underpin his famous ladder of inference, twenty years later (see below).

Despite the differences between Petrie's and Randall-MacIver's description of archaeological reasoning, there is an underlying point of agreement: that any act of reasoning depends to an extent on background assumptions relating to the material. With Petrie, these were defined as forms of evidence, but for MacIver, they acted as limits on interpretation. For both, however, these background assumptions also acted as a bridge between the contemporary archaeologist and past people. This was not explicit, but rather more implicit in their argument and based on a sense of shared cognition or rationality – which, in MacIver's case, was seen as sometimes limited in extent. The archaeologist who drew this issue out explicitly as the basis of his philosophy of history was, of course, R.G. Collingwood, who began his career as a philosopher but turned his interest in archaeology from a hobby to a vocation. Collingwood offers us the most explicit and extended discussion of epistemic issues in archaeology in Britain during the first half of the twentieth century, and he became a philosophical role model for a generation of British prehistorians during the 1940s and 1950s. Although most of his writings on this topic were published posthumously, his influence in lectures and talks should not be under-estimated.

What is perhaps striking about Collingwood is the way he blended models of English Baconian science with historical idealism. In his autobiography, he argued that archaeology was a much clearer example of a Baconian science than history – even though his whole goal was to transform history into such a science (Collingwood 1944: 90). His conception of the Baconian method made explicit reference to the idea of eliminative induction through his 'question and answer' approach. Through that, Collingwood also drew strong analogies with the law, as Petrie had done earlier (Collingwood 1946: 266–268). Thus, there remained a strong continuity with the nineteenth-century ideal of inductive science where sources are treated as evidence to be subject to inference. Now if this was all that Collingwood had to say, his influence and importance might not be worthy of further comment. For what he did was couple this Baconian method to a philosophy of history which essentially argued that any science which seeks to understand human society and history is radically different from the natural sciences, following a common distinction in continental historio-graphy (Collingwood 1946). I should be clear here, though; in terms of method, Collingwood saw no real difference between history and the natural sciences, both using Baconian induction (see Collingwood et al. 1922); rather the difference was more ontological in terms of the object of study.

While the natural sciences studied the external world, history and archaeology ultimately study the human mind, which means that historical knowledge is pre-dicated on understanding past actors and actions from their own point of view (hence his famous concept of historical re-enactment). In this sense he was clearly drawing archaeology back towards its humanistic roots and would have been very sympathetic to Newton's description of archaeological method. For example, in his autobiography he distinguishes the geological from the archaeological record in this way; in the latter, one looks at remains not simply as evidence of what the world was like at a particular point in the past (as in geology) but also to understand the mental life of the people who made and used such remains, as 'expressions of purpose' (Collingwood 1944: 74). Collingwood's philosophy of history (including archaeology) in a nutshell was: "All history is the history of thought" (ibid.: 75).

It is this blending of two very different philosophical traditions – archaeology as both Baconian inductive science and historical idealism – that made Collingwood's work a catalyst for archaeological reflections on epistemology in the 1950s. The influence of the English idealist philosopher Francis Bradley on Collingwood needs to be acknowledged in this context (Bradley 2011 [1874]). And yet, at the same time, he was probably only articulating in an explicit manner what many archae-ologists in Britain tended to work under as a basic assumption. Still, in making this epistemic position explicit, he also opened up a Pandora's box of problems with which archaeologists in the late 1940s and 1950s suddenly had to grapple: most specifically, reconciling the goal of empathetic understanding with the study of material culture in the absence of any textual sources. This was most famously articulated by Christopher Hawkes in his exposition of the ladder of inference in archaeology, where inferring about past technologies and subsistence is relatively easy from material remains but moving on to social organization and religion increasingly hard if not impossible (Hawkes 1954). What Hawkes found so difficult was to put the Collingwood model of history, as a history of the mind, into practice in archaeology without access to other sources of information, chiefly texts. For Hawkes, there existed a real epistemic fracture between text-free and text-aided archaeology, one which constrained how far inductive reasoning could take you (ibid.: 161). Since the human mind was considered to be most active/evident in the areas of social organization and religion, whereas technology and subsistence pertained more to bodily/material needs and functions, the very inaccessibility of these upper rungs of the ladder to archaeology seemed to create a real dilemma.

Hawkes's affinities clearly lay with archaeology as a humanist discipline rather than a science, a point he underlined in various contexts (Evans 1998: 400), so the problem for him ran deep. It was also a sentiment shared by his wife of many years, Jacquetta Hawkes, and in her very personal book on the archaeology of Britain she stresses the duality of archaeology as both a story of material processes and change and a story of the 'growth of consciousness', and these two themes pervade the book and her work in general (Hawkes 1951: 10–11). And the Hawkeses were not alone, of course – many of the leading archaeologists at this time stressed the humanist side of archaeology, such as Mortimer Wheeler and his famous concept that archaeology is ultimately about digging up people, not things (Wheeler 1954) and Stuart Piggott who viewed archaeology as "a branch of historical study" and deliberately used the term 'discipline' rather than 'science' (Piggott 1966: 13).

Glyn Daniel, in his 1950s history of archaeology, also underlined this humanist association: "It is neither helpful nor in accordance with widespread modern usage to call either archaeology or anthropology 'sciences' except in so far as they may claim, with so many of the humanities, to be miscalled the social sciences" (Daniel 1975: 310). Daniel goes on to argue that, even though nineteenth-century archaeologists described themselves as scientists, this is misleading, as is the general association between geology and prehistory; moreover, he warned against conflating the use of scientific techniques with the attribution of science to archaeology (ibid.: 310–311). In short, "prehistory, like history, is humanity – a way of looking at man and his works, not at nature" (ibid.: 311).

But the potential problems that Hawkes had raised in the Collingwood view of archaeology as the study of mind remained and were even pushed further by one his students, Margaret Smith, in her equally famous paper on the limits of inference in archaeology published a year after Hawkes's paper (Smith 1955). Smith even singles out Collingwood as the source of the problem:

> R.G. Collingwood used to say that the way to interpret a piece of archaeological evidence was to try to appreciate the problem of the man who was responsible for creating it. This method is all very well when one already knows, or can guess with reasonable certainty, what that problem was likely to be ... But even if we decide to allow that prehistoric peoples were as intelligent as ourselves – if not more astute – when faced with problems which we know confronted them, we must not make the mistake of assuming that they could have been aiming only at

things which seem justifiable to us. The Western European standards of value which condition our own thought are not absolute.

*(Smith 1955: 4)*

Smith goes on to consider the use of ethnographic analogies as a way round this, but ultimately dismisses these given the massive cultural diversity in the world, past and present. In this paper, Smith is certainly more pessimistic than Hawkes and perhaps most other archaeologists, even those who adopted Hawkes's ladder, such as Stuart Piggott (1966: 21–25). The use of ethnographic analogy and texts (where applicable) was generally seen as a way of mitigating these limits – albeit with caution and only to a certain extent. But for some archaeologists, the problem as framed was itself misguided.

Gordon Childe recognized the problems of different cultural standards referred to by Smith and how these might constrain the archaeologist's ability to understand the past (Childe 1949). Indeed, an awareness of the social context of knowledge production was in fact well developed among many archaeologists in Britain at this time (e.g. Crawford 1932; Childe 1949, 1956; Clark 1957). Like most other archaeologists, Childe also accepted that careful use of ethnographic analogies was a way round this. However, he took it further. In *Social Worlds of Knowledge* (1949), Childe displayed a very sophisticated grasp of the problem, referencing the physicist Niels Bohr's ideas on the impact of observational instruments on the object of study, which applied to both social science and quantum physics:

> Sociologists, whether archaeologists or ethnographers, want to observe cultures. But the instrument of observation is itself culture. The results of observation must be expressed in the categories which we have inherited from our own society. There is an issue which is at once epistemological and sociological.
>
> *(Childe 1949: 5)*

Childe spends most of this paper discussing and endorsing Durkheim's position on the socially derived nature of our categories of understanding, such as those of space and time, only to return to the initial dilemma posed by Bohr: how to understand past modes of thought through modern categories of thought. It is at this point that he mentions and then rejects Collingwood's solution to the dilemma as impossible (ibid.: 24; also see Childe 1950: 1):

> "All history", wrote Collingwood, "is the re-enactment of past thought in the historian's own mind"; and more explicitly, "The historian re-enacts in his own mind the thoughts and motives of the agent". But that, too, is impossible. Empirically – to take what should be an easy case – I cannot 're-enact in my mind' Pythagoras' 'thoughts and motives' when he 'discovered' his theorem. I do understand and use his theorem; I can follow his proof. But that does not make me rush off to sacrifice an ox.
>
> *(Childe 1949: 24)*

For Childe, the issue was not about resurrecting past thoughts but tracing the social origin of our own contemporary categories of thought. Moreover, there was no real need to even attempt to think about past minds, simply because such thoughts had been objectified in material culture:

> To study a past society there is no need to turn its real thoughts into objects for that has already been done. The relics and monuments studied by archaeology are patently objects and need no translation into an alien conceptual framework.
>
> *(Childe 1949: 25)*

In short, the interpretive problem and limits of inference raised by Hawkes and Smith were only really a problem if one held to a Collingwood idealism where the material and the mental were separate. Generously, Childe even implies that Collingwood himself said as much in promoting the idea that all real knowledge is ultimately practical (ibid.: 25), but Childe's 'pragmatism' is not necessarily all it seems. His idea of objectified knowledge is closely linked to the idea of cumulative knowledge and human progress, for one of the reasons why we can understand past societies through their material culture is that the very efficacy of that objectified knowledge also guarantees its transmission over the centuries. In short, we have inherited their epistemological successes – only their failures remain a mystery – and these successes constitute a shared set of categories of thought:

> Now this tradition, this heritage, what I should call our culture, already incorporates the real thought of past societies. The best results of their thinking are already embodied in, and indeed constitutive of our culture. They do not have to be translated into alien logical forms or fitted into foreign frames … Thereby they suffer no relativity distortion …
>
> *(Ibid.: 26)*

This is not the place to go into an extended discussion of the problems of Childe's views; rather enough has been said to underline the complexity of thinking at this time in Britain. If, in the United States, the earlier part of the twentieth century was a gradual move towards making theory respectable – and inevitable – in Britain, theory had largely remained integral to archaeology and was a necessary partner, so long as it was wedded to the data (e.g. see Clark 1953). The issue in Britain that emerged was not whether to use theory or not, but rather the crack that was opening up between archaeology as a humanist discipline and archaeology as an empirical science. This difference had always existed, but under the surface; it was only with Collingwood's explicit attempts to wed the two that the problems this posed for archaeology were suddenly exposed in terms of the limits of inference. This crack only widened as developments in theory in North America reached the shores of England and a brasher version of archaeology as empirical science was encountered. Before I continue with this story, however, it is important to make some observations about the different way history was perceived in North America and Britain.

In Britain, as just related, history for most archaeologists was closely linked to an idealism (e.g. Hawkes, Piggott), although materialist perspectives also existed, whether broadly Marxist (e.g. Childe, Crawford) or ecological (Clark). In many ways, what was at stake in the 1950s was precisely what view one took of history, ontologically speaking. In the United States, however, history was largely seen by archaeologists as simply a sequence of events. Archaeologists typically viewed their discipline as both historical and ethnological, but one where the historical aspect was almost solely about reconstructing chronologies while the ethnological one pertained to more comparative, generalizing interpretations (e.g. Taylor 1948; Ehrich 1950). Walter Taylor offered one of the most extensive discussions of this, distinguishing four different meanings of history, but even in the most interpretive and synthesizing sense (which he defined as historiography), it was still ultimately a particularizing historical narrative (Taylor 1948: 30–36). Willey and Phillips discussed the same issue but framed it in terms of the dichotomy of history and science, and, while recognizing that archaeology is both part history and part science, emphatically argued that archaeology, as anthropology, "is more science than history" (Willey & Phillips 1958: 2). For them, this was an ontological issue as well insofar as they regarded culture and society as part of the same realm as the material world, and not a separate super-organic entity as might be attributed by historical idealists (ibid.: 3). In this, they no doubt shared common ground with Childe.

But the key point I want to stress is that history in North American archaeology was more commonly linked to a phase in an epistemic hierarchy which ascended from the interpretation of particular events or sequences to the explanation of general processes or laws (a.k.a. processual interpretation) as in the scheme of Willey and Phillips (1958: 4). In other words, history was easily assimilated into archaeology as a phase of work because of the way it was defined, unlike in Britain where its primarily ontological definition was a potential source of rupture. All this is perhaps well known but it is worth remembering as the difference between the two views of history and its relation to archaeology on opposite sides of the Atlantic is crucial to understanding subsequent events. That and the different conceptions of induction (eliminative versus enumerative) held by archaeologists in the two nations. Because of the complexity of discussion and the explosion of literature after the 1950s, I will now separate my discussion of North America and Britain into two sections, In the first, I follow the story over the latter half of the twentieth century in North America where the philosophy of science becomes drawn into the debate; in the second, I trace developments in Britain where continental philosophy, especially the hermeneutic tradition, was the main influence. After that, I will bring the two streams back together for a final section discussing the clashes and reconciliations of the two streams, ending with a review of the current status of epistemology today.

## Explanation and the philosophy of science

The link between theory and data which became an emerging concern in North American archaeology in the 1950s remained a hot topic into the 1960s but really exploded during the 1970s. What was particular to North America, however, was the explicit connections forged with the philosophy of science – both by archaeologists drawing on the literature of this field and, perhaps more importantly, by philosophers of science entering archaeological debate. A central thread of this debate revolved around the issue of confirmation – that is, how to arrive at valid or justified inferences from the data. In 1962, Gordon Lowther published a rather turgid paper on epistemology and archaeological theory, framing his discussion in terms of the opposition between correspondence and coherence theories of truth (Lowther 1962). The former implies that the truth of a theory or explanation lies in its correspondence to reality, whereas the latter in its coherence within a general system or framework. Lowther's purpose in drawing on this opposition, however, was to develop criteria for verifying archaeological claims – and whether such criteria should be based on correspondence or coherence, which he linked to positivist and idealist philosophies respectively. Lowther clearly favoured the latter – though observing that most archaeologists tended to assume the former as a 'common-sense' view (Lowther 1962: 501).

What is interesting about Lowther's paper is the emphasis he lays on the theory-ladenness of facts under the coherence theory (although, again, he phrases it differently): "facts are not given. Facts are themselves conclusions" (ibid.: 502). Albert Spalding's response to this paper and this issue in particular, as a card-carrying positivist, is equally revealing:

> [A] healthy awareness of the filter of predilections, prejudices, theoretical biases, sensory imperfections and so on through which sensory impressions are strained is by no means inconsistent with a positivist view. We do indeed see the world through a glass darkly …
>
> *(Spalding 1962: 508)*

In effect, theory-ladenness – or, less anachronistically, the role of background beliefs and prior assumptions – was regarded as a non-issue and certainly did not jeopardize the nature of verification. A point also made by the English archaeologist Glyn Daniel in his commentary (Daniel 1962: 504).

Another paper which stressed the importance of verification was by Robert Butler who raised the distinction between the way archaeologists talk *post hoc* about the logic of their inferences (conceived or reconstructed logic) and the way they actually make their inferences (operational logic or logic in use; Butler 1965: 1123). Butler suggested that the conceived logic in relation to the particular case he discusses in the paper (the Old Cordilleran Culture concept) generally follows the hypothetico–deductive method, whereas the actual operational logic is more intuitive (and presumably inductive), heavily influenced by pre-existing theoretical expectations and commitments (ibid.: 1124–1126). Butler recognized that the former was an idealization of the process of inference, but nonetheless suggested that it could and should be made to align more with actual practice, and especially supplant the conventional model of 'inductive-enumerative generalization' – that is, amassing enough data until the pattern emerges. There is also a sense in which it supplies the only way to validate intuitive hunches and act as a corrective against pre-existing theoretical commitments, something which an inductive method cannot do.

Discussions about the role of background assumptions as raised by both Lowther and Butler reoccurred in the literature for the next few decades but never garnered any great concern until the 1980s because they were assumed to apply only to the context of theory formation, not theory-testing. Instead, all the momentum gathered around the positivist hypothetico-deductive model for archaeological interpretation and verification, culminating in the Binfords' *New Perspectives* volume (Binford & Binford 1968). In its wake, though, the papers by both Lowther and Butler were swiftly forgotten and have very rarely been cited since. In 1968, Lewis Binford explicitly argued for the need to move from an inductive to a deductive epistemology; the problem with conventional archaeological interpretation was that it was focused on how to *draw* inferences from evidence, whereas for Binford the issue was rather how to *test* inferences against independent evidence (Binford 1968: 17). Quoting the positivist philosopher Carl Hempel, Binford argued that the process of building an interpretation does not really matter since it would always fall foul of the problem of induction; rather one needed to subject any given interpretation to a test against independent evidence in order to support or falsify it. For Binford, "The shift to a consciously deductive philosophy, with the attendant emphasis on the verification of propositions through hypothesis testing, has far-reaching consequences for archaeology" (Binford 1968: 18). Among these consequences was, of course, the ability of archaeologists to overcome the perceived limits of the archaeological record for interpretation and to fulfil the programme laid out by Willey and Phillips in the 1950s for processual explanation.

Binford's adoption of Hempelian positivism was due to the influence of his former teachers Leslie White and Albert Spalding, the latter who, in the same 1968 volume, gave a more detailed rendering of this philosophy, espousing the deductive-nomological (DN) or covering-law (CL) model of Hempel's version of positivism (Spalding 1968). It was Spalding's paper that set in motion the train of publications on a positivist epistemology in the following decade. At this point, it is crucial to distinguish between two separate concerns about the relationship of theory to data in the United States: generalization and confirmation. The increasing desire for theory in the United States was also a desire for a particular kind of theory: one which produced generalizations about cultural process and development, hence the revival of neo-evolutionary theories. It was this that the DN or CL models of explanation sought to exemplify. Alongside that, however, was also an interest in developing more rigorous methods of archaeological inference or interpretation, which would help to justify such generalizations. This is what the hypothetico-deductive (HD) model was meant to achieve. The HD and DN/CL models usually came bundled together because they were both part of Hempel's philosophy of science (Hempel 1945a, 1945b; Hempel & Oppenheim 1948; Hempel 1965), although it is important to remember they served different aims. One concerned what constituted an appropriate explanation, the other, an appropriate confirmation of any explanation. These two aspects do not necessarily have to be related; issues of valid inference pertain to any kind of interpretation or explanation, whether they aspire to be generalizing or not. At the same time, the two became increasingly bundled together through their alignment with scientific method and the adoption of the natural sciences as a role model, so that during the 1970s the waters often became very muddied.

Fritz and Plog's brief paper on "The Nature of Archaeological Explanation" (Fritz & Plog 1970) was one of the first to follow Spalding's lead (1968) in adopting the view that a scientific explanation in archaeology is of the form that it relates two or more phenomena together by subsuming them as particular cases of a universal law, hence the term covering-law (CL). In one of their rather banal examples, the classification of a feature as a hearth is viewed as a form of such explanation insofar as it assumes a link between certain physical attributes (e.g. pit with burned sides and charcoal fill) and certain behaviour (fire-making) under a general model which is universally true (ibid.: 408). Though banal, that was part of the point: archaeologists make these kinds of interpretations all the time – this is a hearth, or a house or a projectile point – but without ever being explicit about the generalizations they imply. Fritz and Plog argued for the necessity of drawing these generalizations out into the open and subjecting them to proper testing. However, that was only one part of their ambition; the other involved explicitly generating new laws. To achieve this, they outlined a model for archaeological explanation which involved the creation of a hypothesis (by induction, for example – or abduction, as they termed it), formulating test implications (by deduction) and then testing the hypothesis with fieldwork specially designed and data specifically collected for this purpose. This model is what became known as the hypothetico-deductive (HD) method, although they did not use this term in the paper.

Their paper elicited a great deal of reaction, where a number of criticisms were aired. One common point concerned the way they conflated generalizing assumptions (such as those used in interpreting a feature as a hearth) with laws; if such assumptions have not been tested, how can they be called laws (Tuggle et al. 1972: 4)? Such conflation was also seen to mask the fact that generalizing assumptions are not explanatory in the same way a law purports to be; the links made are inferential rather than causal (Levin 1973: 391–392). But criticisms such as these did not dent the enthusiasm for logical positivism among its adherents and 1971 saw a book-length treatment of the subject by Patty-Jo Watson, Steven LeBlanc and Charles Redman in their *Explanation in Archaeology* (Watson et al. 1971). There, the authors follow the same Hempelian epistemology as a guide and argue for explanation as the subsumption of particulars to a law (Watson et al. 1971: 4–5). Like Fritz and Plog before, they laid emphasis on the importance of drawing out implicit generalizations used in archaeology and testing them, although they regarded Fritz and Plog's approach as more about testing explanations which employ laws rather than directly testing the laws themselves (ibid.: 26).

In this context, however, they do suggest that, in most cases, archaeology is more reliant on generalizations developed in other social sciences (e.g. ethnology) and so its primary function is to test such inherited laws rather than generate new ones, *contra* Fritz and Plog. The chief exception is with long-term processes which they see archaeology as uniquely suited and positioned to address and thus develop laws for (ibid.: 163–165; also see Watson 1976). This was also a position that Binford was soon to adopt, arguing that no inferences made about the archaeological record could generate laws since they were always reasoning from observed phenomena (static archaeological record) to unobserved phenomena (past cultural systems). Theory-building or the generation of laws could only come through middle-range research where both sides of the equation were present (Binford 1977, 1983: 13–17; Binford & Sabloff 1982).

Watson, LeBlanc and Redman also adopted the HD model of inference and confirmation, considering archaeological knowledge to proceed through three conceptual stages: generation of hypothesis, collection of relevant data and testing of hypothesis against data. In many ways, though, the book was more cautious about its claims than one usually gives credit for. Its authors recognized the provisional nature of all archaeological knowledge and that certainty is an impossible ideal; they also did not reject the use of induction but rather contextualized it as part of a longer chain of reasoning where induction was used in the formulation of hypotheses, but deduction in their testing: "The logic of empirical science in its completeness is a combination of inductive and deductive forms and procedures" (Watson et al. 1971: 12). Nevertheless, their main stress lay on testing through confirmation or falsification, and one of the main weaknesses of the book was its lack of proper discussion of what constituted confirmation. Even accepting their stance on confirmation as always provisional, they never gave very clear indications of when a hypothesis is at least provisionally confirmed except insofar as it was not falsified in any given test, although subsequently Steven LeBlanc tried to remedy this (LeBlanc 1973; see below). Another advocate of the HD method, who gave an extended treatment of the approach, was James Hill whose empirical work formed a key exemplar for Watson et al. Hill also hinted at the importance of multiple competing hypotheses as way of strengthening a confirmation, anticipating what was to become a major theme in the late 1970s (Hill 1972: 95–96).

The first half of the 1970s thus saw a torrent of papers in support of or opposition to the CL and HD models. In many ways, the issue that had the greatest resonance initially with archaeologists was the status of laws in archaeological explanation. Leroy Johnson argued that archaeology was not a nomothetic science and so the covering-law model was simply inapplicable. Rather, as a behavioural science, archaeology dealt with empirical generalizations, not nomothetic regularities and operated through a form of induction, akin to the method of Sherlock Holmes. It used what Johnson called a mix of analytical narrative and inferential statistics (Johnson 1972). Kent Flannery was especially critical and sceptical of laws in archaeology, regarding some of them as examples of the worst archaeology on record:

> From a Southwestern colleague, I learned last year that "as the population of a site increases, the number of storage pits will go up." I am afraid that these "laws" will always elicit from me the response, "Leapin' lizards Mr. Science!"
>
> *(Flannery 1973: 51)*

In response to such criticisms, Steven LeBlanc argued that, collectively, such trivial generalizations are crucial to building up more interesting and important laws (LeBlanc 1973: 206).

The real novelty of the period, however, was the arrival of philosophers on the scene. The philosopher Michael Levin, who had commented critically on Fritz and Plog's 1970 paper (Levin 1973; see above), was joined by Charles Morgan and Merilee Salmon (Morgan 1973, 1974; Salmon 1975, 1976). Both focused on what they saw as a misguided and confused application of the covering-law model to archaeology. Morgan, in commenting on Watson et al.'s book, based his critique on four grounds: first, their inadequacy in articulating the covering-law model, both in terms of its different variants and its definition of a law (many of Watson et al.'s so-called laws did not conform to the definitions given by Hempel); second, their lack of consideration of alternatives – Morgan pointed out that the covering-law model was already discredited within the philosophy of science by this time as a plausible description of explanation; third, a lack of correspondence between their examples of archaeological explanation and the covering-law model they were supposed to illustrate; and fourth, their appeal to authority figures (such as Hempel) and the rhetoric of 'science' and 'scientific' to justify the correctness of their position (Morgan 1973, 1974).

Watson et al.'s response to Morgan's critique was to counter-attack by claiming he was unfamiliar with the specific issues and problems in archaeology and so had missed their main point – which was to make archaeology scientific and to do so using the covering-law model of explanation (Watson et al. 1974). But their response was in many ways equally off the mark insofar as they seemed to completely ignore the core of his criticism: first, there are many different types of covering law whereas Watson et al. appear to assume the DN model is synonymous with the covering-law model; and, second, there are also other forms of scientific explanation besides the CL.

While Morgan's engagement with archaeology was brief, the same cannot be said for Merilee Salmon who built on several articles to ultimately write a book on the philosophy of archaeology (Salmon 1982). Salmon was more sympathetic to the ambitions of archaeologists like Watson, LeBlanc and Redman and shared most of their basic positions: a commitment to a scientific archaeology and an acknowledgement of the importance of hypothesis testing and that laws are an essential component of any explanation (Salmon 1975: 464). However, she strongly disagreed with how the New Archaeologists had characterized these ambitions and their adoption of the hypothetico-deductive (HD) method of inference on the one hand and the deductive-nomological (DN) model of explanation on the other. Indeed, a recurrent thread of Salmon's argument is that there was a major discrepancy between the way New Archaeologists described what they did and what they and in fact other archaeologists actually did in terms of making inferences and explanations.

In this regard, she points out that although Watson et al. accepted that most laws or generalizations in the social sciences were statistical in nature (Watson et al. 1971: 7), they failed to see that the covering-law model they used (i.e. the DN model) could not logically work with statistical generalizations. If a law was true under this model, *all* instances had to be confirmed (Salmon 1975: 459; 1976: 380).

Statistical generalizations admit of exceptions whereas the deductive logic of the DN model does not. As Morgan had earlier pointed out (Morgan 1973) and as Salmon repeats, there are various types of covering-law model of which the DN is only one – and not a very appropriate one for any science dealing with statistical regularities (Salmon & Salmon 1979: 64). As an alternative, she proposed the adoption of the statistical-relevance (SR) model developed by her husband, the philosopher Wesley Salmon. She discussed this model only briefly in these critiques of the covering-law model but provided a more detailed account in a joint paper with her husband at the end of the 1970s (Salmon & Salmon 1979) and in her book from the early 1980s (Salmon 1982a). As she summarizes it:

> Briefly, the SR model says that to explain an event is to assemble a total set of conditions relevant to its occurrence and to assess the probability of the event's occurrence, given those conditions. The total set of relevant conditions must include at least one law-like generalization.
>
> *(Salmon 1975: 463)*

The fall-out from all this criticism was twofold: on the one hand, to reaffirm the notion of archaeology as a science and, on the other, to fix some of the initial gaps and inconsistencies in the original program, prompted by the critique. Of the original three authors of *Explanation in Archaeology*, it was Steven LeBlanc who led the counter-charge, both in his "Two Points of Logic" paper (1973) and chiefly in a joint paper with Dwight Read (Read & LeBlanc 1978). In the latter, they admit that "the covering law model, by itself, is inadequate as a paradigm for what can be termed an intuitively satisfactory explanation" (ibid.: 307–308). In short, the reason was that the CL was considered to be too focused on the *form* of an explanation and did not take into account the actual *content* of hypotheses. One important element of the content relates to the causal processes involved in a law-like generalization as opposed to its purely formal structure. For example, the law-like generalization 'All Swans are white' entails certain formal or logical consequences, but to be a real empirical law as opposed to a purely logical one, it must be underpinned by causal reason such as Darwinian selection (see Read & LeBlanc 1978: 310). Formally, 'all swans are white' is identical to 'all swans are blue'; empirically, however, only one is relevant. This critique of formalism is ironic given that it was precisely this issue that Morgan had critiqued them for and which they originally denied (see Watson et al. 1974).

Despite this, Read and LeBlanc still regarded the covering-law model as a necessary component of explanation, once the issue of content has been properly acknowledged. Moreover, for the same reason, they rejected Salmon's argument for statistical laws; although they admit most empirical regularities in archaeology will be statistical, to explain them requires their subsumption to a universal (i.e. non-statistical) law, since only these can properly deal with causality (ibid.: 311). In ending their paper, they highlight what they see as one of the chief goals for future work: theory-building, which they illustrated in an appendix by Read who developed a model relating population size to habitation area. It was this aspect of theory-building that also seemed to take up most of the attention from commentators on their piece, including Morgan and Salmon, although the issues of covering laws and testing cropped up in a subsequent comment and response (Read & LeBlanc 1979; Stickel 1979).

Although much of the initial energy of debate focused on the covering-law model, it is the critique of the hypothetico-deductive model of inference that has arguably had the greater lasting impact for archaeology. Merilee Salmon first attacked the use of the HD model of inference in her rebuttal of LeBlanc's attempt to shore up gaps in the discussion of this issue from the co-authored 1971 book. In his "Two Points of Logic" (1973), LeBlanc had proposed several criteria for the strength of a confirmation, two of which were most important: the *number* of instances where a law was found to be confirmed (i.e. not falsified) and the *independence* of each confirmed instance. In the case of the former, Salmon argued that one is clearly back in the territory of induction and its attendant problem – how many instances is enough? (Salmon 1975; also see Salmon 1976: 377) Moreover, she criticized the rather naïve notion that any hypothesis in archaeology is so simple that it does not incorporate multiple auxiliary hypotheses or implicit background assumptions, and so even if a hypothesis is falsified, it may in fact be one of the auxiliary hypotheses that is to blame (Salmon 1975: 460; 1976: 378). Regarding the issue of independence, Salmon argued that this was a qualitative issue not a logical one as it required familiarity with the data to enable an assessment of what constituted a relevant level of diversity or variety. Testing a law which purports to have universal applicability through numerous cases all drawn from the same cultural and linguistic region fulfils the criteria of logical independence but not data diversity (ibid.: 461).

Salmon's critique ultimately rested on the recognition that testing is dependent on induction, not deduction as it had been portrayed by LeBlanc and other New Archaeologists. In a later paper, she sums this up well:

> All scientific knowledge about the past, the future, the unobserved in general, is based on induction … Deductive reasoning is employed … but its role is a very limited one. It can protect us from contradiction but not from error. It can guarantee consistency but not truth.
>
> *(Salmon 1976: 377)*

For Salmon, there were two primary forms of induction: by enumeration and by analogy. Induction by enumeration proceeded by generalizing from multiple instances (e.g. in excavated examples of Neolithic pottery from a particular region, the vessels are all coil-built, therefore all Neolithic pottery from this region is coil-built), whereas induction by analogy works by extrapolating on the basis of similarities between two things (e.g. two stone implements look the same; one was used as an arrowhead and so the other probably was too). Both are ampliative – that is, they say more than is contained in their initial premises or observations and hence are inductive (Salmon 1976:

376–377). However, what Salmon adds to this is also the probabilistic nature of any inductive inference – *probably* all Neolithic pottery is coil-built, *probably* this stone tool was used as an arrowhead. But it is a probability of a very specific kind: one which attempts to assess the *prior plausibility* of any hypothesis, a probability which can only be effectively gauged in the presence of alternative or competing hypotheses.

The issue of multiple or alternative hypotheses had rarely been raised by the New Archaeologists up to this point (but see Hill 1972), but essentially the HD method gives no basis of discriminating between two hypotheses, both of which might be confirmed by the same test data but which nonetheless give contradictory explanations for that data. It is related to the similar problem of equifinality, where the same effect could be the product of quite different causes. For example, a scatter of potsherds on a floor could have resulted from accidental drop or deliberate smashing – the same data could be used to confirm two very different explanations. What Salmon argued is that we need to assess which of these two explanations has greater prior probability (and thus plausibility) and to do this, required drawing in other relevant data about the context in which these sherds were found – the type of floor or room, the type of site and our prior knowledge about the society involved. In her later book, she even draws on a Bayesian approach to show how one might even quantify such prior probabilities, though she also admits this is not essential (Salmon 1982a: 51–56). In short, relevance becomes one of the key qualifiers for any method of confirmation and as such, reveals the limitations of any model of explanation which is based solely on formal structures of logic or reasoning. Substantive issues of content matter as much as formal issues of logic when assessing the validity of an inference, a point which is underlined by recognizing the close link between explanation and causality (see W. Salmon 1982). Any explanation which purports to invoke causality will always go beyond pure logic or formal structures of reasoning, a point made by David Hume in the eighteenth century.

Merilee Salmon's views were brought together in her book *Philosophy and Archaeology* (1982a), which provides a very readable and extended discussion of most of the key issues discussed by archaeologists in the 1970s and is arguably the culmination of her contribution to epistemological issues in archaeology. Her subsequent work connected to archaeology has generally been less engaged and includes elaborations of earlier statements (e.g. Salmon 1982b) or attempts to deal with the implications of postprocessualism (Salmon 1992; 1993). However, her earlier work did have an impact on archaeologists. Some grudgingly acknowledged the inductive nature of confirmation while others embraced the larger implications of Salmon's critique. Among the former was Steven LeBlanc who, as we saw in a paper with Dwight Read (Read & LeBlanc 1978), acknowledged the problems around the inductive nature of confirmation, citing many of the same issues as Salmon. It is perhaps telling, though, that he did not cite her work, but rather that of Mary Hesse (1974), another philosopher of science (one who later had a brush with archaeology (Hesse 1995) but who at this time was not involved in any of the archaeological debates).

Among those more positive to Salmon was Bruce Smith who focused on the exposed inadequacies of the HD method of confirmation as discussed by Salmon, and proposed an alternative, the hypothetico-analog (HA) method, drawn – as Salmon had done – from the work of Salmon's husband, Wesley Salmon (Smith 1977). The HA method essentially encapsulates the same position as that of Merilee Salmon, specifically arguing that the problem is not so much confirming any given hypothesis as finding which hypothesis is the most plausible (Smith 1977: 603–604). Thus Smith endorses the function of prior plausibility and the need for multiple working hypotheses, from which one generates testable outcomes – but using induction, not deduction. Smith also highlighted the critical component of bridging arguments which link any hypothesis to its test implications, offering a list of five criteria by which the relative strengths of each hypothesis could be assessed in relation to test data.

The question of bridging arguments became the primary focus of another archaeologist, Alan Sullivan. In particular, he highlighted the distinction between data or evidence on the one hand and archaeological observations of material remains on the other (Sullivan 1978). To use such observations as data or evidence entails important theoretical considerations around formation processes, and thus a Binfordian programme of middle-range theory or Schiffer's behavioural archaeology acted as critical elements of such bridging arguments. Although formation theory occupies the core of Sullivan's discussion, interestingly he frames the whole issue more broadly in terms of information transmission and thus situates it in relation to David Clarke's approach which identified different theories for dealing with different stages in information transmission such as formation, recovery and analysis (Clarke 1973).

What ultimately emerges from these critiques of the HD model of archaeological inference is that assessing the validity of an interpretation cannot be separated from the conditions of its generation. That is, the logic of discovery and logic of justification were intertwined through the issue of relevance or what Salmon called prior plausibility. Once this distinction started to crumble, so did the whole edifice of positivism. This was to take a new twist as Thomas Kuhn's philosophy of science and the paradigm concept entered archaeological discussion, making the issue of theory-ladenness the central topic of concern during the 1980s as archaeologists switched their focus from theory-testing to theory-building. However, before I pick up this thread, we need to situate this against a set of parallel developments in British archaeology, specifically the emergence of postprocessualism and its adherence to a different view of explanation: interpretation.

## Interpretation and hermeneutics

In Britain the response to these developments in North America was divided between an aversion to the jargon of 'science' and heavy use of statistics on the one hand (e.g. Hawkes 1968; Hogarth 1972) and on the other a more welcoming attitude (Clarke 1972a, 1973, 1978). Jacquetta Hawkes's famous defence of archaeology as a humanist discipline against the wave of scientism flooding the shores of England reveals the persistence of the view of archaeology as history in Britain (in the Collingwoodian sense, not the North American sense):

> The greatest danger in the narrow scientific outlook is the assumption that because analytical and statistical methods cannot properly be applied to values that most differentiate man from the other animals, those values must be ignored. Only that counts that can be counted.
>
> *(Hawkes 1968: 259)*

Many British archaeologists of the 1960s and 1970s echoed Hawkes's views. Glyn Daniel approvingly cites her paper in his revised history of archaeology, linking the scientism of the New Archaeology to a new antiquarianism by which he meant an obsession with data collection and data crunching epitomized by the increasing use of statistics (Daniel 1975: 371). Even Bruce Trigger in Canada, though not opposed to the idea of laws of cultural development, saw archaeology as better suited to a more particularizing science (Trigger 1970; see Watson 1973 for further a rebuttal of these views).

In this regard, I think one should point to the fact that Watson et al. do make a distinction in the preface to their 1971 book between scientific and humanist archaeologies, being explicit that their work is not intended to collapse this distinction but rather just focus on one side of it:

> Further the separation between anthropological archeology on the one hand, and classical and humanistically oriented archeology on the other, is almost universally accepted. The purposes and objectives of classical archaeologists and art historians have traditionally been different from those of archaeologists or prehistorians who have been trained in anthropology. It is only the latter archaeologists who consider themselves to be social scientists, rather than historians, and it is primarily this group with whom we are concerned.
>
> *(Watson et al. 1971: ix)*

Watson et al. spend no further time discussing the distinction between the two archaeologies, and yet perhaps it is precisely this failure which may have caused so much misunderstanding – on both sides. Trigger's discussion (1970) of nomothetic versus ideographic science is tied up with this distinction, although Watson et al. treat both as types of science and thus fail to see this. For those in Britain, what was at stake was the very definition of *any* archaeology as a science (also see Bayard 1969).

However, there was at least one British archaeologist who clearly was out of step with his colleagues: David Clarke. Clarke is interesting because, on the one hand, he was very sympathetic to many of the ideas emerging from the States and especially the role of systems theory. However, he was quite opposed to the way New Archaeologists had adopted the Hempelian DN model, because it simply assumed that a philosophical model developed on the natural sciences ought to be applicable to a social science like archaeology – or indeed even the life sciences (Clarke 1972b). In his review of Watson et al.'s 1971 book on explanation, he considered it an error of extrapolation which no philosopher of science would condone. Archaeology is not like physics, and models of explanation cannot be imported from one to the other without great confusion ensuing. Not that Clark was averse to generalization; rather the law-like nature of the DN model was simply inapplicable to a social science such as archaeology, where generalizations were more probabilistic. Clarke, in fact, was a great believer in each discipline developing its own specific model of explanation, even if external sources could be used to aid such development. His own multi-staged approach to archaeological theory was an attempt to do just this (Clarke 1973).

Clarke was also critical of the HD method of inference. In his major work, *Analytical Archaeology*, he "follows Bacon's conception of the necessary development of scientific theory by 'anticipations, rash and premature'" (Clarke 1978: xvi). Clarke explicitly rejected the deductive view coming out of North America, arguing that "most archaeological propositions are made by inference and induction rather than by classic deduction" (Clarke 1978: 16). Even though Clarke admits the generation of hypotheses, these are induced rather than deduced. In many ways, then, despite his ontological break with the British tradition of archaeology through his adoption of systems theory, epistemologically he continued this tradition of invoking Bacon and induction as a role model.

The reaction by other English archaeologists to Clarke's work is interesting; many, for example, found his language and jargon highly alienating (e.g. see Daniel 1973, editorial), as they did for the New Archaeology. Christopher Hawkes, in responding to Clarke's work, also laments his language, calling it elitist (Hawkes 1973: 176). Reading Hawkes's commentary, however, there is a clear sense of him struggling to have anything to say; every criticism is softened by an expression of deeper sympathy and, at the end of the day, one senses that, for Hawkes, their common goals and ambitions override the differences – although maybe he was just being polite. Indeed, Hawkes deflects the whole issue away from persons to ideas, raising the pitfalls for an archaeology which clings to outdated concepts such as the equation of archaeology with prehistory and the meaning behind the culture concept. For Hawkes, these are the true 'dinosaurs' of archaeology, not people – such as himself, no doubt.

It is difficult to know the impact Clarke would have had on the discipline in Britain if he had not died so young, aged just 38 (see papers in Malone & Stoddart 1998). But one of his contemporaries, Colin Renfrew, very much held the banner for processual archaeology in Britain from the late 1970s onwards and his view of an archaeological epistemology was presented at the Theoretical Archaeology Group (TAG) conference in Southampton in 1980 (Renfrew et al. 1982). Although Renfrew considered that archaeology was now in a 'postinductive era', his discussion of explanation in archaeology largely invoked Clarke's 'typological' approach where a number of different '-isms' or explanatory paradigms were outlined (Renfrew 1982a; also see 1982b). Renfrew suggested that there was a mismatch between the prescriptive programmes of explanation (such as the cover-ing-law model) and what archaeologists actually did, and this led him to conclude, in a preliminary manner, that explanations in practice relate more to whether archaeologists were attempting to explain *specific* events (such as the Classic Maya Collapse) or *classes* of events (such as the origins of agriculture).

One might note the irony of Renfrew adopting an inductive approach to analyse explanation in archaeology in an ostensibly 'postinductive era', but of more significance is his concluding remarks on two basic forms of explanation: "It must simply be recog-nized that there are two paths here – one towards the general and hence the compara-tive; another towards the specific analysis of context and hence ultimately to the unique" (Renfrew 1982a: 21). Renfrew was explicit that his interests lay with the former, while the latter he labelled as "hermeneutic" explanations (ibid.). Although there were no representatives of this hermeneutic approach in the published volume, the tone of other papers clearly reflects the presence of this other epistemology, as a "specter haunting Cambridge" (Gellner 1982: 97). Of course, this was the emergence of what became known as postprocessual archaeology, centred on Ian Hodder who was a student of Clarke and initially worked within a similar framework (e.g. Hodder 1978). The same year as the Southampton volume came out – 1982 – saw the publication of both *Symbols in Action* and *Symbolic and Structuralist Archaeology* which outlined the agenda of this new archaeology (Hodder 1982a, 1982b).

In a key early statement on his theoretical position, Hodder explicitly made links between his view of archaeology as a 'cultural science' and the British tradition as exemplified in Childe, Clark, Daniel and Piggott who stressed archaeology as a histor-ical and humanist discipline (Hodder 1982c; but for his retrospective on this issue, see Hodder 2008: 31). Hodder also highlighted the problems these earlier archaeologists faced when attempting to interpret past ideas and beliefs through Hawkes's ladder of inference but argued they lacked the necessary theory to make these inferences work – theory such as structuralism (among others) could provide. However, he did not really address more specific epistemological issues until a couple of years later where he cri-tiqued the presumption that theories can be tested against the data (Hodder 1984, 1986). Hodder takes as his starting point the recursive relation between theory and data as diagrammed by Renfrew (1982b) and argues that data are never independent of theory in such a way as to permit the data to act as a test of any interpretation:

> To summarise, the dilemma apparent for archaeologists is that there is a widespread desire for science and objective tests, a fear of speculation and the subjective, and yet we want to say something about the past. In particular, in recent years it has become clear that if we want to say anything interesting about the past, we must include statements about prehistoric ideas. Yet to say anything about the past, and about past ideas, involves moving beyond the data to interpret them, and there can be no testing of these interpretations because the data themselves are formulated within and are part of the same argument as the theories. Speculation and the subjective are therefore part of the 'scientific' process.
>
> *(Hodder 1984: 28)*

Hodder goes on to argue that this result is only a problem if one assumes that science should be completely objective and separate from the social context in which it is conducted – which, for him and many others, it was not.

Now Hodder's recognition of the theory-dependence of data is not really new, as should be clear from earlier discussion on the issue. What is new is how he uses it to critique the idea of testing, but especially Binford's claim for middle-range theory as a way to safeguard some independence between data and theory (Hodder 1986: 16). Nonetheless, Hodder's critique has itself been critiqued as missing an important difference between paradigm-dependence and inferential circularity. More on this in a moment. But for Hodder, there were other ways to frame this whole discussion – ways which already existed in the British tradition of archaeology based on Collingwood's views of history. In *Reading the Past*, Hodder spends several pages reviving the Collingwood version of Baconian method:

> The 're-living' of the past is achieved by the method of question and answer. One cannot sit back and observe the data; they must be brought into action by asking questions – why should anyone want to erect a building like that, what was the purpose of the shape of this ditch, why is this wall made of turf and that of stone? ... The response to such questions is dependent on all the data available ... but also on historical imagination, something which is very much affected by our knowledge and understanding of the present.
>
> *(Hodder 1986:94–95)*

Hodder then goes on to argue that justification of any interpretation is based on both internal coherence of an argument and correspondence with data, which are still real and tangible, even if they can never be defined as objective in any absolute sense. Hodder's use of Collingwood here is inevitable given his commitment to an archaeology which argues that to understand past material culture, we need to understand something of the mindset of the people who made and used it. At the same time, Hodder grew dissatisfied with this Collingwoodian epistemology and began to dig deeper into the continental tradition of historical interpretation for a more sophisticated position, specifically the philosophical field of hermeneutics (see below).

Although Renfrew had alluded to a hermeneutic form of explanation as distinct from a generalizing mode (see above; Renfrew 1982a), the first extensive discussion of hermeneutics in archaeology came with Hodder's students, Michael Shanks and Christopher Tilley, who devoted a chapter on hermeneutics and interpretation in their *Re-Constructing Archaeology* (1987), where they affirm its role as an alternative to positivism and explanation. They argue that interpretation moves in a circular or spiral fashion in that archaeologists always bring certain assumptions or analogies from other contexts into their understanding of archaeological data, and it is through a dialectical interplay between data and pre-conceptions about that data, that interpretation develops and moves forward (Shanks & Tilley 1987: 104–105). Drawing on the work of Gadamer (1975, 1977), they emphasized the interpretive basis to human experience, anticipating subsequent articulations by Bjørnar Olsen and Julian Thomas.

In the early 1990s, the Norwegian archaeologist Bjørnar Olsen with Harald Johnsen published an important paper addressing the lack of more sustained discussion on hermeneutics, specifically focusing on Hodder's contextual archaeology (Johnsen & Olsen 1992). They highlighted many of the parallels between Hodder's theory and hermeneutics, especially the emphasis on an 'inner' understanding of material culture, but they also criticized what they saw as an outdated conception of meaning, and pointed out inconsistencies and contradictions within Hodder's writings. In ending, they argued for the need to engage with more recent and theoretically sophisticated hermeneutic writings, singling out Gadamer as the key figure. They argued that archaeology needs to appreciate better the dialectical relation between past and present so that our study of the past should act back on our perception of ourselves and that modern hermeneutic philosophy can provide a stronger basis for understanding the production of archaeological knowledge. Their paper was published at one of those ironic moments, for, after it had been written but before it was published, Hodder, as if anticipating this critique, published a paper in the same journal addressing exactly these concerns (Hodder 1991). In a postscript, Johnsen and Olsen acknowledge this, and while unable to comment at length, they do question Hodder's characterization of hermeneutics as a method as opposed to a philosophical theory about human existence, an aspect taken up later by Julian Thomas (2004a).

Hodder's paper 'Interpretive Archaeology and Its Role' engaged with the hermeneutic tradition in a more direct and explicit manner than previously (Hodder 1991). In part, this was driven by Hodder's need to distance himself and his brand of postprocessualism from the excesses of post-structuralist archaeology (e.g. Bapty and Yates 1990) which many critics from within the processual core were lambasting as a descent into pure relativism, crippling archaeology from making any kind of authoritative statements about the past. For Hodder, the recent hermeneutic philosophy of Gadamer and others provided a way to counter these criticisms, avoiding, as he saw it, the excesses of both positivism and post-structuralism. Archaeological data thus provided a *guarded objectivity* insofar as they represent a reality partially independent of our interpretation and can resist as much as agree with such interpretations. At the same time, our interpretation of such data is not guided by external methods of validation, but needs to adhere to a principle of *internal* coherence between any particular part and the whole – which includes seeing archaeological remains as the product of human intentionality and agency (see Hodder 1992 for a classic case study illustrating this approach; also Hodder 1999). These are clearly modified versions of his emphasis on coherence and correspondence in *Reading the Past*. Additionally, though, interpretation should also be *reflexive* and *critical* of the wider set of background assumptions and traditions within which archaeologists make their interpretations. These three facets of interpretive archaeology – objectivity, coherence and reflexivity – combined to make a powerful alternative to the processual account of explanation.

Hodder's notion of interpretation was drawn from the concept of the hermeneutic circle, conceived on the lines of a part–whole relation in terms of textual
interpretation. Parts can be anything from words to text sections (translated into
artefacts and ditch sections, for instance), while wholes can be anything from sentences to a language (e.g. social practices). The circle describes the necessary
working back and forth between the two so that an accurate understanding of
meaning can be achieved. Thus, to understand an unusual word in an ancient text
may require not only assessing it in the context of its sentence, but also considering
how the word is used in other sentences, and how this usage might differ between
different authors, literary traditions and even time periods. It is an ever-widening
circle, but one that is also always a back and forth between part and whole.
Expressed this way, it describes a method of interpretation and it was this part–
whole relation that Hodder adopted in his uptake of hermeneutics and which he
illustrated so clearly in his interpretation of a Neolithic enclosure (Hodder 1992,
1999: 32–40). In this case study, he narrates how his interpretation of the excavation changed over seasons as it shifted back and forth between the evidence and his
expectations based on prior knowledge of such sites. He describes this process not as a
circle but a spiral, to emphasize that the interpretive process is always forward moving,
not locked as in a closed loop, a point also made earlier by Shanks and Tilley (1987:
104). At the same time, however, in the process it is not only the interpretation of the
site that has changed, but also the general background knowledge about such sites, and
perhaps the Neolithic in general. This is why Hodder (and others) often also describe
the process also as a *dialectic*, because in moving back and forth between part and
whole, *both* are transformed in the process.

During the 1990s, Hodder's contextual archaeology thus morphed into an
interpretive archaeology; indeed, one might talk more generally of an *interpretive
turn* within postprocessualism during the last decade of the twentieth century. Two
volumes appeared making explicit reference to this development: one called *Interpreting Archaeology* (Hodder et al. 1995) and the other called *Interpretative Archaeology*
(Tilley 1993). Shanks and Hodder suggested that the label 'interpretive archaeologies' supersedes postprocessual archaeology as a way of avoiding polarization in
debate. The concept of interpretation was elaborated further in both volumes, in
similar and yet different ways. Ironically, though, neither volume gave much
explicit attention to hermeneutics, but rather remained closer to a mix of post-
structuralist and Marxist theory.

In one volume, Shanks and Hodder defined interpretation as the understanding
of meaning; this process of understanding, they emphasized, is a dialogue in which
both sides (the archaeological record and the archaeologist) are active (Shanks &
Hodder 1995). As a process, it is also always ongoing; it never reaches a conclusion
or closure. Indeed, even those statements which appear factual or uncontroversial
are still interpretations; only the interpretive aspect has been black-boxed. This in
itself is necessary to enable interpretation to move forward, but at the same time
such statements are potentially open to revision, like any other interpretation. In
the other volume, however, Tilley took quite a different view. Tilley gave a broad

definition of interpretation as an activity undertaken only in situations where were are unsure, where something is not immediately obvious (Tilley 1993). If one sees a figurine of a frog, one does not *interpret* it as a frog – it is just perceived directly as a frog. If the figurine exhibits an ambiguous form, on the other hand, we might say it looks like a frog to me, and in that case we are interpreting the object. For Tilley, this is why interpretation always remains open to change, lacking finality, and its 'truth' remains dependent on agreement between people rather than on the evidence – in other words, the figurine is a frog if we *all* interpret it as a frog.

Tilley's volume occupies an important moment within postprocessual archaeology, subtly marking the transition from post-structuralism to phenomenology as a guiding philosophy for its two leading contributors – Tilley himself and Julian Thomas. In many ways, it also marks the end of explicit discussion on interpretation within post-processual archaeology; though short-lived, the series of papers and volumes mentioned here from the first half the 1990s effectively comprise most of what has been written on interpretation in archaeology in relation to the hermeneutic tradition. The fact that little has been written since is perhaps largely due to the fact that epistemic issues in archaeological theory in general have greatly diminished in importance, at least for those working out of the postprocessual tradition. For others, especially in North America, however, a chance was seen to start building bridges by suggesting that perhaps the processualist and postprocessualist epistemic positions were not as different as they had been portrayed. This is an issue I will come to in a later section.

However, one of the points made by Johnsen and Olsen in their review of hermeneutics and Hodder's version of it is that interpretation is not simply an epistemological concept about the method of knowledge acquisition; it is an ontological concept defining something fundamental about human beings. This was taken from Gadamer's philosophical hermeneutics which blended Heidegger's phenomenology with the hermeneutic tradition. For Gadamer, Heidegger marks a turning point in the theory of interpretation, transforming the hermeneutic circle from a methodological concept to a metaphysical or ontological one. In *Being and Time* (1962), Heidegger described the process of interpretation in terms of the relation between fore-understanding and understanding, where fore-understanding represents our implicit way of seeing the world inherited from the particular historical tradition we were raised in. In one sense, Heidegger *temporalized* the hermeneutic circle – instead of being about the part–whole relation of words to texts, it became a past/future to present temporal relation between fore-understanding/ expectation and interpretation. Gadamer adopted this stance in his key work *Truth and Method*, using the term 'prejudice' for this fore-understanding (Gadamer 1975).

Julian Thomas developed this ontological view of the hermeneutic circle in archaeology, citing Gadamer who characterizes humans as *interpreting beings* (Thomas 2004a: 24). For Thomas, interpretation is thus something we are always doing and it applies to all experience; thus, in Tilley's example cited earlier, when we unhesitatingly see the figurine as a frog, this is just as much an interpretation as when we consciously decide it is a frog. All acts of experience are enframed within a pre-understanding: we always see things *as* something; there can be no raw, unprocessed or uninterpreted experience. Even if we are uncertain it is a frog, we at least see it *as* a figurine. For Thomas, this aspect of human existence – what Heidegger called the as-structure – contradicts Hodder's notion of even a partial or guarded objectivity. Quoting Gadamer, Thomas argues that interpretation is a circle we cannot escape; however, it is not necessarily a vicious circle. While implicit pre-understanding always informs any experience, any explicit act of interpretation can also alter that pre-understanding and thus alter our experience of the world. This is a basic issue of contention with the hermeneutic circle; some see it as a vicious circle, allowing no grounding in any stable or solid point; it is another version of the post-structuralist play of endless difference. However, the position taken by Gadamer and Thomas is that the circle actually *enables* understanding or interpretation in the first place.

It is important to stress that this turn to hermeneutics initially only elevated the increasing tension between processualism which saw archaeology as a science, and postprocessualism which saw archaeology closer to history. It is a divide that had grown since the 1960s, especially as many New Archaeologists started to denigrate and misrepresent what history was, almost equating it with description devoid of interpretation (see Trigger 1970 for a very astute, contemporary discussion of this). However, the divide of the 1980s hinged on ontological rather than epistemic grounds. This is because, with hermeneutics, a very fundamental division was made between the human and natural sciences in terms of their intellectual approach methods. This is epitomized in the distinction between interpretation (*verstehen*) which lies at the core of the human sciences (*Geisteswissenschaften*) and explanation (*erklären*) as exemplified in the natural sciences (*Naturwissenschaften*). This difference is predicated not so much on method as the object of study; for Dilthey, who largely provided the philosophical foundation for hermeneutics in the early twentieth century, the methods of natural science and human science operated under very similar logical processes of induction, deduction, generalization and comparison (Rickman, in Dilthey 1976: 13). The difference lay in how these processes were operationalized. With explanation, the particular was subsumed under the general (i.e. what later became known as a covering-law model), while, with interpretation, particulars were related together in the form of complex wholes but, in doing so, still drew on generalizations to make these connections. The different methods were, however, largely dictated by the different nature of the objects of study – nature or the material world in one case, and mind or culture in the other. Thus interpretation was further defined as a form of knowledge which emerges from a first-person or internal perspective on the world – that is, the world as seen from a human being's point of view as they are immersed in a world constituted by meaning and value. Such a first-person/internal perspective underlined the fact that we can understand other people because we are one of them. In contrast, explanation involved a third-person or external perspective. Here, one understands trees or rocks in a different way; because we are not trees or rocks, we can only ever understand them from an external or outsider's point of view.

Although it was Dilthey who developed this concept of interpretation, it was popularized by the sociologist Max Weber in the early twentieth century and used to promote an interpretive sociology which was to contest the French positivist sociology of Comte and Durkheim. The French sociological tradition, unlike the German, adopted a much less divided view on the relation between the natural and social sciences, seeing them more as sharing a similar methodology and philosophy. However, the German hermeneutic tradition, especially after Weber, impacted the way sociologists and anthropologists saw their disciplines, and by the middle of the twentieth century, many scholars within the social sciences in the Anglophone tradition increasingly reflected on the special character of their methods and forms of knowledge. One of the earliest studies was Peter Winch's investigation into the nature of social science, linking Weber to Wittgenstein and which had a massive impact on subsequent social theory (Winch 1958). It provided the philosophical foundations to the interpretive turn in many of the social sciences such as anthropology represented in the work of Clifford Geertz from the 1970s and archaeology through Ian Hodder from the 1980s.

In adopting hermeneutics and the concept of interpretation, then, the contrast with the concept of explanation carried connotations of two very different ways of acquiring knowledge, ones which entailed ontological as well as epistemological differences. How well these ontological differences were appreciated is hard to assess, but there is a common ontological thread that runs from Dilthey to Heidegger and Gadamer, which also explains the close connection between hermeneutics and phenomenology, a connection which one also sees developed in archaeology through the work of Bjørnar Olsen, Christopher Tilley and Julian Thomas. This ontological dimension was largely eclipsed in subsequent attempts to reconcile hermeneutics with post-Kuhnian philosophies of science (e.g. Kosso 1991; also see below). Indeed, for the most part, the wider epistemological debates in the 1990s still revolved around the tense poles of positivism and relativism, for it was the relativist implications of postprocessualism that seemed to cause most concern in the wider archaeological community. The connection between hermeneutics, which stressed the socially embedded nature of understanding, and post-positivist philosophies of science, especially Kuhn's concept of paradigms, was not missed by archaeologists. Although the concept of paradigm was much more widely used by processualists than postprocessualists, the spectre of relativism was an issue everyone recognized, regardless of philosophical terminology. It is this story I now want to pick up.

## Theory-ladenness, paradigm-dependence and relativism

The concept of paradigm as a way to characterize scientific practice was used by Thomas Kuhn in his seminal book *The Structure of Scientific Revolutions*, first published in 1962 (Kuhn 1970). The book was a critique of a view of science that presented the development of scientific knowledge as a series of cumulative and progressive improvements; in contrast, Kuhn suggested that science rather developed discontinuously through paradigm shifts, where paradigms represented incommensurable conceptual frameworks within which scientists worked. As a model for characterizing developments within academic disciplines, it became very popular, and not just in archaeology. However, it did come at a very timely moment, at least in North America when the New Archaeology was proclaiming a major theoretical and methodological advance for the discipline. One of the earliest papers to link the New Archaeology to Kuhn's model of a paradigm shift was Robert McC. Adams's paper in the journal *Science* from 1968, but this was followed by many others, notably Martin (1971), Leone (1972) and Zubrow (1973), while in the UK David Clarke (1972a) provided yet another perspective on the applicability of Kuhn's work to archaeology. All of these authors translate the concept of paradigm into archaeology slightly differently, and, in particular, both Leone and Clarke discuss the existence of multiple paradigms in archaeology existing at that time.

What is interesting is that all these papers were published at the height of debates on explanation and confirmation, yet seemed to be strangely disconnected from them. I have previously suggested that the reason for this lies in the fact that the paradigm concept in the 1970s was largely used historiographically rather than epistemologically (Lucas 2017). Thus, in Kuhn's work, the paradigm concept functions in two related yet still distinct ways: one concerns its historiographic function as a way to mark disciplinary development (i.e. paradigm shifts and revolutions), the other its epistemological function as a way to understand how scientific knowledge is constructed (i.e. paradigm-dependence). Even though these two functions are closely connected, it is also quite clear that it was the first function that appealed mostly to archaeologists, especially as a rhetorical device to authorize the claims of New Archaeology. Conversely, while Kuhn's model of science was adopted historiographically, almost none of the New Archaeologists adopted its epistemology. This is, of course, the deep irony and one of various contradictions found in the philosophy of the New Archaeology, as others had already observed (Wylie 2002: 20–21; Gibbon 1989: 94).

It was mainly David Clarke and later Lewis Binford who recognized the epistemic function of paradigms. Thus Clarke explicitly acknowledged the theory-laded nature of facts: "all observations, all perceived facts, depend on the observer, his frame of reference and personal idiosyncrasies" (Clarke 1972a: 14). Indeed, Clarke was one of the few archaeologists to adopt a sense of Kuhn's paradigms as a conceptual framework which directed the nature of archaeological investigation and meshed well with Clarke's use of the concept of models (Clarke 1972a). Thus he argued that there were several models or paradigms operative in archaeology at that point in time including morphological (i.e. typological), anthropological, ecological and geographical. Similarly, although Binford critiqued the vocabulary of the paradigm, it was chiefly its historiographic function he disliked (but see his earlier writings for a more receptive view, e.g. Binford 1972). Thus, in the 1980s, he began to acknowledge the theory-dependent nature of data using Kuhn's concept of the paradigm: "Archaeological knowledge of the past is totally dependent upon the meanings which archaeologists give to observations on the archaeological record. Thus, archaeologically justified views of the past are dependent upon paradigmatic views regarding the significance of archaeological observations" (Binford & Sabloff 1982: 149).

At the same time, Binford was especially wary of the dangers of paradigm-dependence in leading archaeologists down a path of relativism – particularly in the context of an emerging postprocessualism from Britain where it was commonly perceived that archaeologists were dancing on a razor's edge of interpretive nihilism (Watson & Fotiadis 1990; see below). Indeed, it was because of this threat that Binford regarded middle-range theory as so essential as it was the key to breaking the epistemological vicious circle raised by the paradigm concept: using the independence of non-archaeological contexts to test archaeological interpretation (ibid.; also see Binford 1982). Thus Binford argued that even though middle-range research was conducted within its own paradigms, what mattered is that these were different from those framing archaeological study. As an example, he gave the relation between radiocarbon dating and archaeological studies on agricultural intensification: both draw on paradigms which frame their respective data, but the theory behind radiocarbon decay is effectively independent from the theories of agricultural intensification (Binford 1982: 134–135). In short, Binford argued that paradigm-dependence was a red herring, a bogeyman used to justify relativism and strip archaeology of any basis of accountability (Binford 1987, 1989).

Binford's rebuttal was in many ways quite germane, and in fact similar attempts to mediate between the issue of theory-ladenness and objectivity were swiftly taken up by a number scholars in the late 1980s and early 1990s, both philosophers and archaeologists. However, not everyone was that worried by the implications of Kuhn's work and in fact the core Hempelians, Watson, LeBlanc and Redman, published a revised version of their 1971 book essentially holding fast to the Hempelian programme, albeit modified in the light of critiques, notably from the Salmons (Watson et al. 1984). Thus, although they acknowledged Kuhn's work and the subjective element in all science, they upheld the distinction between the logic of discovery and justification, and argued that objectivity could still be guaranteed through testing (ibid.: 40). This is a position that increasingly became hard to maintain and the twilight positivism expressed in such work seemed to fade gradually into more general commitments to a critical and evaluative attitude (e.g. Watson 1986; Hill 1991).

In its place, more developed views became increasingly common towards the end of the 1980s, views that took the problems of paradigm-dependence much more seriously. As I have already related, part of the impetus to maintain some form of objectivity against the potential relativism of paradigm-dependence grew out of a simple acknowledgement that the conventional positivist account based on the hypothetico-deductive model of inference was simply inadequate. Questions of relevance and the connections between theory-building and theory-testing meant that 'subjective' factors could not be ignored. However, it was not simply the inadequacy of the HD method that caused the debate to shift in this way. It was also the fact that, in Britain, some archaeologists were embracing a view of knowledge that seemed to imply that any kind of objectivity was impossible. It was the discussions on the nature of interpretation by Hodder, Shanks and Tilley, and others, outlined in the last section, that seemed to imply a dangerous relativism to many (e.g. Watson & Fotiadis 1990; Bell 1991; Kohl 1993; Trigger 1989) and thus added to the incentive in the United States to redefine objectivity in ways that nonetheless incorporated the theory-laden nature of all data.

In 1988, the philosopher Marsha Hanen and archaeologist Jane Kelley offered a detailed analysis of the philosophy of science for archaeologists in a post-Kuhnian era in their book *Archaeology and the Methodology of Science* (Kelley & Hanen 1988). The book is a magisterial review of the issues that were central to archaeological debates on epistemology in the United States during the 1970s and adopted a qualified version of Kuhn's paradigm-dependence model. Accepting that archaeological interpretations are framed by consensual paradigms, they argued nonetheless that such paradigms were not all-enclosing but rather had gradations of consensus. They used the notion of a core system (CS) which comprised a central set of beliefs widely shared, while other beliefs that resided outside this core were more equivocal. They also explored in great detail various dimensions of the sociology of knowledge active in determining archaeological research such as nationalism and sexism, issues that others had already started to raise (e.g. Trigger 1980, 1984; Conkey & Spector 1984; Gero 1985). Offset against this, however, Hanen and Kelley were also keen to maintain some form of objectivity against a purely sociological account of archaeological knowledge, as, for instance, exemplified in the Edinburgh Strong Programme of the sociology of scientific knowledge (e.g. Bloor 1976). To achieve this, they adopted the model of inference to the best explanation as an alternative and more accurate depiction of how archaeologists reason (also see Hanen & Kelley 1989).

Inference to the best explanation (IBE) was explicitly used in contrast to the hypothetico-deductive model and essentially crystallizes the same issues raised by Salmon: the dependence on induction and the issue of multiple hypotheses. For Hanen and Kelley, IBE was essentially a process of eliminative induction which, ironically, brings us full circle back to Bacon – that is, ruling out competing interpretations to arrive at the best or most plausible. They, of course, did not develop IBE but rather drew on more recent developments within the philosophy of science and epistemology where the term had first been proposed by Harman (1965; see Lipton 1991 for the classic exposition). IBE has its problems, of course, which Hanen and Kelley openly acknowledge – especially the fact that sometimes one simply cannot determine which of two or more explanations best accounts for the data. Despite this, they felt it still captured closely the way archaeologists reason and also provided a tenable means to maintain some form of objectivity in a post-Kuhnian environment.

Another approach to the problem was offered by the archaeologist Guy Gibbon, who also gave an important review of the positivist model of explanation in archaeology and proposed a realist theory as a solution to the inadequacies of positivism (Gibbon 1989). Like Hanen and Kelley, Gibbon shared a commitment to objectivity, but his approach, which draws largely from the works of Roy

Bhaskar (1975, 1979), mostly focuses on the ontological conditions of knowledge and the positing, specifically, of hidden or underlying structures of reality behind the flux of the actual world. Gibbon's programme was, in the end, somewhat tangential to the issues that most other archaeologists were dealing with. Moreover, while Gibbon acknowledges the socially constructed nature of scientific knowledge, he never really offers a viable account of how to square this with a commitment to objectivity.

The most sophisticated accounts to deal with this problem in archaeology ultimately came from philosophers, specifically Alison Wylie but also Peter Kosso. It was Alison Wylie who emerged as the key voice of mediation in the 1980s and it is Wylie who remains today the most important philosopher engaged in sustained archaeological debate. Especially in two papers from the end of the 1980s, she laid out her signature arguments for a mitigated objectivity (Wylie 1989a, 1989b). In a paper addressing the interpretive dilemma of safe-but-trivial versus speculative-yet-interesting interpretations, she argues there is no safe option anymore in the wake of Kuhn's work. The real dilemma is to accept that all data is both theory-laden – yet not so laden that it cannot act as a brake on wild speculation (Wylie 1989a). Wylie's solution to this dilemma involves recognizing that the requisite tension comes not from between theory and data, but between different lines of theory-laden data. Drawing on a metaphor adopted by the philosopher Bernstein (who in turn took it from Peirce), archaeological inferences are not like linear chains of reasoning, but rather interwoven cables of multiple lines of reasoning which mutually strengthen (or weaken) the whole argument (Wylie 1989b).

Wylie's core argument has more or less remained unchanged since these papers, although it has been greatly elaborated upon and deepened (Wylie 2002) including in her most recent work (e.g. see Chapman & Wylie 2016), which I will address later in the chapter. However, perhaps the most important and innovative addition came when she injected contemporaneous work in feminist epistemology into her argument. Her 1992 paper on the interplay of evidential constraints is a landmark in this debate, since it directly engages with the issue of whether an avowedly positional epistemology linked to feminism can be objective (Wylie 1992a; also see Wylie 1996). She argues, in characteristic fashion, that the choice between objectivity and relativism is false, and that the relative independence of different theory–data couplets means that each can mutually act as a check on the other. Data is neither completely neutral nor completely constructed, but always moderated through its multiplicity. Thus feminism – through enhancing such multiplicity – ultimately makes archaeology more objective, not less. Wylie's arguments became very important, especially for other feminist archaeologists (e.g. Brumfiel 1996), but, more generally, her papers provided a common go-to model for many archaeologists, both processual and postprocessual.

Indeed, Wylie's generally conciliatory approach was to set the tone for a gradual rapprochement between processualism and postprocessualism over the 1990s – at least in epistemic terms. Another paper from 1992 speaks of red herrings and rhetorical positioning, as she recognized that both sides of the debate admitted theory-ladenness yet eschewed relativism (Wylie 1992b). For her, the problem lay not in any fundamental difference about knowledge production, but how they articulated (or not) their response to this tension between paradigm-dependence and objectivity. Against this, Wylie offered several specific suggestions which could act to create what she called a mitigated objectivity (ibid.: 276–279). The most important was perhaps the relative independence of different theories and data which she linked to the independence or 'disunity' of the sciences, since archaeology drew heavily on other sciences for much of its data construction (also see Wylie 2000).

Finally, one should mention the work of Peter Kosso, another philosopher active in archaeological issues during the 1990s. Kosso is perhaps best known among archaeologists for his argument which drew parallels between hermeneutics and middle-range theory, a point I will come to in a moment (Kosso 1991). However, his basic position on objectivity echoed Wylie in suggesting that the most important factor that guarantees objectivity is independence. Kosso, however, frames this rather differently, in terms of a distinction between evidential claims and accounting claims; the former refer to the particular lines of evidence used in an interpretation while the latter refer to what might be called supporting or background evidence for an interpretation. For Kosso, middle-range theory and hermeneutics both function in the same way, as accounting claims; for him, the critical measure of objectivity was that such accounting claims were independent of the evidential claims (Kosso 1991; also see Kosso 2001).

No doubt partly in response to such a reaction, the issues of relativism and objectivity were also reassessed by postprocessualists in Britain. Although Shanks and Tilley remained unapologetic about their stance and in fact argued that they had never embraced relativism, they did clarify their position in a later paper (Shanks & Tilley 1989, 1992), arguing for the role of mediated resistance by material culture to archaeological texts: "So the past is real, it did happen, it is not just our fiction, and can be used in and against the present, *in its difference*" (Shanks & Tilley 1992: 256). Hodder was even more extensive in his reassessment, acknowledging the importance of a guarded objectivity provided by the data (Hodder 1991), while in a later publication Shanks and Hodder together argue for a distinction between epistemic and judgemental relativism: accepting that knowledge is socially constructed does not entail that all knowledge claims are equally valid (Shanks & Hodder 1995).

However, it was perhaps the political implications of such relativism that stung postprocessualists the most, given that the political dimension of archaeology was a central facet of postprocessualism. The idea that a lack of objectivity could lead to fascism, that without an epistemological safeguard any version of the past is as good as another, was thrown back at postprocessualists relentlessly (Trigger 1989). Such claims prompted a joint response from archaeologists at the University of Lampeter in Wales in the late 1990s, at that time a creative haven for postprocessualists in Britain (Lampeter Archaeology Workshop (LAW) 1997). Included in the group were Michael Shanks, Cornelius Holtorf, Yannis Hamilakis, Mark Plucenniek, Sarah Tarlow, Michael Tierney and Bill Sillar. After all, it was not just archaeologists in the United States who felt threatened by the implied relativism of postprocessualism; many archaeologists in Britain were equally unsympathetic (e.g. Bintliff 1988, 1989; Renfrew 1989).

The response of the Lampeter group is interesting; at one level, they reassert relativism against objectivity, returning the charge of fascism against the authoritarianism of any position which claims objectivity and monolithic views of the past. At another level however, they qualify this relativism by characterizing it as pluralism rather than 'anything goes'; recognizing that there are various grounds on which to evaluate archaeological claims, but this variety still has constraints, repeating Shanks and Hodder's distinction of epistemic and judgemental relativism (LAW 1997: 169). Such constraints were both empirical but also socio-political. The commentaries that followed the paper – and indeed the individual statements by members of the group that followed the joint text – reveal a diversity of positions. Fundamentally, the core of the issue revolved around the distinction of relativism from pluralism; for the Lampeter group and indeed most of the discussants, pluralism was seen as a virtue in archaeology (also see Holtorf & Karlsson 2000). The problem was rather how to distinguish pluralism from relativism and, for many, the Lampeter group still did not seem to do this effectively, while they in turn suggested their critics were being too restrictive in their demands for such criteria.

It was in the wake of such debates and reassessments, as well as the reconciliations, that one sees the start of what could be seen as a tentative rapprochement between processual and postprocessual archaeologies – epistemologically speaking at least (e.g. see Preucel 1991; VanPool & VanPool 1999). However, a less charitable conclusion would be that people simply got tired of going round in circles and just agreed to disagree. Indeed, by the end of the 1990s, the heated debates on objectivity and relativism had all but petered out, resulting in a tacit acceptance of theoretical pluralism and an 'epistemic silence' by the turn of the millennium (Hegmon 2003: 230).

## Archaeological epistemology in the new millennium

Discussion of epistemological issues in archaeology since 2000 are certainly noticeable by their near absence, for reasons alluded to at the end of the last section. But this is not to suggest that no one has written on such topics, and in concluding this chapter, I want to briefly discuss three of most prominent of these: indigenous archaeology, neo-empiricism and evidential reasoning. For reasons that will become apparent, I will devote most attention to the last of these. Indigenous archaeology in many ways shares the strongest link to earlier discourses, which, in accentuating the value of pluralism by extending the debate outside of Western epistemologies, has forced archaeologists to consider the problem of epistemology yet again (Watkins 2000; Atalay 2006, 2012; Habu et al. 2008). However, since I covered this in the last chapter, I will not repeat myself here. In many ways, the chief strength of this stream has been to reinforce and expand the importance of pluralism to knowledge practices. The second stream, which I call neo-empiricism, is arguably the most original development and needs a little more discussion.

Neo-empiricism or empiricism 2.0 are terms used broadly to refer to a rethinking of the empirical within the wave of a 'return to things', also known as the new materialisms (Siapkas & Hillerdal 2015; Witmore 2014). Without trying to summarize this broader movement, the key aspect of neo-empiricism is that it tries to avoid the dichotomy of knowing subject and known object implicit in conventional empiricism or empiricism 1.0 (see Witmore 2015 for one of the clearest expositions). The roots of the neo-empiricist position are found in the work of science and technology studies which saw knowledge production as the work of multiple agents: trowels, GPS, archaeology professors, institutions, potsherds, and so on, seeing all as (potentially) equal actors in the constitution of knowledge rather than a monolithic bifurcation of epistemology into the archaeologist (knowing subject) and archaeological remains (known object). This distribution of epistemology on to multiple agents thus avoids the subject–object language of conventional empiricism. Certainly a great deal of important work has been done in archaeology along these lines, especially in the context of knowledge production in the field, as already discussed in Chapter 1. But through the lens of speculative realism, neo-empiricism has an added twist. It is not just humans knowing about potsherds, but potsherds also 'knowing' about the soil in which they sit, of the soil 'knowing' about the trowel which scrapes at its surface. Knowing, in fact, becomes a term for the way any agent comes to apprehend (or prehend, in the language of Whitehead) another (e.g. see Olsen et al. 2012; Edgeworth 2016).

This is undoubtedly a very different way to understand knowledge, offering what one might call a non-anthropocentric epistemology. But in reducing knowledge to a form of prehension, neo-empiricism also becomes a form of hyper-empiricism; our knowledge or understanding of things, of objects – in order to be faithful to them – has to remain as concrete as possible. We must never lose sight of the thing itself by wrapping it up in symbols, in meaning, in interpretation; for neo-empiricism, description remains the truest form of knowledge and this is borne out in their writing. At the same time, even description has its limitations or at least needs rethinking, which is why a lot of attention is devoted to issues of sensation and affect (Marila 2017; Sørensen 2015, 2016; Hamilakis 2017) and why other forms of representation such as photography play an important role. Although such an approach has obvious parallels with Geertz's notion of thick description, the philosophical basis of each could not be more different.

There are two problems which such a position raises, only one of which, I think, is really cause for concern. The first is a danger that neo-empiricism becomes indistinguishable from the most vulgar notion of empiricism, where the 'things speak for themselves'. Matthew Johnson has argued that such vulgar empiricism actually still underwrites the vernacular imagination for the majority of archaeologists (Johnson 2011), although comparing, for example, a description written under neo-empiricism and vulgar empiricism would clearly reveal the sharp differences. If nothing else, it would expose the deeply theoretical and contrived nature of description under vulgar empiricism. In contrast, the theoretical nature of description is fully acknowledged under neo-empiricism, where theory and things are seen as mutually entangled, whereas under conventional empiricism, even the more sophisticated, philosophical kind, theory is an imposition on things (Johnson 2011). We only have mediated access to the world through intervening concepts – what speculative realists call correlationism (see Edgeworth 2016; Marila 2017; Witmore 2014)

In a recent paper, Þóra Pétursdóttir and Bjørnar Olsen have countered this conventional view and argue that just as things don't speak for themselves, neither does theory; against the view that sees theory as enabling things to speak, they argue that things just as much enable theory to speak (Pétursdóttir & Olsen 2018). This folds us back into the same issues with STS and the multi-agent nature of knowledge production, and through their argument, I see no difficulty distinguishing neo-empiricism from vulgar empiricism: they are not the same. Pétursdóttir and Olsen's paper should make this abundantly clear. It is rather another problem connected to neo-empiricism that I find more troubling. The hyperempiricism and trend towards reducing all interpretation and theory to a form of description seems to limit the scope of both the objects and practice of archaeology. Intentionally or not, such empiricism would seem to want to constrain archaeological knowledge to experiential objects on the one hand (i.e. tangible things), and to practices which involve direct interaction with such objects (i.e. fieldwork), on the other. The genealogical links between phenomenology and neo-empiricism are too obvious to need pointing out, while the focus on fieldwork as the chief characteristic of studies influenced by STS is equally evident.

Despite the avowed symmetry that all things count as things, it does seem clear that some things gain more attention than others under neo-empiricism. Both Matt Edgeworth and Irene Garcia-Rovira, drawing on Timothy Morton's concept of hyper-object, suggest that the study of large-scale and long-term processes, which are often seen as the hallmark of archaeology, cannot be easily accommodated by such hyper-empiricism, though, of the two, Garcia-Rovira is more explicit on this point (Garcia-Rovira 2015; Edgeworth 2016). Citing Morton is important because of his links to speculative realism; such reductionism then may not be as faithful to things as one thinks. In terms of objects not immediately evident to our experience, Garcia-Rovira in particular argues that archaeology needs inference and interpretation and that the current epistemology of the new empiricism is not enough.

The question of archaeological entities or objects ordinarily inaccessible is also central to Sandra Wallace's recent attempt to resurrect Bhaskar's scientific realism. Wallace's book *Contradictions of Archaeological Theory: Engaging Critical Realism and Archaeological Theory* is far removed from the theoretical stream of neo-empiricism and new materialisms, but nonetheless shares some of the same ambitions. It is by far the most sustained attempt to link Bhaskar's realism with archaeology and argues that the apparent pluralism of contemporary archaeology actually masks deep contradictions and inconsistencies in archaeology (Wallace 2011). This I find an interesting argument and in fact quite opposite to most other archaeologists who have tended to argue that such pluralism masks a deeper, underlying unity. What is less convincing is Wallace's suggestion that the problems lie with a failure to engage with ontological issues as she seems to ignore all this new work on the new materialisms just discussed. This is especially ironic since much of it has link-ups with Bhaskar's transcendental realism, especially his concept of objects in terms of their tendencies and his distinction between the actual and the real (Bhaskar 1975, 1979; DeLanda 2006, 2016). However, Wallace's case for critical realism, like Gibbon's before her (see above), offer no new insights on the epistemological dimensions of adopting a realist approach.

In raising the question of accessing the inaccessible, one also then raises the question of other forms of archaeological practice that are not directly engaged with things themselves – at least archaeological things. Sitting at a computer working through a database, or writing up a paper – what kind of knowledge practices are these? It seems to me that this is where neo-empiricism, taken as a form of object-interaction, really fails us. The question of whether such failures are intrinsic to the basic arguments of neo-empiricism, or just a contingent product of the way it has unfolded in archaeology, is certainly pertinent but not an issue I want to pursue. The end result is the same, which is to draw our attention away from the quite real and tangible practices of writing and its link to knowledge production, which is the core focus of this book. To address these concerns, I have actually found it more helpful to engage with the third stream of work in archaeological epistemology, one which, ironically, is perhaps also that with the most orthodox pedigree: evidential reasoning and evaluating knowledge claims about the past.

One of the first attempts to revisit these old issues was a resurrection of the model of inference to the best explanation (IBE), originally suggested by Hanen and Kelley in the late 1980s as an alternative to the hypothetico-deductive model of inference. Lars Fogelin explicitly evokes IBE as an ideal 'middle ground' model of reasoning between the extremes of processualism and postprocessualism, and, like many before him, employs the argument that archaeologists have been using IBE without knowing it for decades now, using examples from Alfred Kidder, Lewis Binford and Ian Hodder to support his case (Fogelin 2008). Fogelin's paper offers a more detailed and prescriptive treatment of IBE than that given by Hanen and Kelley, and is certainly very lucid and engaging, though essentially similar: IBE is a form of eliminative induction whereby competing interpretations are evaluated and the best one wins. Where Fogelin improves upon Hanen and Kelley is in offering specific criteria for making such evaluations which include: empirical breadth (diverse data), generality (diverse cases), modesty, refutability, conservatism (compatibility with existing knowledge), simplicity and multiplicity of foils (i.e. competing interpretations).

A more extended discussion of evaluation, however, is given by Alison Wylie, who continues to work on issues of archaeological epistemology; her recent volumes with Bob Chapman indicate a revival of interest in this topic (Chapman & Wylie 2015, 2016). Chapman and Wylie's volumes offer far more detailed and in-depth engagements with epistemic issues than the other examples I have outlined. In particular, their book *Evidential Reasoning in Archaeology* (Chapman & Wylie 2016) is a very compelling and readable discussion of epistemic issues in archaeology and for that reason I will spend more time discussing it. It is largely a modified and elaborated version of Wylie's position staked out in the late 1980s and early 1990s, but it remains ever relevant, nonetheless. As Chapman and Wylie point out, despite the collapse of the processual–postprocessual wars of the 1980s and early 1990s, epistemological issues of knowledge production have not been resolved so much as buried underground. Theoretical pluralism may reign on the surface, yet the tacit consensus of knowledge being not-quite-relative yet not-fully-objective either probably survives only through lack of scrutiny. The acceptance by processualists that data is always theoretically laden, while for postprocessualists a guarded objectivity has to be retained, seemed to melt together in a middle ground where both sides could agree—so long as neither probed the matter much further.

Like Wallace, then, Chapman and Wylie are suspicious of the supposed consensus that emerged at the end of the 1990s, but, unlike Wallace, they stick to an epistemological line of enquiry. They see their task as to build from the recognition that knowledge is always partial, contingent and imperfect, yet ask how such knowledge is nonetheless still successfully developed in practice. Central to their approach is to view knowledge production as a form of argument. They are not the first to suggest this (e.g. Stutt & Shennan 1990), but they do develop it in the most interesting way. Drawing on the work of philosopher Stephen Toulmin, specifically his book *The Uses of Argument* from 1958, which provides the classic account of 'logic in use' (Toulmin 1958), they attempt to dissect the elementary structure of archaeological arguments, as they are actually framed in real contexts. Critical to this structure is the concept of scaffolding, which secures the connection or inference between a claim and its evidence. Once you adopt the idea of scaffolding, clearly what matters is how well it performs – that is, does what it is supposed to do. To measure this, Chapman and Wylie use the concept of 'robustness' which they define in some detail, linking it to one of Wylie's famous metaphors of cabling (Wylie, 1989b). Arguments work best not as linear chains but as multiple strands which work to triangulate around the same claim.

I give a more detailed description of their approach in Chapter 4, but for now I want to raise what I see as one of the problems entrained by using argument as a model of archaeological reasoning. As I will suggest in Chapter 4, argument is linked to a particular mode of knowledge construction rather than a universal feature of all knowledge, and subsuming such diverse practices as excavation and lead isotope analysis (as they do in their case studies) under the same mode of reasoning may be glossing over too much epistemic diversity. In other words, there is a potential contradiction or tension here between a recognition of pluralism in knowledge practices – something which Wylie has been and is an ardent supporter of – and the reduction of archaeological reasoning to a single model, namely argument. The same basic stance is taken by Fogelin in his adoption of IBE and ultimately in all similar earlier attempts to provide a reconciliatory path through the processual–postprocessual wars (e.g. Kosso 1991). What is happening here?

In a sense, this is a natural or inevitable response to diverting the threat of relativism, once epistemic pluralism has been accepted. While multivocality, different ways of knowing and so on are all fine, this still leaves open the question of how one adjudicates between different accounts or claims on a basis we can all agree upon. Instead of invoking some abstract model of scientific method, rather the stress is now on more general, shared patterns of reasoning which are visible in IBE or, simply, 'argument'. But does this not just repeat the same error as before, only at a deeper level? Is this not just another version of a single rationality? Can it really avoid all the same issues of being politically and socially charged as those levelled at 'western science'? But then again, if we do not believe in some underlying principles of reason which we can all share (regardless of cultural background), we become drawn again into the vortex of relativism.

These are lots of questions but I think one needs to stop the spiral right at its root. *Pluralism does not lead to relativism but is its strongest bulwark against it.* Wylie has said as much on numerous occasions, as have many others. Pluralism takes many forms. The very disunity of science – the fact that its various practices and specialisms are irreducible to each other – means that any claim about the past is strengthened if it draws on such diversity. The physics of radiocarbon decay, the osteology of animal bones, the stratigraphy of deposition, the ethnography of gift exchange – because all these different domains work from different sets of background theory, if they work together in an archaeological interpretation, then they increase objectivity. Multivocality – implicit in feminist, class-based or indigenous archaeology – means that our views of the past are constantly being checked against our social biases of the present. Whether it is about our excavation methods, research questions or interpretations, such multivocality only increases objectivity. Why, then, invoke some underlying, shared mode of reasoning to guarantee objectivity when the very pluralism itself is what safeguards this?

I suppose the missing ingredient here is: what makes these different perspectives or knowledge practices come together? How do we show (or know) when different knowledges work together or against each other? This is one way to look the recent work of Chapman and Wylie, but I am troubled by the tacit reunification of knowledge it seems to imply. Why cannot pluralism also exists here too? What if such pluralism can be maintained all the way down? Thus I would rather suggest that different knowledge practices can be brought together in different ways, that there are multiple modes of reasoning, not just one – whether it is IBE or 'argument' or something else. Archaeology has never operated under a single epistemic register and it does not need one.

I framed the historical review of this chapter in terms of two epistemic cultures: that in Britain and that in North America. The very epistemological issues debated were themselves caught up in two, different epistemic perspectives – differences especially between how British and North American archaeologists perceived induction and the concept of history. They worked with very different meanings of these concepts, which often led to deep misunderstanding. It should be clear that I in no way consider these perspectives as 'incommensurable paradigms'; we need a better term to refer to these disciplinary matrices or traditions that carries none of the burden of these older concepts ('repertoires' is one candidate recently offered; Ankeney & Leonelli 2016). Communication, dialogue and debate were all clearly quite possible across the Atlantic and increasingly common as the twentieth century progressed, and, as a result, the differences in these two epistemic cultures started to break down – or, rather, new bridges began to be built. And, ironically, it is precisely over the issue of epistemic pluralism that the two cultures found the most fertile meeting ground. Between Kuhn's notion of paradigm-dependence and the hermeneutic circle, epistemic pluralism was a solution that banished the threat of relativism hanging over both.

I think we can make such epistemic pluralism continue to work for us, even at the level discussed by Chapman and Wylie. I can readily accept that IBE or 'argument' can act as a means to mediate and even adjudicate between different knowledge claims and perspectives. But I am less ready to see it as the *only* way to do this. Part of the problem here is the still abstract or disembodied nature of concepts like 'argument'. One of the strengths of Chapman and Wylie's approach to argument is that they eschew the idealization of models of reasoning that dominated so much of the twentieth century. Their view of argument is strongly wedded to its conception as a 'logic in use', how archaeologists actually do reason, rather than how they should, based on some abstract principles of logic. Yet I would suggest they do not go far enough in embedding argument in practice. Although they use case studies to embed their study of argument, the case studies are still offered as distillations of actual practice. Can we not contextualize argument even more? How does argument relate more specifically to a case study on lead isotopes; indeed, what is a case study – and how does an argument figure in it? This takes us into the realm of epistemic genres (Morgan 2014a).

As I mentioned in Chapter 1, one of the important shifts in the last two decades has been to move the whole debate around knowledge production from a purely epistemological issue to one centred around practice, where the stress has been much more on the social and material conditions of knowledge production (e.g. Gero 1996; Edgeworth 2003, 2006; Olsen et al. 2012; Lucas 2001a, 2012). What most of this work largely bypasses is any engagement with the traditional concerns of epistemology as portrayed in the bulk of this chapter and in Chapman and Wylie's recent work. But, as I have argued in the introduction to this book, I find this lacuna somewhat troubling and the whole rationale for this book is to try to connect these traditional epistemological issues to the more recent work on knowledge production in the field. At the same time, recent texts such as those by Fogelin and Chapman and Wylie, while clearly developing the epistemological discussions of the late 1980s and early 1990s, seem to largely ignore this work in science studies. How to bring the two together?

This is where I think the function of writing and textual composition becomes so important. Because the 'arguments' that Chapman and Wylie so convincingly unravel in their case studies are all embedded in texts. Certainly those texts are connected to multiple other practices that have taken place in the field, in laboratories, classrooms and conference halls, and no doubt 'arguments' can be discerned in many of these contexts. But it is in the written text that an 'argument' is most cogently and clearly made. But, by the same token, texts also construct other forms of knowledge than 'argument'. Arguments are not the only fruit. Narratives, descriptions, expositions are all somewhat different textual (and epistemic) forms, and I think it is dangerous to conflate them or reduce them all to 'argument' (or 'narrative' as was the custom in the 1990s). This approach has some resonance with Joyce's use of Bakhtin's concepts of polyphony and heteroglossia, which also argues for textual diversity (Joyce 2002). But where Joyce puts great emphasis on the genre of conversation or dialogue as a textual form, I think we can explore such heteroglossia in even the most conventional texts. It is on that note that I move in the next chapter to a discussion of different text types in archaeology, before drawing out their epistemological implications in Chapter 4.

# 3

# TEXT TYPES AND ARCHAEOLOGY

## Introduction

Towards the end of the last chapter, I discussed the recent work of Wylie and Chapman on evidential reasoning, especially their use of Toulmin's model of argument. This is a very compelling study as it tries to situate many of the traditional epistemological issues that archaeologists have engaged with within a less formalized framework. Instead of the classical logic of induction or deduction, Toulmin's informal logic offered an account of how people actually reason, rather than some idealized version of it. The issue of an idealized logic of inference cropped up several times in my story in the last chapter, but often it became another way to compare induction (as what archaeologists do, such as inference to the best explanation) versus deduction (as what some archaeologists would like to think we do – or should at least aspire to, through the hypothetico-deductive method). The advantages of Toulmin's approach breaks with this classical deadlock, and when I was first sketching out ideas for this book, the concept of argument seemed to have a great appeal, precisely for this reason.

And yet as I read about how scholars have discussed argument (including Toulmin's book), it quickly became clear that an argument was used not just to refer to an informal approach to logic, but also to refer to a particular type of academic prose or rhetoric. Toulmin's book was not well received within philosophy. Indeed, the current of philosophical logic was moving too fast for his book to have stopped it. Yet it did find a home in North America among communication studies where it fitted well into the fields of rhetoric and composition, where argument was one of the four modes of discourse alongside exposition, description and narrative (Toulmin 2003: vii–viii). As such, it quickly became a well-known text and the 'Toulmin model' of argument entered into textbooks of critical thinking (e.g. see Reinard 1991). In 1978, Toulmin co-authored a more extended version of his approach to fit into this new environment and, by now, whole new typologies of argument were being developed, such as argument by analogy, argument by example or argument from authority, as well as major fields of argument which had their own specific criteria of validation, such as law, ethics, science, management and art criticism (Toulmin et al. 1984).

However, it is not the variations of argument that concern me as much as the idea of argument as one of several rhetorical strategies. The connection between rhetoric and text types will become clearer as this chapter progresses, but it was the idea that argument could be linked to a specific form of textual composition that grabbed my attention, and that, by implication, if argument entailed one form of informal logic, what other informal logics did other text types embody? But here I am anticipating issues developed more fully in the next chapter. For now, it is sufficient to acknowledge that academic prose is produced in different ways, that there are various different types of textual composition – with argument being just one of them. Moreover, in terms of how archaeologists have discussed texts and textual composition, argument has not really figured highly. Rather the main emphasis has been on another type of prose altogether: narrative. As a prelude to the next chapter which grapples directly with the issue of relating epistemology to textual composition, the rest of this chapter will lay out the more general issue of composition and text types in archaeology.

## Archaeology and narrative

Interest in the nature and form of archaeological texts started to emerge in the late 1980s, but the 1990s was the decade that saw a peak of writing about this topic, culminating in Pluciennik's seminal review paper (Pluciennik 1999). The new millennium began with what remains perhaps the most original and insightful study, Joyce's book *The Languages of Archaeology* (2002), and although discussion of archaeological writing has continued, it is fair to say that its popularity as a topic has greatly diminished, even if the subject still inspires some important work (e.g. see the recent volume edited by Van Dyke and Bernbeck, 2015). I want to try to summarize the broad outlines of this archaeological discourse on writing before going on to suggest taking it in a new direction, one that will reconnect with the issue of archaeological epistemology as outlined in the last chapter.

As a way of framing this summary, I want to suggest making a distinction between those works which offer an analysis of the nature of texts in archaeology and those which experiment with new forms of text. The distinction is somewhat forced, as some of this work – most particularly, Joyce's book already cited – clearly engages with both of these fields. However, for the sake of my exposition it will help nonetheless to make this distinction, and certainly many of the works I discuss more clearly fall on one or the other side of this divide.

## Textual analysis

The analysis of archaeological texts is often traced back to two papers published in 1989: Hodder's discussion of site reports and Tilley's analysis of the Cambridge inaugural lecture (Hodder 1989; Tilley 1989). Hodder's paper traced the changing ways in which archaeological site reports have been written from the eighteenth century, especially the shift from a first-person narrative of events to a third-person, objective description. Hodder, drawing on Foucault, linked this shift to the changing power relations embedded in knowledge production, specifically the association between archaeology as an elite or 'gentlemanly' pursuit in the eighteenth century to its anonymous institutional context in the twentieth century. Hodder concludes his paper with some suggestions for rethinking the structure of archaeological site reports by invoking the concepts of narrative and dialogue, which, although remaining undeveloped in this paper, nonetheless anticipate future developments, as I will discuss below. Tilley also drew on Foucault's concept of discourse and its connection to power structures to situate his analysis of four inaugural lectures given by new incumbents of the chair of Disney Professor of Archaeology at the University of Cambridge. Using the concept of the inaugural lecture as a genre, Tilley argues that, as a genre, each lecture is largely constrained and dictated by the social and political context of its presentation: "What defines the importance of the statements actually made is not their propositional content, but the fact that their conditions of enunciation involve the status of the Disney Professor and his or her institutional site" (Tilley 1989: 60). Tilley offers a detailed analysis of the discursive strategies employed in his four examples which illustrate this, such as citations to previous Disney Professors, and the overall sense of his study is that of a very detailed, close reading of these texts.

Hodder and Tilley's texts both came at the end of a decade which saw them as key figures in the development of postprocessual theory, much of which drew inspiration from or was part of broader developments in the humanities where language was a central motif. From the key postprocessual strategy of seeing material culture as text, it was inevitable that archaeological texts themselves would come under scrutiny, especially as a similar move was evident in anthropology, epitomized in the landmark volume *Writing Culture* (Clifford & Marcus 1986). Pluciennik situates this development in more detail, so I will not dwell on this further. At the same time, however, studies such as Hodder's and Tilley's were not to develop into a more sustained field of research. Tilley published a few similar papers in the early 1990s (Tilley 1990, 1993; also see Johnson & Coleman 1990), but that decade saw a turn away from the framework of Foucauldian discourse towards narrative as the key concept in analysing texts as anticipated in Hodder's concluding remarks. Again, this was partly just following wider trends, but, what-ever the reason, the concept of narrative became the dominant way of looking at archaeological texts, a shift which still largely informs current debate.

This 'narrative turn' was inaugurated at the very start of the 1990s with a paper by Terrell exploring the nature of storytelling in prehistoric archaeology (Terrell 1990). His paper addressed four different aspects of narrative including the reasons why archaeologists use stories in their accounts, what kind of structure these stories have, what pitfalls are involved in adopting a narrative structure and finally the question of how narratives related to the scientific method. His examination of the structure of such narratives is, in some ways, the most detailed, as he draws on Landau's exploration of the narrative structure of stories of human evolution to analyse some texts on Pacific prehistory (Landau 1984). Landau's study, developed into a book published the year after Terrell's paper (Landau 1991), had used Propp's classic work on the morphology of folktales, which reduced all narratives to combinations and permutations of 31 generic narrative elements (Propp 1968). This kind of archetypal or typological approach to narrative became a recurrent theme in later studies of archaeological narrative, although such studies have tended to be more influenced by Hayden White's tropological schema than Propp's morphology. I will come to White in a moment, because his work on historical narratives has perhaps had the greatest influence on archaeology (White 1973). But first it is important to qualify they key difference between Propp and White.

One of the key issues here is whether narratives are categorized by their content or their form; Propp's analysis largely focused on narrative content; thus, in Landau's analysis of human evolution stories, she identified nine key chapters or scenes through which the story unfolded. This kind of approach is also seen in another famous study, Joseph Campbell's analysis of myths, which offered a much more simplified version than Propp's, reducing all myths to a single narrative form: the monomyth (Campbell 1968). Here the basic story is of a hero going out to battle supernatural forces and coming home a victor. The success of the *Star Wars* movies has been partially attributed to the fact that George Lucas largely constructed the storyline based on Campbell's work. In contrast to studies such as Propp's and Campbell's, Hayden White's analysis of narrative was more structured around the form than the content; rather than seek generic narrative elements, White was more interested in the overall structure of the plot which encapsulated a general aesthetic or moral position; thus he proposed four basic plot types: Romance, Tragedy, Comedy and Satire (White 1973). These he linked with specific linguistic tropes, types of argument and ideological positions. There is no need to go into any detail about these here; they have been well discussed in the archaeological literature (Pluciennik 1999; Hodder 1993, 1995; Rudebeck 1996; Solli 1996). Perhaps because Propp's narrative elements – drawn as they were from folktales – do not always so easily fit archaeological narratives, White's scheme had more appeal for archaeologists. White's analysis was also based on scholarly historical narratives, not myths or folktales, which made it closer to archaeology.

Although widely cited, there were nonetheless few attempts to actually apply White's approach to archaeological texts. Hodder drew on White's scheme but in a very original way, by translating it into a tool for analysing material culture sequences (see Chapter 5 for further discussion of this; Hodder 1993, 1995). However, this seemed to run out of steam very quickly. A more conventional use of White and the most cited example is Rudebeck's analysis of archaeological narratives of the transition to agriculture in Scandinavia (Rudebeck 1996, 2000).

Rudebeck discusses these archaeological texts in terms of their mythic structures and cites the work of Landau as well, but then primarily draws on White's fourfold typology to suggest that three of his four plot types can be discerned in the archaeological texts she analyses. Rudebeck supplements her use of White with other schemes, but the overriding message of her work is that archaeological narratives are broadly determined by conceptual frameworks which can be analysed in terms of these basic narrative plots. There is a strong aura of constructivism pervading her analysis and, as with White's own work on historical narrative, there is the feeling that the actual content – the data, the evidence – is almost irrelevant.

This unease surrounding the privileging of form over content was expressed by Pluciennik in his review paper (Pluciennik 1999). Pluciennik offers his own analysis of archaeological texts which deal with the Mesolithic–Neolithic transition, and although he characterizes the different accounts in a way that tries to mediate between form and content, the result is an ambiguous blend of archetypal or meta-narratives (especially that of progress) in the style of Propp and a tropological emplotment after White. Pluciennik's concern with keeping form and content together is one of the most important points in his paper, but his own analysis ultimately fails to do this convincingly. The problem is that even an analysis which focuses on content, such as Propp's, is still ultimately constructivist. Chris Ballard, in his discussion of narrative through examples of prehistory in New Guinea, is also wary of the way constructivism or formalism creates a sense of determinism in narrative, and suggests that what he calls a more phenomenological approach to narrative (e.g. in the work of Ricoeur and Carr) can allow more nuanced accounts which incorporate contingency as well as have real explanatory potential (Ballard 2003).

One of the most recent analyses of archaeological texts brings us full circle; Lesure's study of the site monograph evokes Hodder's 1989 paper on site reports, but is quite different in its approach (Lesure 2015). Lesure explicitly takes White as his starting point but finds his fourfold typology restricting, especially when considering the narrative structure of site monographs. Thus he adds the plot type of Epic to White's scheme and argues that the site monograph has all the qualities one normally attributes to such a genre, such as vast scope and multiple storylines. Indeed, Lesure even suggests that the Epic characterizes other archaeological texts and is, in many ways, the archetypal narrative form for the discipline. Comparing Lesure's paper with Hodder's is instructive insofar as it reveals how much the discourse around texts in archaeology has congealed around a rather singular and simplified focus. Although Hodder's paper situates the site report within the broad concept of discourse and power, he raises at the end the potential of looking at archaeological texts in terms of narratives. Twenty-five years later, Lesure's discussion takes for granted that the site monograph is a type of narrative and that the issue is really about what type of narrative it is.

I find this development very problematic, but one can see the change happening in Pluciennik's review. Whereas Terrell had quite explicitly accepted that narratives were just *one* mode of exploration or model-making as he put it (Terrell 1990), Pluciennik essentially argues for extending the narrative concept to cover *all* archaeological writing. Drawing on other work on narrative in related disciplines, including the philosophy of science, Pluciennik even argues that something like a chemical formula can be seen to be a narrative insofar as it has a configuration, like a plot (for more constrained views on narrative in science, see papers in Morgan & Wise 2017). This inflation of the concept of narrative did not go unremarked (see comments section which follow Pluciennik's paper), but the fact is that it seems that the assumption that all archaeology is ultimately a form of storytelling or narrative quickly became the new consensus. This is most evident when one looks at some of the experimental writing that was emerging in the 1990s, a topic I want to briefly turn to now.

## Textual experimentation

Exploring new forms of writing in archaeology emerged around the same time as archaeologists started to analyse the texts produced by their discipline. Michael Shanks and Christopher Tilley were among the first here, both of whom developed a 'poetics of archaeology' (Shanks & Tilley 1989), yet with very different styles, as their independent works from the 1990s attest. Shanks, in particular, has made a specific writing style almost his signature, with a philosophy of archaeology that was expressed as much through the style of his writing as its content. Often composed of fragmented, short text sections with equally short, fragmented sentences, Shanks's writing explicitly articulated the need for what he called an archaeological poetics. Discussed in the penultimate chapter of his book *Experiencing the Past* (1992), Shanks discussed a variety of elements to such a poetics, including narrative. But narrative is clearly just one component here and, in a way, more characteristic of Shanks's writing is that of montage. Mickel recently took up this idea of montage to suggest that most archaeological texts – at least the informal, everyday texts that archaeologists produce such as through field diaries – have always taken on this form. Narrative, she argues, may actually damage attempts by archaeologists to communicate what they do to the general public, as the narrative structure itself perpetuates the common mythologies surrounding archaeology encapsulated in popular culture through icons like Indiana Jones (Mickel 2013).

Mickel suggests that contemporary forms of media technology actually work in the discipline's favour; the internet and its forms of text are almost tailor-made for montage rather than narrative, which is tied to the traditional media technology of the printed page. Shanks's work is a clear expression of this insofar as so much of his output in the past few decades has been web-based through his Stanford metamedia and personal websites; indeed, websites and blogposts are a forum through which many archaeologists now routinely write. Shanks's interest in archaeological modes of expression has remained a key theme throughout his later work, especially exploring non-textual modes such as photography and performance (Pearson & Shanks 2001; Shanks & Webmoor 2010). This was also a concluding point of Pluciennik's paper on narrative insofar as he suggested a greater need for 'anti-narrative' narratives as well as other media of expression (Pluciennik 1999: 667). It is telling, though, that the only way Pluciennik can talk about non-narrative texts is still to call them narratives.

Exploring the potential of new media technologies like the internet have had wide appeal and Shanks is by no means the only archaeologist to have exploited this. Indeed, pioneering work came from Ruth Tringham in the 1990s and her Chimera Web, which used the non-linear structure of hypertext to develop new modes of writing archaeology (Joyce & Tringham 2007). Importantly, though, Tringham sees her writing as still essentially narrative in form; the difference being that rather than offering a single, coherent storyline, the hypertext format allowed for multiple stories, fragments that she calls vignettes or microhistories which could be read in many different permutations. Tringham calls this kind of approach recombinant histories, after Anderson (2011), and has recently developed it in the context of her work as part of the Çatalhöyük Project (Tringham 2015).

Tringham's focus on narrative is perhaps more in line with the general trend in experimental writing in archaeology. Throughout the 1990s, archaeologists started to explore the potential of fictive storytelling, but triangulated against archaeological data. This was not conventional historical fiction, especially as the narratives were often short and fragmentary, and, more importantly, contextualized against traditional archaeological reportage, as the bibliographic essays that were often appended to such stories underline. The use of fictional stories was not completely new, of course; Flannery's Golden Mar-shalltown has become a classic text, although written in the early 1980s, and set a model for using fictional characters and dialogues to communicate archaeological theory (Flan-nery 1982; Johnson 2010; A. Praetzellis 2000). But a definite wave of interest in using fictional stories emerged in the 1990s, exemplified in works by archaeologists such as Janet Spector (1991, 1993) and Mark Edmonds (1999). It was within North American historical archaeology, however, that it received its widest appeal, perhaps because of the close association between texts and material culture (Joyce 2006).

Experimental writing in historical archaeology, especially narrative writing, had earlier pioneers such as Ivor Noël Hume and Carmel Schrire, who both used autobiographical techniques, albeit in very different ways and with very different politics (Noël Hume 1991; Schrire 1995). But it was two sessions on storytelling at the annual conference of Society for Historical Archaeology in 1997 and 1998 which proved to have huge appeal, and papers from the first session were subse-quently published (M. Praetzellis 1998). Mary and Adrian Praetzellis's narratives in particular became widely cited and praised, especially as their stories often emerged from archaeological research conducted under development-led conditions, but many other major historical archaeologists explored this format (see the papers in M. Praetzellis 1998; also Wilkie 2003; Mytum 2010).

In 2000, Gibbs published a review of this genre of storytelling in historical archaeology and expressed what has been perhaps a recurrent but muted concern about such fictional stories: what value do they have? (Gibbs 2000; also see McCarthy 2003) The obvious answer, and one generally cited by those creating these stories, is their function in actually engaging people with archaeology; as Adrian Praetzellis indicated, most archaeological writing is simply boring – not just to the public but even to the profession (A. Praetzellis 1998: 2). Stories liven things up – they make it personal – and, as Deetz commented, can even draw attention to the questions that really count. But Gibbs also suggested another answer – one, in fact, also raised by Terrell in his early paper: creating fictional stories from archaeological data can work as a heuristic tool for thinking about that data in new ways, and even suggesting questions which might be subject to further testing (Gibbs 2000; Terrell 1990).

From this latter point, one senses in Gibbs review that the ultimate value of storytelling to archaeology must somehow rebound back on to traditional forms of representational knowledge. The bottom line about fictional narratives, even if based on real data, is that they are still fictional. So long as the function of a narrative in archaeology is being judged by standards of representation and correspondence with what really happened in the past, such narratives will always remain suspect. However, as Pluciennik pointed out in his review, narratives can have other functions beyond representation and it is clear that although storytellers like the Praetzellises do not consider their stories to be anything more than fiction, they still see them serving a function. Like any historical fiction, they can evoke something about the quality of life, the experience of living in a certain place at a certain time, even if the actual events or dialogue are made up.

I suppose one could still call this a form of representation, but if we do, then we run the risk of blurring the boundary between fiction and history – which, in some ways, is what many intend to do. Arguably, even the dullest archaeological description contains elements of fiction, those creative or imaginative leaps needed to join the dots. But this is to conflate imagination with invention. In many ways, one could argue that a subtle and very conventional scale of interpretation is at play here, with the boring basic facts at the bottom and fictional stories at the top, with orthodox archaeological narratives lying somewhere in between – part fact, part fiction. But I think we need to keep a clear line between fiction and archaeological narratives which purport to some kind of representation of the past. As Lamarque has argued, the referential and ontological commitments of fiction are very different to historical narratives such as those written by archaeologists (Lamarque 1990).

In many ways, Rosemary Joyce's approach to the value of these fictional stories is the most compelling as it underlines an element common to all archaeological texts, not just fictional stories: their dialogic nature (Joyce 2002). Drawing on the work of Bakhtin, Joyce argues that all archaeological texts should be seen primarily as modes of communication between people – they have an inherently dialogical structure, whether they actually employ dialogues or not, as a lot of the fictional stories do. Through citation and the general fact that any text is always partially a response to previous texts while also eliciting a response from future texts, archaeological writing is dialogical in nature. This dialogic character means that archaeologists should be striving for what Bakhtin calls heteroglossia and polyphony: using different language registers and multiple voices to capture the diverse nature of human experience. Moreover, this is how it should be, simply because the archaeologist (like any other social scientist) is not ultimately engaging with mute, inanimate objects but other human beings; for Bakhtin, this underlines the unique nature of the methodology of the human sciences (Bakhtin 1986).

Of course, this position sustains a distinction between the human and natural sciences – an old argument developed in the late nineteenth century – and implies that the nature of texts in these two fields will inevitably be different. The danger here is in forcing on archaeology that old choice between two forms of knowledge construction – explanation and interpretation – as I reviewed in the last chapter. And implicitly aligned with this is the idea that interpretive texts will generally have a narrative structure. Indeed, this probably goes a long way towards accounting for the inflation of narrative as the paradigm of any archaeological text; narrative is not just being understood as a text form, but it is also a mode of reasoning, an epistemology. Archaeology, insofar as it is part of the humanities, will embody a narrative mode of explanation and thus narrative mode of expression. A similar opposition is hinted at in the recent volume on narratives in archaeology edited by Ruth Van Dyke and Reinhard Bernbeck who contrast traditional expository texts with alternative, experimental narratives, even if their book is an excellent testament to the diversity of narrative form (Van Dyke & Bernbeck 2015: 1). However, the concerns of that volume are also somewhat different to mine, with a much greater focus on the politics and ethics of archaeological representation, and while issues of epistemology are raised, these are filtered through a concern for the wider social context in which such narratives are produced.

## Rethinking archaeological texts

My review in the last section of archaeological approaches to text has ultimately tried to draw out one salient feature: the reduction of all archaeological writing to narrative. Not everyone was or is guilty of this; as a wave of 'alternative narratives' started to emerge in the 1990s, narrative was sometimes used to refer explicitly to these alternative texts in contrast to conventional expository texts or scientific writing, a distinction which many still maintain (e.g. see Van Dyke & Bernbeck 2015). However, the ease with which the term 'narrative' slips from being a very specific form of text to a general label for all texts is problematic, and my sense is that the general usage has been more dominant. This occurred gradually and almost without notice, but it has resulted in a very constrained and arguably myopic perspective, which is not without problems. At one extreme, one sees the idea of narrative being stretched to encompass such diverse textual forms as excavation monographs and experimental fiction so that the term loses any real value; the only way to mitigate this is to draw on typologies which tend to focus on broad differences in form, usually based on the typology of Hayden White.

A similar problem is entailed if we preserve the idea of narrative as a fundamentally exclusive form of text associated with the human sciences since all texts are then referenced against the narrative form. Even those discussions which focus on the idea of montage do not really stand in opposition to narrative, for fragmentary texts can still embody a narrative form (e.g. Tringham 2015). Indeed, the issue in these discussions seems to be between textual and non-textual forms of representation, where texts are understood as narratives and non-texts include (most commonly) visual media and performance. However, some recent work suggests that archaeological writing that is more faithful to archaeological material might actually offer an antidote to narrative; reflecting on the work of archaeologists Bjornar Olsen, Þora Pétursdóttir and Chris Witmore, literary scholar Jeff Love and historian Michael Meng comment:

> For the archeologists at Svæiholt these objects or things are precisely what they seek to uncover, not as placeholders in narratives, but as challenges to narrative assimilation: they refuse to be transformed into wholes that give us a sense of a past well understood. As such, they are reminders of a past we can neither assimilate to narrative nor place into a greater whole or even understand secularly as a part thereof.
>
> *(Love & Meng 2016: 235)*

What is being alluded to here is an alternative history, one closer to what Walter Benjamin sketched and which archaeologist Laurent Olivier has used to construct an anti-historicist view of archaeology (Olivier 2011). Implied here is the intimate connection between narrative and history, where archaeology is not history and therefore where narrative has little place (also see Mickel 2013).

In this section, I want to explore other possibilities for looking at archaeological texts that escape the framework which assumes all texts are basically narrative in nature. Doing this will help us find a way out of the problems just mentioned but, more importantly, allow us to integrate epistemic concerns with textual composition in a way that the narrative debate has prevented because of the way all epistemic issues seem to be caught in the fiction/history dichotomy. I also want to counter the often overly negative portrayal of conventional texts that discussions of alternative narratives engender. One criticism, for example, is that conventional archaeological texts are boring. Well, yes, some are, but some are not. There are some jaw-dropping, mind-bending expositions out there which, frankly, are far more engaging than some of the narratives I have read. Narratives do not have any monopoly on excitement. But also one has to bear in mind that some archaeological texts are not really meant to be read in the same way as a narrative. Of course site reports are usually boring; who on earth sits down and reads a site report from beginning to end like a novel? You read it more like an encyclopaedia or dictionary; it is a resource for consulting. You might well read individual chapters with more interest than others, but this just demonstrates that a text like a site report is not homogeneous – I point I will belabour later on.

While the accusation of being 'boring' is, then, not a valid critique, that mainly leaves the more substantial issue that conventional texts are somehow limiting. What is usually meant here is that scholarly prose does allow us to really capture the human dimension of our subjects – people's past experiences, feelings and so on. I think this is a more reasonable comment, but it does beg the question: is this a limitation in our writing or our source material? It does seem to me that it is precisely for this reason that the whole anxiety around the fact/fiction has become amplified. I should be clear at this point that I am not arguing against alternative narratives, the use of fiction or attempts to inject a bit more 'humanity' into our accounts of the past. What I am doing is arguing that these issues have nothing to do with the limitations or deficiencies of conventional texts. The question of fiction can apply to an exposition just as easily as to a narrative – think about the Sokal hoax which involved the publication of a purely fictive exposition (Sokal 1996). In many ways, the hang-up on the fiction/fact divide is a red herring – it is not that I think the distinction is irrelevant; it is more that we are looking in the wrong place for the basis of this distinction.

With these preliminary remarks, let me now move on to the main point of this section: how to rethink archaeological texts in such a way that it goes beyond this binary divide between conventional and alternative or scientific and narrative. One of the characteristics of almost all the archaeological studies on texts that I have been outlining in the last section is that they have largely taken inspiration from within literary theory and literary studies. As a consequence, it is perhaps no surprise that narrative became the key concept for analysing such texts. However, a somewhat different tradition of textual analysis is met with in discourse analysis and especially textual linguistics, which generally adopt a much broader view, one where narrative is regarded as just one kind of text. This difference comes out clearly in the way the concept of genre is used in the two fields.

In literary studies, genre generally refers to literary genres which typically derive from Aristotle's *Poetics* and the division into three types of Epic, Lyric and Drama, the latter of which is usually subdivided into Tragedy, Comedy and Satire. It is these literary genres which, via Northrop Frye (1957), structured White's model of narrative forms (White 1973). In text linguistics, however, the concept of genre has a very different meaning and rather relates to the culturally specific purpose or situation in which texts are produced (see Matsagouras and Tsipilako 2008 for a useful summary). Genres are primarily seen in terms of historically and culturally contingent forms of communication and include, for example, business letters, newspaper articles, sermons, poems and so on. One of the first scholars to redefine genres in this sense was Bakhtin who explicitly looked at non-literary genres to understand the broader social discursive nature of literature (Bakhtin 1982). However, it was the work of Roman Jakobson on the communicative functions of language as well as developments in ordinary language philosophy, especially the work of Austin and Searle on the performative nature of language and speech acts, that became the primary influence, especially within North America during the 1980s (Austin 1962; Jakobson 1960; Searle 1969). Scholars linked to the field of New Rhetorics articulated the idea of a genre as a form of social action (Miller 1984), and classifications of texts – like classifications of speech acts – were perceived as modes of communication, ways of doing things with words. Some scholars even promoted the idea of text acts, analogous to speech acts and/or tried to draw very close parallels between the classification of speech acts and those of text acts (e.g. Horner 1981; Adam 1992; and, most recently, Tsipilako and Floris 2013). A similar, social conception of genre was developed in Australia during the 1980s and 1990s, although this approached the concept of genre from a more strictly linguistic and grammatical perspective, known as systemic functional linguistics. Both North American and Australian versions of genre theory, however, had close links with pedagogy and writing composition, a theme I will come back to later in the book (see Matsagouras and Tsipilako 2008).

The idea of texts as forms of social action has become the standard approach to genre since the 1980s, but actual approaches to the classification of genres have varied greatly. Some of the initial work, especially in the Australian tradition centred around Halliday (Halliday 1994; Halliday & Hassan 1991; Martin 1997), produced a very defined, closed list of general types (e.g. Martin 1989); however, on the whole the consensus has been that the range of genre types is open-ended: the number and variety of genres can expand indefinitely simply because genre is connected to the social context of their production and is therefore dynamic, not static. Part of the problem was that because speech acts were often classified into a few, limited types (e.g. Searle's classification), it was assumed that genres might largely follow this. But while some genres can be mapped into specific speech acts – for example, the prayer as a genre follows the specific act of praying – many genres were much more complex and could not be so easily reduced to a single speech act, such as the novel (Todorov 1976). So genres – while they might still be broadly understood in relation to speech act theory – cannot so easily be reduced or linked to typologies of speech acts.

However, this very diversity and open-endedness of the genre also means that it loses a lot of analytical and explanatory potential. Consequently, a new concept – the text type – emerged in text linguistics as a way of classifying texts that was closed, limiting the range of types (Moessner 2001). One of the earliest works along this line was by Kinneavy who classified texts according to their discursive intentions, essentially seeing texts as modes of communication or discourse, drawing inspiration from neo-Aristotelian divisions of language use into four classes: scientific, dialectical, rhetorical and poetical (Kinneavy 1969, 1971). Kinneavy used this to develop his own fourfold typology of textual composition types: expressive, referential, literary and persuasive. A whole series of other typologies followed (e.g. Werlich 1975; Longacre 1983; Chatman 1990; Virtanen 1992; Fludernik 2000), with fewer or more types, but all more or less based on the same approach (Table 3.1). One well-known study even used cluster analysis to examine the language of a whole range of texts and developed a classification along similar lines (Biber 1989).

There remains no general consensus on text types, although on the whole the four most commonly cited types remain description, narration, exposition and argument, and are typically related to rhetorical strategies. However, one of the reasons why there is no agreed-upon classification of text types is due to the way the classification is conceived. Although some scholars, especially Biber, have argued that their classification is based on internal linguistic features, all the classifications, including Biber's, actually reveal a close affinity to language function and the texts' external context of use – that is, a sense of what the overall *intentions* of a text are, which brings us back to texts as modes of social action. If text types are ultimately defined in the same way as genres, what real value is there in making a distinction?

**TABLE 3.1** Examples of different text typologies after author

| Werlich | Longacre | Chatman | Vitnanen | Fludernik | Biber |
|---|---|---|---|---|---|
| Text types (ideal) | Deep structure genres | Text types | Text types | Macro-genres | Text types |
| descriptive | – | descriptive | descriptive | reflective | reportage |
| narrative | narrative | narrative | narrative | narrative | narrative |
| expositive | expository | – | expositive | – | expositive |
| argumentative | hortatory | argumentative | argumentative | argumentative | persuasive |
| instructive | procedural | – | instructive | instructive | – |
| – | – | – | – | conversational | conversational |

It is no wonder, then, that the distinction between text types and genre is often confusing, and, for some, it raises questions over the utility of the text type concept (e.g. see Trosberg 1997; Matsagouras and Tsipilako 2008; Lee 2001). One way of preserving the distinction between genre and text type is to think about how their classifications are constructed. Thus, in the related field of translation studies an analytical distinction is made between text kinds (*textsorte*) and text types (*texttyp*) which largely correspond to the difference of genre and text type respectively; the former is generally seen as an empirical classification, based on observations of the different forms that exist in any society, whereas the latter is seen as a theoretical classification. In his review of genres, Todorov made a similar point suggesting there are two ways of approaching genres – as a historical, empirical phenomenon and from a theoretical perspective (Todorov 1976). However, as Todorov points out, these two approaches should be seen as a single, working process rather as separate methods of classification and much the same view is taken in translation studies.

An alternative way of keeping the concept of text type alive is to recognize that it is defined on the basis not solely of its function but also its structure. Virtanen distinguishes between discourse type and text type where the former refers to the overall, general function of a discourse and the other to its specific form (Virtanen 1992, 2010). Thus a narrative discourse mode might employ a descriptive text type as well as narrative text type. For Virtanen, narrative is a very ecumenical discourse mode – and thus a very basic and primary text type, simply because it can use multiple text types to achieve its function, whereas an argumentative mode is usually restricted to argumentative text types. However, it seems to me that precisely because a narrative can serve multiple functions – that is, it can be used to explain, to elicit emotions, to instruct, to entertain – that defining it solely in terms of a function seems rather vacuous. What Virtanen's argument does point to, however, is that text types might perhaps be best thought of in terms of their structure as well as their function.

But defining texts by their structure is equally problematic. This is nicely illustrated by the philosopher Elizabeth Anscombe in an example that was later used by Searle (Anscombe 1957; Searle 1969). Anscombe described a list of objects and

**TABLE 3.2** Is this a shopping list, stock list or checklist?

| | |
|---|---|
| 12 | trowels |
| 15 | hand shovels |
| 15 | buckets |
| 6 | shovels |
| 4 | spades |
| 2 | wheelbarrows |

pointed out that to understand what this list means involves understanding its intention or function in relation to social action. Is it a shopping list or an inventory? It can be either: structurally it has an identical form (see Table 3.2). However, what this means is that the structure of a text – like a list, but also like a narrative – can be read or intended to perform different functions, depending on its social context. In this sense, a list could be viewed as a text type, like a narrative. However, reducing the concept of a text type to a structural definition is limiting, because while one can see how a list or even a narrative might be defined structurally, other text types like description or argument seem to involve a more purposive definition. Argument, for example, is typically defined as a form of persuasion which returns us to a rhetorical dimension.

There is no easy resolution to these issues and in fact it might be best to retain both function and structure as relevant dimensions of what it is that defines a text type. For now, let us keep this question open; I will return to it again in the final section of this chapter when I discuss the structural and performative dimensions of texts in the context of the digital humanities. Before addressing this, however, it is probably useful to pause at this moment and reflect on how all this discussion within text linguistics impacts our understanding of archaeological texts.

If one thinks about the variety of archaeological texts, one can easily come up with a diverse list from journal articles to student dissertations, from monographs to edited volumes, from book reviews to field notes. However, some clarification is needed to try to relate this to the previous discussion. First, one needs to be clear that the medium of the text is, in all cases, not an issue here. By medium, I am referring to the material form the text takes and that links texts to media technologies (e.g. see Gitelman 2014; Kittler 1990, 1999). So, for example, a journal article or a book is neither a genre nor a text type – these refer to texts as material objects. Moreover, there is an increasing distinction between online articles and books and their print versions, which makes the question of textual media even more complex. I will come back to this point later in the chapter; but before I do, I want to clarify some of the other distinctions touched on.

An excavation report – which might appear online, in a journal article or even a monograph – is clearly part of a different classification; arguably, it is an example of a genre (e.g. see Bradley 2006). It is a genre because it is directly related to an archaeological act: excavation. Both act and text are deeply conventionalized within the discipline, so we have no difficulty recognizing them as types – of acts or texts. However, two excavation reports – say, as journal articles – can still differ quite substantially, as we saw in Hodder's analysis of the site report (see above). Hodder's study, of course, focuses on the political reasons for the differences between an eighteenth-century and twentieth-century site report, but, linguistically, we would say these differences are about language styles or registers. A register in linguistics is another contested term (e.g. see Trosberg 1997; Lee 2001), but generally it refers to the form or style of language used in a text. For example, texts written for a scholarly readership will differ from those written for a general audience. Popular books which draw on archaeology might belong to a different register than an academic monograph intended primarily for archaeologists, although such distinctions are by no means always clear. On the whole, though, genres and registers often overlap – most modern site reports adopt the same register. But what about text types in archaeology? If we stick with our current example, a genre such as an excavation report might incorporate multiple text types in its composition – description (e.g. of a structure), narration (e.g. of a site sequence) and argumentation (e.g. that the site was only seasonally occupied). Similarly, a text type can recur in multiple genres and even different registers – for example a narrative can be written in both academic and more literary prose styles, while it can be used in site reports, topical essays or other genres.

Thus, when thinking about archaeological texts, it is important to keep in mind the differences between medium, genre, register and text type as I use them here (Table 3.3, see p. 80). They may frequently overlap and they certainly mutually influence each other, but they are basically different ways of looking at texts. The latter three have been subject to intense discussion within textual linguistics and related fields. Genre is easily conceived as being linked to specific practices in archaeology: excavation reports, the inaugural lecture, a student dissertation – these all have obvious social contexts of production which are linked to the organization of social practices in archaeology, whether in commercial or university settings. Indeed, a commercial excavation report is arguably a different genre to a research excavation report in this sense. The concept of register is somewhat less clear, but in many ways one could argue that most archaeological texts adopt a very similar register today – that of academic or scholarly prose with its own technical language. It is only with more experimental texts, especially those using fiction, that a different register is employed; nonetheless, even within a single text, the register can shift from high academic prose to a more informal or personal tone, while arguably the language of a theoretical text is very different to that of an archaeological science paper. Finally, there is the medium. Given the current importance of the digital humanities and its relation to archaeology, this dimension of a text needs a little more discussion, especially on the distinction between digital and print text. This is something I will save for a later section in this chapter.

I think it is important to think of these four elements as involving different, cross-cutting typologies; while a common trend has been to create an overarching scheme where genre, register and text type (or variants of these terms) are all incorporated within a single, hierarchical model, with one term sub- or super-ordinate to another, I prefer to think of them as separate dimensions of texts. For

**TABLE 3.3** Text dimensions with examples

| Medium | Genre | Register | Text type |
|---|---|---|---|
| Printed Book | Excavation report | Academic prose | Description |
| Online article | Book review | Vernacular | Narration |
| Lecture notes | Literature review | | Exposition |
| Website | Case study | | Argument |
| | Interview/dialogue | | |

my purposes in this book, however, it is the category of text type that will remain my focus, not medium, genre or register, let alone any overall model. In the next section, I will explore in more detail how text types manifest themselves in archaeological writing.

## Text types in archaeology

To illustrate the nature of text types, I want to briefly examine a small selection of archaeological texts and parse them into the four principal types that recur in most classifications: narrative, description, exposition and argument. For the sake of clarity, it will help if I define, roughly, what I take these four types to involve (also see Table 3.4); this rough sketch will be elaborated in much more detail later in this book. Narrative involves a story, which means there has to be a 'plot' of some kind, involving actors or characters and events, and it will unfold over time, typically having a beginning, middle and end. Description involves an observed object or event, whose basic qualities or attributes are presented for the reader, whether as facts/data or in more aesthetic prose; descriptions are usually of limited length and rarely define a whole text, but tend to be part of larger texts. Exposition is about explaining or clarifying a topic or issue; unlike narrative or description, exposition generally has a more abstract idea as its subject, although this can relate to empirical phenomena. Arguments also have a similar abstract subject matter, although they differ from exposition in that this subject matter will also be contentious and thus involve a claim or thesis which will be supported or critiqued by drawing on lines of evidence.

Choosing which texts to analyse using these four rhetorical structures is not easy and certainly no pretence is made to be exhaustive here – my sole aim is merely to elaborate on the discussion in the previous section with some concrete examples. To that end, I decided to select texts that will be well known to most readers, at least within the Anglophone archaeological tradition, and I will focus on the two most important textual media: journal articles and books. According to two recent searches, the most cited archaeology papers today are Binford's "Willow Smoke and Dog Tails" (based on a search by Michael Smith; http://publishingarchaeology.blogspot.is/2008/10/most-heavily-cited-archaeology-articles.html) and "Radiocarbon age calibration" by Stuiver et al. (based on a search by Doug Rocks-Macqueen; https://dougsarchaeology.wordpress.

**TABLE 3.4** Text types and their characteristics

| Text type | Subject | Salient features |
|---|---|---|
| Narration | Story/Plot | temporal structure, 'actors', events |
| Description | Object/Event | observable qualities, phenomena, facts, data |
| Exposition | Topic/Issue | definitions, classifications, summations, results |
| Argument | Claim/Thesis | justifications, warrants, evidence, critique |

com/2011/08/26/highest-cited-archaeology-journal-papers). Both searches used the same software (*Publish or Perish*), but entering different parameters will return different results. I used the same program to include a search on archaeological books and at the top came Tilley's *Phenomenology of Landscape* followed by the third edition of Hodder's *Reading the Past*, co-authored with Scott Hudson. One can, of course, debate how accurate these searches are or even whether 'most cited' means 'most well-known', but since this is not the goal here, but rather a means to an end, I will use these four texts as principal exemplars. I will not go into any detail about the content of each text, but rather present an outline of their rhetorical strategies and how that relates to the com-position of the text. I will begin with the journal articles.

## Journal articles

Binford's paper opens with an explicit statement on its intentions in the first paragraph: an exposition of the archaeological patterning relating to the mobile lifestyle of hunter-gatherers (Binford 1980). However, the following paragraphs shift register to a more argumentative stance, as Binford lays out his theoretical background assumptions (systemic conception of culture) and his familiar epistemic position about the role of middle-range theory. This is clearly a personal position being presented, and although he does not actually argue his assumptions and approach in this paper, they would be well known to readers. The main, middle section of the paper then reverts to an expositional form as Binford elucidates two basic mobility patterns – foragers and collectors – based on ethnographic exemplars. In discussing the two patterns, his text occasionally draws on ethnographic descriptions, but its overall tone is expository, drawing out generalizations both within and between each mobility pattern, especially in regard to their potential archaeological signatures. In his following discussion, Bin-ford brings his paper back into argumentative mode as he explores explanations for the two different strategies of foraging and collecting, offering various claims or postulates which carry certain implications which he then 'tests' against various lines of evidence. The paper concludes with a summation of the argument, drawing out its connections to the nature of assemblages as they might be observed in the archaeological record.

If we tabulate Binford's paper section by section in relation to the parsing of dominant text type employed, it is clear the paper largely oscillates between an expository and argumentative mode, although descriptions occur occasionally in the middle section (Table 3.5). Is the paper as a whole, then, an exposition or

**TABLE 3.5** The rhetorical structure of Binford's "Willow Smoke and Dog Tails" (1980) as defined by its principal text types.

| Section | Pages | Text type |
|---|---|---|
| [Introduction] | 1 | Exposition |
| [Introduction] | 2 | Argument |
| Collectors and Foragers | 8 | Exposition |
| Discussion | 5 | Argument |
| Conclusion | 2 | Argument |

argument? I am not sure one really needs to make such a decision, and in fact I would say that the paper begins chiefly as an exposition (but with a brief argumentative section), but then switches in its discussion section to an argument. In terms of page length, both modes get more or less equal weight.

Let us now turn to the second paper, "Radiocarbon age calibration" by Stuiver et al. (1998). In many ways, this is a much more straightforward albeit far more technical paper, presenting a set of calibration curves for radiocarbon dates. The main text of the paper is largely an exposition of the methodology and associated issues used to produce these curves which are appended to the last 20 pages of the paper. The calibration is based on three different materials – dendrochronologically dated tree rings, uranium-thorium dated corals and varve-counted marine sediment. Various problems such as the marine reservoir effect are discussed, but there is no real thesis or claim being made in this paper; those problems that are addressed are subordinate to the basic exposition of method. There is also some basic description of data and laboratories in some of the sections, but again although a great deal of data lies behind the work of this paper, the main focus of the text is methodological exposition rather than detailed description of data. Thus, there is no need to break this text down as I did for Binford's article as this is essentially an expository text from start to finish.

These two papers I have just briefly analysed are very different, both in the language and style (i.e. register), but also their rhetorical structure (i.e. text type). However, they also largely illustrate only two of our four text types – exposition and argument. Fragments of description can be found in both, but of narrative there is no real trace. Whether this reflects the dominant rhetorical modes in archaeology, I cannot say; indeed, this would require a more in-depth and focused study, which is beyond my scope here. As ostensibly the two most cited archaeological papers, it could be argued they embody a paradigm of what a proper archaeological paper should look like. And yet 'most cited' does not necessarily mean 'most common', and thus while it has been a useful starting point to select texts for analysis, I feel we need to supplement this with an additional example in order to get a more rounded picture of textual composition in archaeology today. To that end, I will take one more journal article, somewhat at random but in the hope that it elucidates better the diversity of text types present in archaeology. The paper I have selected is called "Archaeology Dreaming" by Nick Shepherd (2007) and deals with a politically charged case of development-led excavation of a burial ground in Cape Town, South Africa, and the conflict that emerged in its wake between various interest groups. I have chosen it because it illustrates the narrative mode extremely well, a form starkly absent in the previous examples.

The paper starts with a broad summary of the topic in what is best described as exposition, but then switches to a narrative mode to retell – in greatly abbreviated form – the story of a famous South African novel whose moral is then linked to the topic of the paper through further exposition. The next section opens with a descriptive account of the area where the burial ground was located, but description quickly morphs into narrative as the events around the discovery, excavation and public response to the burial ground are told in considered detail. This takes up several pages, and leading characters in the events are named and their role in the affair made explicit. After this, Shepherd offers his reading of these events, which revolve around 'points of fracture' between competing groups; in other words, he reverts to an exposition of the complex and diverse groups caught up in this case and a characterization of the tensions emergent from them. In the next section, he then shifts the exposition on to a more academic plane by linking the debates around the burial ground to a broader perception of science and the history of archaeology in South Africa. Following from this, Shepherd then turns back to the burial ground affair and discusses the cleavages in terms of the different languages adopted by different parties – that is, the terms in which a debate was conducted and how this was linked to very different conceptions of heritage and material remains from the past. This thread is picked up in the subsequent section which narrates how the developers viewed the site through the reading of a glossy brochure. The paper ends with some general reflections on the nature of heritage in post-colonial contexts.

Tabulating Shepherd's paper in the same way we did for Binford shows, again, a paper which switches between two main text types, narrative and exposition. Although in terms of sections, exposition dominates, by page length, the ratio is more even. As with Binford's paper, then, we should not succumb to the need to define this by a dominant rhetorical mode, but accept that the paper works, precisely because it tacks back and forth between two forms.

**TABLE 3.6** The rhetorical structure of Shepherd's "Archaeology Dreaming" (2007) as defined by its principal text types.

| Section | Pages | Text type |
| --- | --- | --- |
| Six Feet of the Country | 3 | Exposition/Narration/Exposition |
| Time-Line Prestwich Street | 7 | Narration |
| Points of fracture | 3 | Exposition |
| An Image of Science | 2 | Exposition |
| Rival languages of concern | 3 | Exposition |
| Post-apartheid urban imaginaries | 2 | Narration/Exposition |
| In the post-colony | 2 | Exposition |

As I mentioned before, in taking these three papers as exemplars, by no means is this meant to convey the full range of rhetorical strategies used in textual composition in archaeology; it is more about revealing their complexity and hybrid form in terms of the 'ideal' text types of narration, description, exposition and argument. To complete this discussion, I want to now turn to some books and analyse them in the same way. Books are, of course, much larger and more complex constructs than articles, so my analysis will be necessarily truncated and will focus on only the broadest of outlines.

## Books

The two books I have chosen to study are, as mentioned earlier, selected because they came up on a search as the top two most cited archaeology books today. One is what you might call an extended essay or monograph, Tilley's *The Phenomenology of Landscape*, while the other – Hodder and Hutson's *Reading the Past* – is effectively a textbook of archaeological theory. They thus offer a nice contrast, but, as with the journal articles, I have decided to supplement these with one more book, an excavation monograph chosen somewhat at random.

To begin with Tilley (1994). This is a short book, just over 200 pages, and is a seminal text of postprocessual and especially phenomenological archaeology. The book is divided into two parts, the first a theoretical discussion covering two chapters, the second part consisting of three case study chapters, with a concluding sixth chapter. I will not analyse the book in detail but rather take the first chapter from each part. Chapter 1 opens with an exposition about theoretical convergences between archaeology and geography, but on the fourth page the beginning of an argument emerges as a claim is put forward about a phenomenological approach towards space in archaeology. The nature of a phenomenological approach is then outlined in a return to an expository mode as the work of relevant key philosophers and social scientists is summarized, elaborated through various concepts/dimensions such as place, politics, landscape, movement and narrative. Essentially, this chapter lays out the theoretical groundwork for the book, elucidating various key concepts; however, it is essentially expository and not argumentative. There is a claim made about moving archaeological studies of space into a more embodied and phenomenological mode and away from the disembodied abstract notion of space characterizing earlier work in archaeology; however, what follows this claim is not a set of arguments or warrants to justify this so much as a general exposition on what a phenomenological approach entails. One could contrive to make this exposition the equivalent of a set of warrants, but this is not how Tilley writes it – and that is a crucial point I want to underline.

Chapter 3 is the first of three case studies in the second half of the book and presents a phenomenological account of prehistoric monuments in south-west Wales. The chapter opens with a description of the landscape, followed by a description/exposition of the current state of knowledge on archaeological remains dating to the Mesolithic in the area. I use the two terms description/exposition here because sometimes Tilley is simply enumerating sites and finds and at other times making some generalizations about the locations of these sites. He then moves on to discuss Neolithic remains in much the same way but in a more extended manner and drawing on personal fieldwork in the area. The text is very descriptive, being attentive to details of landscape and monument appearance; it is very visual/visually oriented, a fact underlined by the many photographs which are a key counter to conventional distribution maps. Interspersed between descriptions are expository remarks, which culminate in a brief concluding section to the chapter stressing the locational aspects of the sites in terms of paths and movement.

I think it is fair to say that Tilley's book as a whole is largely a combination of description and exposition, the first part being more expository, the second more descriptive, although exposition is interwoven throughout the case studies. The final chapter, however, takes on the contours of an argument; it begins with an exposition that is a summation of basic differences between Mesolithic and Neolithic relations to and perceptions of the landscape, as discussed in the individual chapters. But the chapter then goes on to make several claims about the ideological basis of these differences, especially for the Neolithic and its monuments – claims that are usually provided with brief warrants based on the case studies. The concluding chapter is short – only seven pages – and in many ways it is an attempt to retrospectively cast the case studies and book as a whole, as an argument.

The second book I want to look at is more textbook than monograph. Hodder and Hutson's *Reading the Past* (2003) is a primer in archaeological theory, with more than 250 pages divided into ten chapters. Each chapter takes a different theme, but they are more or less all very similar in textual structure and rhetorical strategy; as an example, I will just analyse chapter 5, which deals with the topic of agency. At 16 pages, there are three sections. The first outlines the practice and structuration theories of Bourdieu and Giddens, explaining their basic approaches and key concepts, illustrated with archaeological examples. This is pure exposition. The subsequent sections explore the topic of power and resistance, and lastly the concept of agency itself; again, these are written in expository mode. Typically, an exposition enumerates the dimensions or aspects of the topic under study; the last section, for example, discusses *three* broad categories of approach to agency, *four* different stages of an action, and makes *six* general points about agency.

Although it is fair to say that most of the chapters in this book are of a similar form, the first chapter – entitled "The Problem" – clearly hints that this is not just a textbook attempting to give a neutral and impartial survey of archaeological theory. This first chapter proffers what is closer to an argument insofar as it makes a claim about the way archaeological interpretation should proceed: with a commitment to meaning, agency, and history as the preface to this third edition also makes explicit. As such, it tells the reader that the exposition you will read on various theoretical approaches and topics should be read against an argumentative framework which is more evident, perhaps, in some of Hodder's other writings. As the preface also indicates, the book is a hybrid – part textbook on theory, part theoretical argument – and yet perhaps time itself may have pushed this more to the textbook end of the spectrum. When I read the first edition (Hodder 1986), I do think I saw this more as a book which argued for a theoretical position, even if an expository mode of textual composition still dominated. Today, this third edition, enlarged to be more ecumenical as well as up to date, has surely morphed more into a textbook than its original incarnation. This reflects as much the changing theoretical environment as it does the actual changes to the text itself between 1986 and 2003.

In ending this section on books, it is appropriate to take what might be considered the paradigmatic text of archaeology: the site report. Here, the selection is endless so I will once again adopt a rather arbitrary choice by taking one that happens to be on my shelf opposite me now: *Power and Island Communities: Excavations at the Wardy Hill Ringwork, Coveney, Ely*, by Chris Evans with contributions from numerous specialists (Evans 2003). The physical appearance of the book immediately marks it out, being A4 size with double column text and smaller font size than either of the other books. At just under 300 pages, the book is divided into six chapters and the first four are almost purely descriptive. Of these, chapter 1 presents the environmental and landscape context including fieldwork methodology, chapter 2 the structural sequence, chapter 3 the environmental data, and chapter 4 the finds. Take chapter 2 as an example; this chapter is divided into sections defined by periods – Bronze Age, Iron Age and historical periods, but with most attention devoted to the Iron Age. Here, sub-sections describe buildings and other features in classic, formulaic fashion (e.g. dimensions, shapes, soils), with accompanying site plans and sections. The section following the Iron Age discusses chronological developments to the Iron Age site and presents a series of arguments about how to read time or site dynamics from the excavated evidence, followed by a suggested phasing. The chapter ends by reflecting on how the site was 'lost' and contemporary local attitudes to landscape history.

One question that immediately arises concerns whether we should call this chapter a narrative rather than a description, unlike the other three chapters already mentioned. It certainly has a very basic narrative structure insofar as it presents the information chronologically, dividing the site into periods and even presenting sub-phasing for one of the periods. However, the text type dominating the chapter is clearly description, with an argument in one section (Iron Age phasing dynamics) and exposition in another (local attitudes to landscape). I think much the same can probably be said about most excavation monographs – they may adopt the general structure of a narrative, but in terms of textual composition they are largely very descriptive. All the same, it should be said that this monograph is unusual in the degree of argument and exposition it contains as most site monographs tend to be far more descriptive. At the same time, the descriptive language used in a site report is very different to that used, for example, by Tilley in his work. Even though we might say both books are predominantly descriptive across large sections, they read very differently; that is because they adopt different registers or languages of description (see above).

The monograph ends with two more general chapters, one returning to the issue of site sequence and the final one addressing broader questions of power and violence. Chapter 5 re-examines the dynamics of change on the site through artefactual and geochemical spatial patterning. It begins by using description and exposition of data patterning, but then draws on this patterning to build up an argument about the settlement dynamics. The final chapter 6 contextualizes the site within broader Iron Age research themes and offers an argument for seeing the site as occupying a key location within the political geography of the area during the Iron Age. To summarize, then, this excavation monograph is one that is heavily defined by description, especially in the first four chapters, but switches into argumentative mode for the final two. However, even within any one chapter, other modes are apparent, although, unlike many of the other texts I have been discussing, exposition is rare. Narrative, though superficially evident as a structuring device, is also more or less absent from the text itself.

What I hope I have demonstrated in these examples of three journal articles and three books is the diversity of text types, even within any given text, and the consequent differences between texts. The permutations and combinations are endless. Thus, glossing all archaeological texts as 'narratives' – as the tendency of recent years has been – is simply misleading. Either the term is broadened so wide as to lose any real meaning, or if it does retain a specific meaning, it is clearly inadequate as a way of expressing the diversity of textual composition. Now, I am sure one could somehow make Binford's text out to be a narrative and even define it in terms of one of White's tropes; equally, one could turn Shepherd's paper into an argument and pull out a claim and various warrants. But in either case this would not be a faithful reading of the text, but rather a rewriting or reconstituting of the text in another mode. In doing this, something is lost – especially any relation between textual composition and knowledge production.

Of course, even my adoption of these four 'ideal' text types is arguably too restrictive, and while I do recognize their potential limitations, they still nonetheless serve a useful purpose, which is to offer a means with which to think about textual composition in a structured yet still faithful way. But I think they can also do much more than that. In the next chapter, I want to put these four text types to work in a very different way to their normal usage in discourse analysis. I want to think about how they relate to knowledge production and therefore consider their ontological and epistemological dimensions. This is important because one of the key issues one faces when evaluating the scholarly quality of a journal article or book is its contribution to archaeological knowledge, and yet if different texts adopt different rhetorical strategies, can we really apply the same measures of evaluation? For example, can we really assess the papers by Binford and Shepherd or the books by Tilley and Hodder using the same epistemic criteria? How deeply embedded is the question of knowledge in textual composition? But before I try to answer these questions, I need to deal with one other, major issue: the material medium in which texts exist.

## Text types and the digital humanities

Thus far, I have put very little emphasis on the role of textual media, although they were clearly acknowledged in the section on experimental texts, especially the digital forms of narrative which drew on concepts like hypertextuality. The question I need to now engage with is the extent to which the increasing use of digital texts in archaeology relates to my previous discussion of text types. What are the epistemological dimensions of textual media?

I think it helps at this point to revisit my earlier discussion of texts in archaeology and fill a gap. In the introduction to this book I mentioned the work of Jean-Claude Gardin and his distinction of two broad archaeological constructs which he defined in primarily textual terms: compilations and explanations (Gardin 1980). The terminology he uses, especially the word 'explanation', is probably misleading and it is much better to think of what he means by explanation as any extended essay or discussion typically embodied in journal articles and monographs, in contrast to the catalogues, inventories and records which make up compilations. In a sense, all the literature on texts and narratives I discussed above was really just focused on what Gardin calls 'explanations'; indeed, for Gardin there was a strong parallel between his distinction of compilations and explanations and the broader dichotomy of science and literature embodied in C.P. Snow's two cultures (Dallas 2016: 318).

Discussion of his category of 'compilations' was not really covered in this narrative literature and indeed there has been very little discussion of this group of texts in archaeology until recently in the wake of the surge of work on digital data networking and preservation. Before addressing this work, it is important to underline what Gardin meant by compilations. For Gardin, the distinction between these two archaeological constructs was critical and had major implications for issues of publication. More crucially, Gardin considered that most archaeological publications actually failed to appreciate the distinction between these two constructs, and hence fell short of what the function of each was supposed to be. For Gardin, the function of a compilation was essentially to act as a database, enabling the retrieval of information about archaeological data; compilations essentially treated the material remains which constitute the archaeological record. The function of an explanation on the other hand was to offer interpretations of that data, interpretations which essentially related to the past peoples and societies in which these material remains once circulated.

Seen in this light, one can better understand Gardin's displeasure with the contemporary state of archaeological literature; on the one hand, there are data–rich texts such as site reports which provide access to data but in a most user-unfriendly manner. Recall my earlier comment about why site reports are largely perceived as boring; under Gardin's scheme, this reflects the fact that they are written as if they are supposed to be read – that is, as prose. If we dropped this pretence and made a clearer distinction between the site report as a database and the site report as an interpretation, this would no longer be a problem. Drawing a sharper distinction would also cure another ailment of the archaeological literature in Gardin's opinion: the inflation of explanations. For, on the other hand, the massive increase in published literature an archaeologist – indeed, any academic – is faced with reading is a problem we can all relate to and has only worsened since Gardin discussed this in the 1970s and 1980s. The proliferation of journals, the pressure on publication output generated by institutional research assessments, all speak to this growth. For Gardin, most of this literature has the surface form of explanation but actually serves as a kind of data dump; the actual quality of the explanatory component is highly variable and often questionable.

A survey done in the late 1980s of the proportion of journal articles which had no citations within five years of publication makes for sobering reading and somewhat underlines Gardin's critique; more than 75% of archaeology papers published in 1984 remained uncited five years later (Hamilton 1991). Un-citation statistics varied between fields but there was a clear trend from the hard sciences at one end (e.g. particle physics with less than 10% un-citation rates) and the humanities at the other (e.g. history at more than 95% un-citation rates). One has to read such figures with caution, of course; citation rates do not necessarily correspond with reading rates and the differences may also reflect different citation practices between disciplines and especially between journal articles and books/monographs – the latter are usually excluded in citation studies. Nonetheless, the statistics should make us sit up and take note. If our publication model is not working – or rather only self-serving an internal production machine of academic capital – then what is to be done? Gardin would like to see conventional publication more a privilege than an obligation, one where a text is worth spilling ink for, one that can and should justify its existence (Gardin 1980: 157). For the rest, archaeology needs to develop digital databases.

I won't pretend there are not problems with this vision: the potential for elitism, for reducing multivocality, and for over-polarizing archaeological knowledge production into two streams. But the issues Gardin raises about archaeological publication, specifically asking us to question its value and purpose, are important. One of the major benefits that have been argued for digital forms of publication is the erasure or at least blurring of boundaries between traditional paper-based archives and print publication (Richards 2002). The relative ease and cheapness with which primary data can now be 'published' online alongside articles and books does suggest that maybe some of our original genres of writing such as excavation reports require rethinking. Indeed, that very term 'grey literature' captures the neither/nor space between compilations and explanations that Gardin found so abhorrent. And yet what Gardin perhaps did not foresee is the potential of the semantic web to retroactively purify this grey literature – to treat anything as effectively a compilation from which data can be mined.

The issue of data mining is in many ways central to the whole contemporary discussion of cyberinfrastructures – that is, about networking multiple, diverse data sets to create interoperability (Kintigh 2006; Kansa et al. 2011; Richards 2006). This goes beyond the problems faced within a single site or project, but deals with how to create a digital infrastructure that will facilitate the integration of data recovered under different projects and conditions, by different teams and even in different countries. It is one of the key issues which projects such as the European ARIADNE was established to address (Niccolucci & Richards 2013). And the rationale behind it is important, since it deals with the interpretive potential offered by such large-scale data: big data can answer big questions (Kintigh 2006; Jones & Levy 2018). The lynchpin of such cyberinfrastructures is the role of metadata, especially that which deals with ontology: the acknowledged set of entities with which an archaeological database operates. The metadata involved in a conceptual reference model (CRM) provides a semantic bridge between different data sets or sources so that when the term 'handaxe' is used in each, we know we are talking about the same thing (or not). It does not so much create definitions for entities as build a map or language linking prior or implicit definitions, which include not only objects but equally their relations to other objects – for example, spatial and temporal context. The most common, contemporary metadata standard in the heritage field is the CIDOC-CRM (www.cidoc-crm.org). In the process, though, a meta-ontology for archaeology is implicit in such systems.

Of course, any individual project or even archaeologist will inevitably work with their own 'ontologies', and even if there is bound to be an overlap due to a shared disciplinary discourse, differences will always exist. One solution would be to try to police this diversity and get everyone to fall in line; but this is unlikely ever to happen and is frankly undesirable. Moreover, given developments in artificial intelligence, such options are becoming unnecessary. Instead, such ontological uniformity only needs to be embedded in the cyberinfrastructure protocols and using algorithms to machine-read any given data or text, a comparable ontology can be retrofitted as metadata (e.g. see Richards 2015). At the same time, this still strives towards some kind of consensual, uniform ontology for archaeological data and raises some serious concerns. Huggett is one of the few who has shown some acknowledgement of this issue and argues for a greater need to conduct ethnographies of these e-ontologies (Huggett 2012). How and on what basis are these ontologies currently being designed? How embedded are they in the practices of what archaeologists routinely do? After all, the group of archaeologists working on these issues form a minor proportion of our discipline, yet the potential impact their ontological metadata may have on its future is great (see Leonelli 2016 for an important study of bio-ontologies in the context of biology).

But there is even more at stake here than simply a need for reflexive, practice-based ontologies. I come back to the issue of uniformity and standardization – a central theme in Huggett's paper already cited. How much uniformity is desirable? Museum databases face this issue in a way that is perhaps far more obvious than one dealing with archaeological data designed primarily for the profession. How do we deal with different ontologies that accompany the different epistemic cultures which might engage with museum collections? The potential conflict between what Boast and Biehl call the classificatory and interpretive practices of knowledge production are drawn out very sharply in museum contexts (Boast & Biehl 2011). This is the tension between Gardin's compilations and explanations which undermines their forced separation. Kansa summarizes the problem in a nutshell:

It does not take much imagination to see emerging theoretical tensions between archaeological knowledge production driven from algorithms and formalized ontologies versus archaeological knowledge constructed from different threads of narrative. In some ways, the tensions between advocates of "deep reading" and advocates for "interoperability" continue long-standing theoretical disputes in archaeology. Some researchers emphasize contextual nuance and particularistic interpretations, while others seek more generalized patterns in more or less interchangeable empirical data. Each different theoretical orientation fits better with a different type of technical style and systems implementation.

*(Kansa 2011: 22)*

It seems to me that the weight of discussion in cyber-archaeology has continued to focus on problems around compilations as if the explanations constructed on them entail less to worry about. It is also quite clear that in all this discourse a subtle substitution is taking place as knowledge becomes synonymous with information. All the issues about digitality, texts and publication are reduced to problems of data handling and networking. It is called information technology for a reason. This is very clearly exemplified in Giorgio Buccellati´s recent book *A Critique of Archaeological Reason* (2017), which mirrors Gardin's distinction of compilations and explanations with his concepts of archaeological grammar and hermeneutics. As with compilations, Buccellati's grammar treats the internal structure of the material record while his hermeneutics, like Gardin's explanation, deals with the broken historical traditions to which these remains refer. As I have already suggested, I think there are serious problems with the way these distinctions have been made, both by Gardin and Buccellati, but I will leave that aside for now. Buccellati, however, is writing in the wake of developments in the digital humanities and his book is more coordinated around the concept of digitality. Specifically, Buccellati argues that archaeology is 'natively' digital, by which he means that its very form – that is, the fragmented and labile state of its data – naturally makes it harmonious with the logic of digital texts.

There is no question of the importance and significance of these developments in cyberinfrastructures for archaeology, but this reduction of archaeology, epitomized by Buccellati's notion of archaeology as natively digital, is I think problematic. Not to mention that of a 350-page book only the penultimate chapter of 30 pages deals with what Buccellati calls hermeneutics. We need to remind ourselves that the digital practices associated with databases are very different operations from writing a story or constructing an argument. We have always conducted data searches, made comparisons and worried about the ontologies of our classifications. The semantic web and digitization in general clearly have the potential to enhance these research strategies at a scale previously unprecedented. But this is still just *part* of the research process. And even if one accepts some of the more radical suggestions for the role of artificial intelligence in the interpretive process, such as Barceló´s vision of an automatic archaeology (Barceló 2007. 2009; also see Stutt & Shennan 1990 for an earlier attempt to formalize archaeological reasoning), this still leaves open issues about how one expresses an interpretation in terms of textual composition.

For me, the wider issue always brings us back to Gardin and his distinction between compilations and explanations. They cannot be so easily separated – and yet at the same time it is important to recognize they are nonetheless different operations. The distinction also has great resonance with current developments in the digital humanities, especially the theoretical distinction between the database and the narrative. This was a dichotomy raised by Lev Manovich in his highly influential work, *The Language of New Media* (2001), where he argued that databases and narratives have two very different logics; for Manovich, it is the logic of the database that structures new media technologies not conventional narrative. By a database, Manovich is not just referring to the highly structured systems of information storage and retrieval that an archaeologist might typically use, but rather to the database as a mode of reading or interaction with texts. More generally, then, databases

> appear as a collections of items on which the user can perform various operations: view, navigate, search. The user experience of such computerized collections is therefore quite distinct from reading a narrative or watching a film or navigating an architectural site. Similarly, literary or cinematic narrative, an architectural plan and database each present a different model of what a world is like.
>
> *(Manovich 2001: 194)*

As the reference to cinema and plans implies, Manovich does not see the database as a new form, exclusively linked to new media technologies; rather that these new technologies have increased the salience and function of databases and reversed the long-standing dominance of narrative: "As a cultural form, database represents the world as a list of items and it refuses to order this list. In contrast, a narrative creates a cause-and-effect trajectory of seemingly unordered items (events). Therefore, database and narrative are natural enemies" (Manovich 2001: 199). At the same time, Manovich acknowledges that narratives still play role in this brave new world, but it is one that has now been redefined by the inversion of this dialectic between database and narrative:

> This formulation places the opposition between database and narrative in a new light, thus redefining our concept of narrative. The "user" of a narrative is traversing a database, following links between its records as established by the database's creator. An interactive narrative (which can be also called "hyper-narrative" in an analogy with hypertext) can then be understood as the sum of multiple trajectories through a database. A traditional linear narrative is one, among many other possible trajectories; i.e. a particular choice made within a hyper-narrative.
>
> *(Manovich 2001: 200–201)*

Manovich is here drawing on other scholars such as George Landow (1992) and Michael Joyce (1995) who have also espoused the transformative effects of hypertextuality on narrative, and, as we have seen, this has also been a dominant theme in archaeological discussion of narrative and new media. Such work has also suggested reconfigurations of the traditional textual philosophy of hermeneutics (Capurro 2010; on material hermeneutics in general, see Ihde 1998, 2009). A great deal of work in the digital humanities also involves effectively converting older, conventional narrative texts into databases – that is, digitizing print texts and making them searchable, facilitating alternative readings through the creation of hyperlinks and so on (e.g. see Folsom 2007). In this sense, quite conventional literary narratives and other texts can be treated more like databases.

There is no doubt that digital technologies are having a massive impact on practices of knowledge production, archaeology included (e.g. see Shott 2014), and are forcing us to consider how archaeology should deal with the data avalanche which it brings in its wake (Buccellati 2017; Kintigh 2006; Jones & Levy 2018). These are themes anticipated by Gardin nearly half a century ago, as we already saw. But the issue I wish to focus on here is this tension or opposition between databases and narrative (or compilation and explanation) which has the most relevance to my discussion of text types. If the digital environment is truly transforming the nature of narrative as Manovich and others argue, to what extent are textual classifications discussed in the last section already becoming superfluous?

I think we need to pause and question this relationship a little more carefully because, as I will suggest, these text types are far from redundant but continue to operate and have relevance. Certainly, much recent literature in composition studies tends to repeat the revolutionary implications of the new media on texts (e.g. Koehler 2017) and within related disciplines, such as history, there is an emerging discourse about how the new digital environment is affecting the practice of writing history (e.g. Dougherty & Nawrotzki 2013; Weller 2013). Much of this work inevitably focuses on issues of facilitating access to primary data and the enhanced potential for exploring different and multiple paths through the historical archive, enhancing collaboration and multivocality. These are, of course, all the same issues that are coming up in archaeology, as discussed above, and in terms of the research and writing process, digital media are having a major impact. And yet in conclusion to a work embracing the digital turn, here is what the historians found:

> Yet we were surprised to discover the degree of continuity in the content of historical writing. The best of digitally inspired scholarship integrates technology into the art of composing works that feature what many consider the finest qualities in our field: a compelling narrative that unravels the past, supported by insightful argument and persuasive evidence.
>
> *(Dougherty et al. 2013: 260)*

It might tempting to conclude from this that it is just business as usual, then. But it is, of course, more complex and even those historians then go on to qualify this statement. One of the key issues is that not all historical writing has to be a closely argued narrative; at the same time, though, when talking about alternative forms of writing, the discussion usually devolves into a dichotomy: narrative versus bricolage (Dorn 2013). We saw the same issue occur in archaeology with Alison Mickel's contrast of narrative and montage (see Chapter 3; Mickel 2013). I have found the work of Katherine Hayles insightful here (Hayles 2002. 2003. 2012); through it, we can connect this opposition of narrative and bricolage/montage to another opposition: that between narrative and database. Hayles questions the sharp opposition that Manovich sets up between database and narrative, and rather sees them as complimentary operations, ones in fact that scholars have always used together and quite happily. Hayles's discussion of this issue in relation to forms or styles of reading is especially instructive (Hayles 2012). Set against the popular debates on how student reading skills have been severely impaired by the new media, especially the perceived demise in close reading in favour of what has been called hyper-reading (Sosnoski 1999) or distant reading (Moretti 2007; also see Guillory 2008, 2010), Hayles suggests that rather than see these as oppositional, they again just represent different, complimentary strategies. Indeed, hyper-reading – which refers to a type of skimming or scanning over a text to pick out bits of information – has always been a practice of scholars, especially working in archives. Certainly, the digital environment has increased its usage, but it did not invent it. Indeed, hyper-reading can also be performed on texts which are meant to be read closely; it is surely no shameful confession to make that in researching for this book I did a lot of hyper-reading of books and journal articles alongside close reading. These are the same issues raised by Gardin in his discussion of how one uses compilations and explanations; you consult the former, but read the latter (Gardin 1980, 1999; also see Buccellati 2017: 209–210, on the distinction between consulting and studying). The only difference is Gardin would have us sharpen the distinction in relation to textual form whereas contemporary theory blurs such boundaries.

This distinction also resonates with that between intensive and extensive reading in pedagogy and language learning, where intensive reading is similar to close reading and an extensive reading typically employs skimming (a quick read to get the gist of a text) and scanning (searching to pull out specific bits of information; e.g. see Brown 2000). Significantly, appreciation of the difference between these reading practices emerged in language education debates of the 1920s and 1930s – long before the era of digital texts (e.g. see Moore 1943). Moreover, alongside close and hyper-reading, Hayles discusses a third type: machine reading, which is the use of algorithms to search for patterns in texts. Machine reading is particularly significant in relation to big data and connects to arguments for a machine epistemology which has interesting repercussions for debates around induction (see Wheeler 2017). Archaeologists are certainly well versed in machine reading – even using a simple sort function in a spreadsheet or database file is arguably a form of machine reading, albeit one under human 'supervision', although the more 'pure' examples would be in the use of agent-based models (ibid.)

What is important in this discussion about the complementary nature of different types of reading is that if one can read texts like databases (i.e. hyper-reading or machine reading), and one can read databases like texts (i.e. using hyperlinks), then why do we need to argue that narrative texts have really been transformed? Especially as these practices seem to predate the new media by centuries. Does it really serve any theoretical purpose, and is it, in fact, an accurate description of the way things really are? Here, Marie-Laure Ryan's critique of the mythologies of the new media is highly pertinent, especially as it is a critique not based on a reactionary position but one which marks out a fault line between the high theory of this new media and its actual everyday use (Ryan 2002). Unpacking the arguments around both hypertextuality and virtual reality in relation to narrative, Ryan argues that narrative is fundamentally at odds with the interactivity that digital media allow. She is not suggesting the two cannot be wedded or work together (although the success of this, she suggests, depends on the particular cybertext genres involved – VR, gaming or hypertext); only that narrative will always still be a narrative, whether it is constructed through digital media or not.

I think many of the problems here can really be traced back to a failure to distinguish between the performative and structural nature of narratives. Performatively, narratives are indeed being reconfigured by the new media, which offer new ways of both constructing and reading such texts – or at least expanding our capacity to read narratives as databases and vice versa. Performatively, the distinction between databases and narratives is highly fluid and weak. But, structurally, the narrative form is the same as it has always been and its distinction from a database is quite obvious. As Hayles puts it: "Whereas data elements must be atomized for databases to function efficiently, narrative fiction embeds 'data elements' (if we can speak of such) in richly contextualized environments of the phrase, sentence, paragraph, section, and fiction as a whole" (Hayles 2012). These notions of atomization and embedding will be quite pertinent to how I will address the epistemological dimensions of text in the rest of this book.

For I will suggest that it is the structural properties of archaeological texts that we need to address in order to understand their relation to knowledge production. This is not to suggest that its performative properties have no epistemological dimension; quite the converse, as part of my goal is to see how performative function is related to structure. Certainly, the computing power of big data and machine reading is opening up new challenges and possibilities, especially in the context of writing long-term histories. Without question, the performative function of database texts is having a major impact on knowledge practices, not least in reviving the status of quantitative data. Moreover, digital books, journals and online articles make accessibility much easier (with all the usual caveats about the hidden political economy of such access), and create more options for both users in the form of searching and for producers in the form of revisions and updating. Furthermore, collaborative authorship is also increasingly facilitated through shared online work spaces and wikis (Bauer 2013; Webmoor 2008), while virtual platforms such as Second Life are being exploited for their pedagogical value (e.g. Forte and Dell'Unto 2010; but also see Harrison 2009 for a more critical perspective in terms of heritage issues). Such technologies surely enhance multivocality and pluralism. However, the extent to which all these performative possibilities are changing the structural nature of archaeological texts is surely debatable.

I think it is to the structural properties of text that we need to attend in order to really come to grips with these epistemic issues, and critical to this process is deciding at what level to analyse a text. One of the key points in my discussion of texts types, which I ought to repeat here, is that these refer to text *sections*, not *whole works*, which are probably better discussed under the concept of genre. Digital media are unquestionably inventing new *genres* of writing, but whether this extends to new *text types* is highly debatable. And the epistemological status of genre is not my concern here. The distinction between database and narrative as these terms have been used in the discussion of new media technologies (and, by extension, Gardin's discussion of compilations and explanations) can therefore, I think, be reconfigured in terms of an epistemic performativity linked to textual structure.

The 'atomization' of database logic can be understood as the ability to break texts down through processes of detachment or deracination, while the 'embedding' function of narrative logic acts, conversely, to sew these elements together. Or, in Deleuzian terms, it is about the process of de-territorializing and re-territorializing textual assemblages and the epistemic function such processes entail. Let us follow a hypothetical example to make this clearer. Presented with an assemblage of faunal remains from a site, the analysis and recording process typically involves a translation of objects into coded strings of numbers and text: measurements, anatomical elements, species identification, taphonomic attributes and so on. At this stage, one still has an atomized or deracinated collection of 'facts'. From the resultant database – which encodes a specific ontology – the faunal analyst may then write a technical report, describing the methodology used, the general composition of the assemblage and, ideally, an interpretive section which draws out any patterns in the data as they relate to their find context. Such reports are typically a mixture of deracinated information (e.g. statistical summaries, often tabulated) and embedded knowledge (e.g. discussion of chronological trends). This report may then get picked up by another faunal specialist who draws out data from it as a comparison with their own material; the report gets mined, treated as a database and information moved into another embedded context. And so on.

For many, of course, the ideal would involve not having to mine 'grey reports' for such information at all, but rather encourage the collation of all such data into accessible, online databases. But even if this happens, archaeologists will continue to work through the same dual processes of deracinating and embedding information as part of the textual practices in knowledge construction. My focus in this book is primarily with the embedding function of texts, and although I address deracination in the final chapter, it deals with quite different objects of deracination. In the next chapter I look to the embedding function and discuss the ways in which four major text types used in archaeology embed or draw together their elements to create a coherent whole and draw out the epistemological implications of this structure. In Chapter 5, I address the ways in which these same elements become detached from their textual context and are able to move between texts. Together, these two performative operations of how texts work, on an epistemic level, illustrate how this dual process of deracination and embedding are constitutive of archaeological writing as knowledge practice.

# 4

# TEXTUAL COMPOSITION AND KNOWLEDGE PRODUCTION

## Introduction

Although there has been a tendency to think of science and especially scientific reason as a monolithic enterprise, consisting of a single, coherent form of rationality, the more recent acknowledged diversity of science and scientific practices has worked against this (Galison & Stump 1996). In Chapter 2, I discussed the philosophies which argued for a difference between natural and human/social sciences and their respective epistemologies of positivism and hermeneutics. However, this cleavage has been since regarded as too dichotomous and various attempts have been made to close the gap (for archaeology, see e.g. Kosso 1991; Salmon 1992), while yet still recognizing the apparent disunity of science (Wylie 2000). In mediating between the need to acknowledge difference while still ceding to the idea that the different scientific disciplines nonetheless form a family, the philosopher of science Ian Hacking, many years ago, proposed the notion of styles of reasoning (Hacking 1992). Hacking was inspired by the work of another philosopher of science, A.C. Crombie, who had been writing since the 1970s on styles of scientific thinking (Crombie 1994), and indeed the idea of styles of scientific thought go back even further to Ludwig Fleck's seminal work from the 1930s and his concept of *denkstil* which was to have a major but albeit delayed impact on historians and philosophers of science in the 1980s (Fleck 1979). Fleck's thought styles were largely very specific to disciplines, however, while Crombie's work attempted to generalize so that he suggested six dominant styles of scientific thought: postulation, experimentation, analogy, classification, statistical analysis and historical reconstruction (Crombie 1988).

In discussing Crombie's work, Hacking more or less followed his classification, but with some revisions and amendments, both to its underlying rationale and to its specific terms. Not least, for example, Hacking refers to his typology as styles of *reasoning*, not *thinking*, because of the distributed nature of scientific practice – that is, it takes place outside the mind as much as inside. More importantly, though, Hacking sees different styles of reasoning as accompanied by different kinds of objects, evidence and ways of constructing knowledge claims. In other words, different styles have different ontological and epistemological commitments. What is also important to recognize is that the divisions between these styles do not align with the divisions between sciences, but cut across them; a single discipline can and will display more than one style and indeed styles can be blended together.

Another paper from the 1970s, which was not picked up by Hacking, in many ways attempts to take a similar approach as Crombie but at a much wider level. Louis Mink used the concept of modes of comprehension rather than styles of reasoning or thinking to address the perceived dichotomy between scientific and historical forms of explanation and thus cover the whole field of academic thought (Mink 1970). Mink wrote his paper in response to the emerging discourse on narrative modes of explanation in history and their distinction from positivist versions of scientific explanation. His paper mostly focuses on the question of narrative. His work became a key text in wider discussions of narrative as I will discuss further below, but what is often forgotten is that Mink regarded narrative as just one of three basic modes of comprehension, the others being theoretical and categorical. Thus narrative is linked to comprehension as a form of understanding which grasps totality through time; the temporal structure of narrative is fundamental to it as a mode of comprehension which is exemplified through the notion of what it means to 'follow a story'. The temporality of narrative is a feature I will return to, as it is of the utmost relevance. As for Mink's other modes of comprehension, the theoretical has a law-like or generalizing character and is most linked to the natural sciences, while his categorical involves processes of classification, analogy and exemplification, which he links primarily to philosophy.

I think the work of Crombie, Hacking and Mink yield very fruitful ideas, but, as they stand, they are perhaps still a little too abstract or rather high-level concepts which combine diverse practices; what, for example, is the link between conducting an experiment and writing about it? Is the same style of reasoning evident during the experiment and in the published paper? My concern in this book is with the very specific practice of writing, as a form of knowledge production. Although one needs to understand how, for example, the writing of an excavation monograph relates to the act of excavation itself, the text itself can still be viewed as a thing in its own right. To put this in Hacking's language, my concern here is with styles of reasoning in relation to textual composition, and in this sense Crombie's list of six types is not so useful. More relevant is the work of Charles Bazerman on the connection between scientific writing and the production of scientific knowledge – or, as he put it, "how language accomplishes the work of science" (Bazerman 1988: 291). Bazerman's papers on scientific writing from the 1980s (collected and expanded in Bazerman 1988) largely focus on the experimental report as a genre, and he takes a long-term historical view from the emergence of journal science in the seventeenth century up to the twentieth century. Bazerman's approach is ultimately about revealing the intimate connections between the formation of writing and the formation of scientific practices and, as such, it does it well.

However, being genre-focused, Bazerman's work still remains too general for my purposes. At another extreme, there is the work of text linguist Halliday who has explored the grammatical features of scientific writing (Halliday and Martin 1993). This work is also insightful, especially in its ideas about the role of grammatical metaphors in the construction of scientific language (which I will briefly mention again in Chapter 5), but it is also far too general, relating mostly to concept formation. Finally, I should also mention Mary Morgan's recent rethinking of the original Hacking/Crombie work on styles of reasoning as 'epistemic genres' in relation to the notion of the case study (Morgan 2014a). Case studies are a critical part of work in the social sciences and Morgan contrasts them with two other common epistemic genres in the social sciences: experiments and statistical studies. Morgan addresses one of the common criticisms of case studies – namely their particularity; whereas experiments and statistics work on large data sets to extrapolate patterns, extrapolation from a single case study is rather risky. For Morgan, however, this only underlines the different epistemologies implicit in different genres and how one cannot necessarily use the same criteria of evaluation for different genres. For the case study, Morgan suggests its primary epistemic virtue is as a vehicle of discovery, not a space for testing generalizations.

Morgan's discussion is interesting but, like Bazerman, it deals with specific genres and is still too broad in scope although it does bring us a step closer to the objectives of this chapter. A case study, for example, is still a wide category that can encompass a lot of diversity and variation in how it is constructed. It is rather with the concept of text type that I find the most potential – especially if we can take Hacking's insight that different styles of reasoning have different ontological and epistemic commitments, and apply that insight to our four text types outlined in the last chapter, of description, narration, exposition and argument. This is what I would like to do in this chapter. The concept of text type more than genre or other linguistic terms works very well with a concern for epistemological issues and in fact the connection has already been made by other scholars (Kinneavy 1971). It has also received concrete investigation in recent studies which analyse instructional or procedural texts, using a classification of textual acts mirrored directly on speech acts (Chemla & Virbel 2015; Virbel 2015). Thus it has been suggested that mathematical texts which incorporate algorithms or medical texts outlining prescriptions can be seen as forms of instruction – how to do something. While certainly an interesting approach, one of its problems is the simple association between speech act types and text types, which I have already critiqued in the last chapter. An instructional text in many ways is a very easy example since it has a clear purpose; other academic texts, however, are less clear-cut in this way and regarding them as performatives in the manner of a speech act is much less straightforward. A more useful approach is to return to the discussion of text types in the non-archaeological literature but now explore its deeper links to the field of textual composition and rhetoric.

One of the things I mentioned in the last chapter is that although the actual classifications of text types varies, most taxonomies seem to make reference to different rhetorical strategies. I also briefly noted that beside the more dominant link to speech act theory or related performative and communicative approaches to textual discourse, another common influence was pedagogy, specifically textual composition and writing. The classical fourfold typology of description, narration, exposition and argument recurs so frequently because of this link to composition studies. Composition studies is a field largely taught in the USA where it is often part of a first-year foundation in undergraduate studies at university level. Composition courses typically present these four text types, or modes of discourse as they are often more commonly known, as four basic writing styles, although the exact number of types vary; for example, description is often dropped as few texts are purely descriptive, even if they include a descriptive element.

Such an approach was very dominant in the early to mid-twentieth century and is generally known as the current-traditional rhetoric (CTR), although it has now fallen largely out of favour (Connors 1981). From the 1960s, composition studies increasingly began to focus on composition as a dynamic process related to the purpose of writing rather than a static set of model text types. Indeed, Kinneavy (1971) was a key figure in this shift, distinguishing his four *aims* of discourse from the traditional four *modes* of discourse, although there were many other people writing about this too. Ironically, though – and confusingly perhaps – his classification of discourse aims is often cited in text linguistics as an early example of text types, whereas most text types in text linguistics actually reference the modes of discourse he was critiquing. However, as a result, although these four modes of discourse – description, narration, exposition and argument – are still cited and used in composition studies, they are much more marginal in theoretical work and the focus is rather on aspects of composition as a process rather than a product, although there is a wide diversity of approaches adopted.

What is interesting, however, is the origin of this fourfold classification, which goes back to a work by the nineteenth-century Scottish philosopher Alexander Bain (Arrington 1986; Connors 1981; Harned 1985). His book *English Composition and Rhetoric*, first published in 1866, became the basic text adopted in US composition studies and outlined five types of rhetoric: description, narration, exposition, argument and poetry, the latter of which was dropped in later compositional studies (Bain 1867). Although there were earlier comparable classifications, none offered such a detailed analysis as Bain. However, what is especially relevant is that Bain's work was largely developed out of a dissatisfaction with the conventional theories of rhetoric which did not seem to work in the context of scientific writing. Moreover, three of his types of rhetoric were implicitly linked to an associationist philosophy of knowledge, most notably exemplified by another, earlier Scottish philosopher, David Hume. Such a philosophy regarded all knowledge as developing through three basic types of mental association drawn between phenomena: similarity, contiguity and contrast (Harned 1985). Thus description was based on spatial contiguities, narrative on temporal contiguities, while exposition on similarities and contrast. Bain also clearly saw narrative as primarily linked to historical writing and exposition to science, with description as a fundamental building block of both and argument as a supplement (Bain 1867: 4–5).

Clearly, then, the roots of this classification of text types goes even deeper than I have originally portrayed it, into nineteenth- and eighteenth-century philosophies of knowledge. In many ways, the key idea of linking compositional rhetoric to knowledge formation is an important insight and one we should keep hold of, even if we jettison an associationist epistemology. This same insight can also help us to rethink the role of the fourfold classification of modes of discourse which have been marginalized in contemporary composition studies. The basic issue at stake here concerns the criteria behind a classification of text types. From the 1960s, modern text linguistics, discourse analysis and composition studies shared a concern to look at texts in relation to their social function; where text linguistics tried to redefine text types on this basis by tying them to speech act theory or Jakobsen's language functions, discourse analysis and composition theory abandoned them altogether in favour of non-taxonomic approaches. However, new life can be breathed back into these text types if we resurrect Bain's original ambition, which was to link textual composition to knowledge production.

In the remainder of this chapter, I will take each of the four text types in turn and attempt to rethink them in terms of their epistemic commitments. In other words, rather than see the four text types as simply rhetorical strategies as they are conventionally portrayed, I want to view them also as epistemic strategies. A general connection between rhetoric and epistemology was resurrected many years ago now by Robert Scott who drew on the work of Stephen Toulmin on informal logic and arguments (Scott 1967; Toulmin 1958). Toulmin's work will figure prominently in this chapter as he seems to be a common source of inspiration for very different scholars. Scott argued that since all knowledge claims exhibit uncertainty – the gap that lies between truth and belief – one inevitably has to take a leap of faith to cross that gap (Scott 1967). Now where conventional philosophers of knowledge have tried to plug the gap with various accounts of justification (hence the classic definition of knowledge as justified true belief, or JTB), Scott suggested that rhetoric is what ultimately closes it. Moreover, knowing that such rhetoric works in the way it does puts a much greater stress on the ethical or moral dimension of argumentation.

Scott's suggestions do not necessarily invalidate the need for justification, of course; rather that even with justification, there will always remain uncertainty. Rhetoric simply becomes an epistemic tool to deal with the limitations of justification. This has the potential to be troubling – especially if rhetoric is seen simply as the art of persuasion. But if one takes a more general view that links rhetoric generally to modes of communication, then I think it is less contentious. To some extent, such an approach has been taken by Steve Fuller in his own brand of a social epistemology which argues for a rhetoric of interpenetrability – that is, the ability of rhetoric to facilitate dialogue and communication between different epistemic positions (Fuller & Collier 2004). However, Fuller's discussion of rhetoric always remains at a fairly abstract level insofar as it not embedded in the concrete forms of knowledge expression such as texts. Fuller's main concern is to situate rhetoric in the wider field of the public accountability of science. Another, more recent approach by William Rehg focuses more on the question of what makes a scientific claim merit our consideration (Rehg 2009). His discussion, which also provides a useful review of other studies connecting argument and rhetoric in science, revolves around defining the cogency of argument – that is, its strength and plausibility. Certainly his work will have some overlap with my discussion of arguments below, although his focus on argument in exclusion to other modes of discourse is, I find, a weakness – especially in a discipline like archaeology.

Because my concern is to think about modes of rhetoric and communication as diverse rather than simply reducible to one form, typically argument, and because my concern is also to think about how these modes are manifest in concrete forms, it is through these four text types that I want to explore further the connection between rhetoric and knowledge practices. I will start with narrative because, in many ways, this work has already been performed, most notably through the work of Paul Ricoeur. It also gives us some distance and pause before we return to a discussion of argument, enabling us to put it in better perspective.

## Narrative: a sense of an ending

I have already briefly mentioned the rise in narrative theory that emerged in the 1980s, one whose effects rippled through most if not all disciplines in the humanities and social sciences, not least archaeology. Its roots – within history at least – go back to the 1960s when traditional narrative history was under attack from the rise of social and economic histories; when graphs and tables of statistical data were replacing stories about kings, politicians and other 'great men'. The debates about the particular nature of historical interpretation typically saw familiar battle lines drawn between positivist accounts drawing on Hempelian models of covering laws and those who argued such models did not fit historical forms of explanation, even of the statistical kind (e.g. see Gardiner 1974 for a useful collection of contemporary papers from this period). The defence of narrative history (understood more broadly than the stories about 'kings and queens') against Hempelian positivism gathered steam and culminated in the widely influential work of Hayden White during the 1970s and 1980s and the central role of emplotment in relation to narrative. However, emplotment, in the sense that Hayden White uses it, is not what I want to draw attention to here; I am not concerned with a typology of plot structures or styles of narration, but rather with the more fundamental relation between plot in general and the concept of time; here the work of Paul Ricoeur is of far greater significance.

Although Paul Ricoeur's work – especially his three-volume *Time and Narrative* (1984, 1985, 1988) – was widely quoted and acknowledged during this narrative turn, it had much less impact than the work of White – at least in archaeology, if not in other disciplines too. In fact, Ricoeur probably had greater influence in stimulating a theoretical interest in time rather than narrative, as it did on my own doctoral studies in the early 1990s. In many ways, the connection Ricoeur forged between time and narrative has somewhat been eclipsed, despite the clear acknowledgement that time is somehow central to narrative. This acknowledgement, however, is a very impoverished version of this connection insofar as it seems to imply nothing more than that narratives typically have a linear structure with a beginning, middle and end. In this section, I want to resurrect the much more sophisticated accounts that exist about time and narrative and that can be largely found in the work of Ricoeur, although others before him had also explored this (e.g. Gallie 1964; Mink 1966, 1970, 1987).

The first thing to stress is that, for Ricoeur, narrative is an ontological issue as much as it is epistemological. For Hayden White – and many others – narrative is something we impose on reality or past events; reality does not in itself have a narrative structure. In contrast, Ricoeur's hermeneutics stresses the close relationship between narrative as an epistemic mode of understanding and narrative as form of being, through the concept of *mimesis* (Ricoeur 1984; also see Carr 1986 for a similar espousal of the narrative nature of reality). Thus narrative 'imitates' human action but not in the sense of a copy or reproduction but as a vital element in human praxis. Ricoeur demonstrates this in terms of the threefold nature of this 'imitation' (*mimesis*): as a preconfigured understanding of human action (mimesis 1), the configuring nature of narrativity (mimesis 2), and the reconfiguration of this narrative back into human action through 'reading' (mimesis 3). This mimetic circle draws upon the typical Heideggerian tripartite analysis of the temporality of human existence (Heidegger 1962).

In many ways the discussion on narrative in the 1970s and 1980s can be seen in terms of this distinction, between those who upheld a sharp separation of narrative from reality or everyday experience and those who did not (e.g. see Meretoja 2014). Although this debate has many dimensions (e.g. see Strawson 2004 for a recent discussion), what interests me is that for those who marked a separation, narrative (and narrative epistemology) could easily be reduced to purely literary terms as it was for White. As a result, literary theory becomes the prime intellectual influence. This is very much how narrative has been adopted in archaeology (but see Ballard 2003). On the other hand, for those who argued for a close ontological connection, more philosophical sets of concerns remain in the foreground, of which the most important is time. I want to follow Ricoeur here, simply because he offers the most sophisticated and extensive analysis of the matter.

In discussing narrative, Ricoeur made two critical distinctions that guide his whole analysis. The first was between the sense and reference of a narrative; its sense is provided by emplotment (*muthos*) and here one can happily draw on all that work in literary theory. In terms of narrative sense or emplotment moreover, history and fiction remain indistinct. Narrative reference (*mimesis*), however, is another matter and also more complicated. Here is also where the second distinction comes in, that which he draws between the primary and secondary reference of narrative. The primary reference of a narrative, according to Ricoeur, is human action – *res gestæ* – hence the concept of *mimesis*, briefly mentioned above; in history this action actually or really happened, while in fiction it has been imagined. Thus, at the level of primary reference, history and fiction part company. However, there is a second level of reference where they reunite: time. Time, for Ricoeur, constitutes the secondary reference of narrative and its ultimate, ontological horizon. This is Ricoeur following Heidegger who makes time the ontological horizon of being or *Dasein* (Heidegger 1962).

Now all this is simply by way of a prelude; since narratives relate human actions (reference 1) and human action is fundamentally temporal in structure (reference 2), it follows that narrative has time as its ontological horizon. Yet time is not an easy idea. For Ricoeur, time had an intrinsically paradoxical character which has been mapped by various thinkers from Aristotle to St Augustine. Its aporetic nature is what produces all those puzzles and paradoxes, and they exist because Western metaphysics operates with two very different conceptions of time: cosmological and phenomenological. Cosmological time is what we often refer to as abstract, physical time – clock time, chronology. It is serial, directional and quantitative. It exists independently of events, it is external to history. Phenomenological time, on the other hand, is time as we experience it, as the concatenation of past, present and future as embodied in memory, perception and expectation. It is inextricably bound up with human existence and internal to us. These two views of time are essentially irreconcilable – at least in any conventional, philosophical way, and here Ricoeur is largely following the important text on time by McTaggart (1908), though without his pessimistic conclusion. In fact, for Ricoeur, the only way they ever reach any kind of reconciliation is through narrative. This is why narrative is so important: it resolves a fundamental ontological aporia of human existence: temporality. And this is where he also parts company with Heidegger, who sought to reduce cosmological time to phenomenological time.

For Ricoeur, history offers a particular form of this resolution which he calls historical time, and which is linked to historical consciousness (Ricoeur 1988: 104–126). Historical time occupies the gap between cosmological and phenomenological time, thus acting as a bridge between the two. For Ricoeur, it takes three major forms: calendars, generational succession and the trace. Using these devices, history is able to mediate between personal and cosmic time; for archaeology, it is particularly the first and last which come into play, and the Museum above all brings both techniques together. In displaying the objects by period, the sense of continuity between past and present is highlighted; by interpreting people's lives and experience as part of a period, an era (e.g. *zeitgeist*), we can juxtapose the personal with objective time. Similarly, the actual presence of artefacts, as traces of the past yet here in the present, is perhaps an even more immediate and evocative conjunction of existential time and the vastness and distance of cosmological time (also see Heidegger 1962 for a similar argument). Yet is conjunction resolution? Ricoeur is aware of this, and indeed in the 'resolution' he recognizes that perhaps the aporia still exists.

This is a very engaging argument, to which my rough summary no doubt does not do proper justice. What I would like to do, though, is use Ricoeur's argument as a platform for thinking about the nature of narrative emplotment in terms of time. In separating sense from reference, plot from action/time, *muthos* from *mimesis*, there is a feeling that the question of time has become very far removed from that of emplotment. However, Ricoeur, in discussing the temporality of emplotment early on in *Time and Narrative* (1984: 66–68), does sketch the idea that emplotment is also about mediating the two views of time by the juxtaposition of a succession of events (cosmological time) with their configuration into a totality (phenomenological time).

The totality of a narrative – that sense of following a story, of grasping it as a whole (as Mink had previously argued) derives partially – according to Ricoeur – from what Kermode called a sense of an ending (Kermode 1967). For a narrative to be considered a whole, a totality, means, *insofar as it is temporal*, it has to end. The importance of the ending to a narrative as a way of providing temporal unity in many ways reproduces the same privilege Heidegger gives to futurity and death as the horizon of *Dasein* – that future end point which unifies the temporal *ekstases* of past, present and future (Heidegger 1962; also see Osborne 2011).

Maybe it's because I read Ricoeur during a very formative period of my intellectual development – my doctoral research – but I have always kept a soft spot for his work. His discussion of the function of narrative in juggling the complexity of time and, more fundamentally, the idea that time itself is ultimately what is portrayed in narrative – I am even tempted to say, *created* in narrative – remains compelling. What this means really is that talking about time gets you nowhere; you have to create time through your practices. Now archaeologists have been very good at creating time – but mostly cosmological time. Stratigraphic excavations, evolutionary typologies, seriation – these are some of the classic means by which we constitute time, and although these can be textual, they are best rendered visually, through section drawings, Harris matrices, seriation charts or dendrograms. When it comes to phenomenological time, however, things are somewhat different. Of course, we *talk* about time as experienced – we talk about social memory, the past in the past or past futures, we uncover all kinds of fascinating insights into the past perception of time which is by no means anything remotely like conventional chronological time. But talking about time in this way does not necessarily *evoke* it in the way a stratigraphic section does. This is about recuperating archaeology as a temporal experience, not just a discipline concerned with time. To put it in rather crude and unfaithful Heideggerian-speak, it is about temporality as ready-to-hand, rather than present-to-hand.

Now, lest I be accused of being unfair, many archaeologists have actually tried to do this – most notably through engaging art with archaeology and exploring, especially in visual media, other ways of evoking time. Archaeologists such as Doug Bailey and Yannis Hamilakis, to name a couple, have been very creative in this regard (e.g. see Bailey & Simpkin 2014; 2015; Hamilakis 2013; Hamilakis et al. 2009). But narrative text is my main focus here, not visual media. Moreover, this really forgets Ricoeur's lesson: a good narrative should do this naturally. It should create a sense of time simply through its structure. If it doesn't, then maybe there is something wrong with our narratives. This is beautifully summed up by the novelist Hilary Mantel in her BBC Reith lectures on historical fiction (Mantel 2017). In her fourth lecture, Mantel succinctly captures the temporality of a good narrative and I would like to quote her on this since she is far more eloquent than me. In the context of discussing why we remain enthralled, even with stories we know all too well, time is everything:

It's the same with the people in history. Our attention is transfixed, as we watch someone stride towards the edge of a cliff, when we can see the edge and the character can't. The reader becomes a small, conflicted god, or a disbelieved prophet. He is in two places at once. He is at the foot of the cliff, wise after the event, and he is also on the path, he is before the event; he is the observer, and he is also the person who steps into air. Only fiction can do this. It's the novelist's job: to put the reader in the moment, even if the moment is 500 years ago.

*(Mantel 2017)*

There you have Heidegger's threefold *ekstases* of time in a nutshell.

I think we can use these observations to model epistemic criteria for evaluating narratives which make the question of time central. What is it that makes a narrative successful – or not? I would suggest that within any narrative the challenge is fundamentally about mediating between time as an open, endless succession of almost random events (cosmological time) and time as a closed, finite chain or network of causation and meaningful connection between events (phenomenological time). Narratives that fail do so because they succumb too much to one or the other of these temporal modes. Thus a narrative that cleaves too closely to succession ends up being what historians have typically classified as annals or chronicles rather than proper, full-blown narratives (e.g. see White 1980). Arguably, excavation reports arranged by phasing are more chronicle than narrative. On the other hand, narratives where the relation between events is too closely stitched together result in a form of determinism where everything almost seems inevitable and predetermined from the very start. Arguably, some structuralist accounts, especially those embracing the idea of the *longue durée*, epitomize these kind of narratives which is why they are often accused of being unhistorical. Similarly with the cruder kinds of social evolutionary narratives where history unravels along a preset course.

In short, if we accept Ricoeur's position that narratives are primordially about mediating two conflicting temporalities, then in terms of emplotment this translates as mediating between inevitability and contingency. Narratives need a sense of order, a sense of a whole, but this must always be punctuated by chance, by randomness if the tension between these two temporalities is to be kept alive. Just as the narrative attempts to close time with its sense of an ending, so it must also acknowledge that time carries on outside the narrative frame. Just as I perceive my life as a totality through the expectation of my death, I also know that the world will carry on after I am gone. This uneasy juxtaposition between time as an infinite, endless series of moments/events and time as a bounded totality of past, present and future is captured beautifully by Thomas Hardy's character Tess of the d'Urbervilles as she reflects on her own death:

She philosophically noted dates as they passed in the revolution of the year. … Her own birthday, and every other day individualized by incidents in which she had taken some share. She suddenly thought, one afternoon … that there was another date, of greater importance to her than all those; that of her own death; a day which lay sly and unseen among all the other days of the year, giving no sign or sound when she annually passed over it; but not the less surely there. When was it?

(Hardy 2005: 111)

If we try to draw out what this might mean for archaeological narratives, it is clear that the two major problems – of reducing a narrative to cosmological time on the one hand and to phenomenological time on the other – can be articulated through the epistemic issue of historical distance.

Historical distance is an issue that has recently come under some scrutiny among historians (e.g. see Ginzburg 2001; Hollander et al. 2011; Phillips 2013) and this body of work offers a useful framework for thinking through the issue in relation to archaeology. To put it simply, historical distance – or hindsight, retrospect – has been generally lauded as a central epistemological condition for objectivity with historical method since the late nineteenth century. It is why, even into the early twentieth century, many historians considered 'contemporary history' an oxymoron; to study the history of recent times was like looking at a painting with your nose pressed to the canvass – how could you possibly see what the picture was of? At the same time, that distance was considered necessary, however; it also defined the primary problem facing historians: how to bridge the gap separating past from present? Hollander et al. (2011) suggest there have been two broad responses within conventional historical theory: the German historical tradition which attempted to get into the minds of people in the past through 'empathy' as developed by scholars such as Ranke and Dilthey; and the Italian/English school which attempted to bring the past into the present through reliving or re-enacting it, in the mind of the historian as exemplified in the works of Croce and Collingwood. Of course, the differences between these approaches are subtle and they share a lot in common in terms of their idealist philosophy.

As the conventional historical theory of the late nineteenth and early twentieth century gave way to the postmodernism of the late twentieth century, so the whole issue of historical distance began to seem more and more irrelevant – as the past and present melted together, both the gap and the distance dissolved. Hollander et al. (2011) characterize this as a shift from seeing historical distance as something given to it being something actively constructed, insofar as the past – as something distinct from the present – is created through the historian's narrative. Historical distance is simply a by-product of the historian's work (but see Bevir 2011 for a slightly different take on this). I am not sure this portrayal is helpful because it conflates two different sets of concerns: historical distance on the one hand, and the separation of past and present on the other. The former issue is far more complex and nuanced than a simple past/present split allows for. This is brought out by Paul's detailed analysis of Bernheim's discussion of historical method in Germany during the early 1900s (Paul 2011), but also more generally in Phillips's important work on historical distance as a form of mediation (Phillips 2004, 2011, 2013). I will come back to these scholars, but first it will help if we clarify some important aspects to the idea of historical distance.

The most important question to ask is, perhaps, distance from what? Is it the events themselves? In some ways this makes sense since it presupposes personal acquaintance with the events on the part of the historian or archaeologist; so long as it happened 'before my time', I can argue that my objectivity is preserved. However, apart from the problems about my perception of those events being coloured by other people I know who did live through the events in question, the larger issue is that it makes historical distance effectively about using sources, or what Hollander calls second-order observations as opposed to first-order observations (Hollander 2011). Indeed, the classic German historical method as espoused by Ranke made this a basis for history; for historians and archaeologists, this is not even a choice, though, but a given. Whether one is studying a Neolithic burial or a Victorian cesspit, the archaeologist has no personal, first-order experience of the events that left these traces; we use the traces themselves as sources to reconstruct these pasts. But whether by choice or default, is the rendering of traces as sources sufficient to answer the demand for historical distance? Is it enough that one uses 'records' of these events rather than my own personal experience, as a guarantee of appropriate historical distance?

Not really and Humboldt's 1821 essay "On the Historian's Task" offers a succinct and condensed explanation for what is ultimately at issue in this question of historical distance: it is all about seeing the form or shape of history (Humboldt 1967; Hollander 2011). As Humboldt himself put it: "Thus historical truth is, as it were, rather like the clouds which take shape for the eye only at a distance" (Humboldt 1967: 58). Hollander (2011) has suggested that this historical form was conventionally seen as something that was the historian's task to draw out of the sources – a goal broadly shared by most historians until the 1970s. This historicism was then upended by a narrativism which argued that such form was imposed by the historian, an argument, of course, best known through the work of Hayden White (1973) but also others, especially Frank Ankersmit (1983). Historical form has been known by many names such as "*Zeitgeist* or *Volksgeist*":

> One may raise one's eyebrows at these ghostly German concepts, but they are in fact no more outlandish than present day equivalents like mentality, ideology, cultural context, episteme, paradigm, or worldview. All these vague and awkward notions do the same: they define ideational wholes, which are indispensable for our reconstruction of the past.
>
> *(Hollander 2011: 56)*

Historical distance is thus quite literally the temporalization of a spatial metaphor; to see 'the shape of the clouds' or the image on a painting requires stepping back; to see the meaning of past historical events requires letting an appropriate lapse of time pass. Of course, there is always an acknowledged trade-off here: the more time passes, the more information is potentially lost. Archives, manuscripts, artefacts all suffer from attrition. However, as more time passes, so historians and archaeologists stand in a position of collating a wider range of sources and information that was not available at the time. Knowing what was happening in many different places allows one to see events in a very different way – as does knowing what happened next. Archaeologists generally like to proclaim the advantages of archaeology as long-term history, arguing that this extended perspective offers them the ability to see patterns in history that would be otherwise obscured. Time perspectivism has pushed this even further to make a virtue of the fragmentary nature of the archaeological record: its low temporal resolution compared with lived experience or historical documents impels us to take a different scale of analysis (Bailey 2007). Although archaeologists have not tended to address the question of historical distance as explicitly as historians, there is clearly a sense that the temporal properties of the archaeological record – whether its resolution or its long time span – has been paraded as a virtue in a manner that would have made Ranke proud.

It is through the notion of historical form – perceptible in historical and archaeological narratives alike – however, that we find a bridge to my earlier discussion of Ricoeur. If historical distance is about seeing the shape of history – or a particular history, to be less contentious – then clearly what matters is that the relation between the archaeologist or historian and their subject needs to be defined by one of closure. It is about the present–past relation, but not in terms of the gap or fracture between them but rather about what they exclude as a couplet: the future. If contemporary history seems to lack the quality of historical distance, it is not really about the nature of the sources so much as the danger that the (his)tory itself has not finished; it is like living in the middle of a story, whose ending we do not know because it lies in the future, even if its beginning happened over a century ago. How can we possibly discern its form when it is still forming? Putting the matter in such stark terms simultaneously exposes the fundamental problem of historical distance and the connection between epistemology and time for any historical discipline: when is the story over? Squair raised this issue many years ago in relation to archaeology, defining it in terms of 'the privilege of retrospect' (Squair 1994). The problem as he identified it is the presumption in archaeology of closure; because the past *is* past, it is assumed to be closed and therefore determined, and this is what endows the archaeologist with a special privilege (Squair 1994: 99–102). As Squair points out, however, just because the past is past does not mean it is over – this ignores the role of the present in constructing the past; it ignores the fact that *the past is only past, by virtue of its relation to the present*. This relation is obscured by a semantic sleight of hand where the present is characterized as the future of the past and thus elides the real future which stretches out before the present.

What is ultimately wrong with the conventional regard for historical distance is the assumption that history runs at an even pace; events 500 years ago, even conceivably 200 years ago, are safe, because they have run their course. The closer we get to the present, the more difficult it is to make that case. But this is simply unsustainable. We are still living with the consequences of what happened 5,000 years ago as our ancestors took up farming, or 100,000 years ago as Homo sapiens migrated from Africa. How can we say when the story is over? The problem is not the gap between present and past, but the cut between the past and the future; where we make that cut surely affects/is affected by the historical forms we want to portray. But more to the point, should we even try to make that cut? We come back to the central dilemma of any narrative – producing an account which has closure, but acknowledging the fact that time exceeds the bounds of any narrative. The problem is this: the only way to characterize such transgressive time is in terms of an external, abstract medium or container for events; as soon as we want to wed time to events, to bring time into the narrative form itself, we are forced also to draw a limit around it, to give it a beginning and especially an end. To not do that then risks creating an incoherent, incomplete narrative.

So where does this leave us? One thing seems certain: historical distance cannot be equated with chronological distance; prehistory can be just as problematic as contemporary history in terms of narrating an 'historical form' and articulating closure. So what form does this historical distance then take? Here the work of Mark Salber Phillips becomes relevant as he discusses the nature of historical distance in terms of active strategies of mediation on the part of the historian. The basis of his approach is outlined in various papers (e.g. Phillips 2004, 2011) and his book *On Historical Distance* (2013). Phillips argues that whatever the chronological distance between a historian and their subject, that distance will always be shaped and mediated by specific strategies which control the degree of proximity or detachment embedded in a work. Importantly, Phillips stresses that historical distance is not an ideal singular point of objectivity, but rather a moveable scale in degrees creating greater or less proximity/detachment. It is an active process of distanciation rather than a given, fixed position (also see Lepore 2001 here for a related discussion). Furthermore, this process operates along at least four different axes or dimensions: form, affect, ideology and cognition/understanding, which translate as narrative form or genre, emotional impact, political or moral commitment and analytic method. For example, in terms of its affect a narrative can offer a very cold and detached description of some event or a more evocative, emotional rendering. Similarly, in terms of method it may present a story in rich, close-up detail like microhistory, or give a more broad-brushed, bird's-eye view of events through statistics. Narratives will mix and blend different levels of distance for each axis.

What is important about Phillips's approach is the recognition of distance as an active strategy with complex, multiple dimensions rather than a simple reduction of historical distance to chronological time lapsed. Of course, as my discussion has, I hope, shown, even this chronological model is not simple, a point even better demonstrated in Paul's analysis of Bernheim's key text on historical method from c. 1900, which links the question of historical distance to scholarly self-distanciation and the cultivation of a specific set of epistemic virtues (Paul 2011). What both Paul and Phillips identify is that the epistemological question of historical distance is bound up with the moral formation of the scholar (Paul) and the textual composition of their work (Phillips). What is also interesting, however, especially in the work of Phillips, is the citation of distanciation as a key concept. For it is precisely the same concept which underwrites Ricoeur's work on *Time and Narrative*, if not indeed his whole œuvre (e.g. see Clark 1990): a reconciliation of the processes of distanciation and belonging. His two temporalities of cosmological and phenomenological time are precisely this: time as distanced, externalized from the subject and time as belonging to, internal to the human subject. In a more basic sense, this is the crux of any hermeneutic philosophy: mediation. What Phillips does is allow us to see how his various mediations of distanciation map on to and thus enhance the mediation of time that lies at the heart of Ricoeur's analysis of narrative.

## Description: a sense of presence

Description has often been contrasted with interpretation, and certainly in older fieldwork traditions there was a clear separation between what affected to be a neutral, objective description of archaeological remains and their interpretation in terms of past processes, events or behaviour (e.g. Barker 1982: 143ff.). This separation later came under criticism where it was argued that even description was interpretive:

> All description involves an interpretive component. But equally, all interpretation involves trying to link sense to data. Interpretation is always interpretation of something. Thus it is always partially a description. ... [W]e need a non-dichotomous approach. The link between description and interpretation is so close that in anthropology an interpretive approach is associated with the idea of 'thick description' ...
>
> *(Hodder 1999: 67)*

Hodder's reference to Clifford Geertz's concept of thick description is testament to the general influence of a hermeneutic or interpretive epistemology on Hodder's own work and postprocessualism in general.

More broadly, though, the opposition of description and interpretation was simply a manifestation of the more general or abstract opposition between fact and theory, which too was subject to the same criticisms where all data was described as being theory-laden (see Chapter 2). To a large extent, the concept of description (at least in archaeology) is closely bound up with the fact–theory couplet, where description is aligned with the idea of facts or factual statements: both purport to offer faithful representations of reality, but ones which strive to bear no relation to any theory or prior interpretation – that is, claim to be disinterested. The only difference is that a fact might be thought of as a simple statement while a description is a more complex text. Now, I imagine some of us might think that because description is interpretive or theory-laden, then the distinction between them is now superfluous, as is that between data and theory. But that would be a mistake and I am not sure many others would argue this anyway. But at the same time, if each is implicated in the other, in what way can we still define them as distinct? To help answer this, it is useful to put the issue in a broader context.

The idea of a fact is usually traced back to the work of the seventeenth-century philosopher Francis Bacon. Facts based on observations or statements – what Lorraine Daston has called deracinated particulars – are those statements purged of any theoretical context, uprooted from any ideological interests (Daston 1991; Dear

1995). Such a history is also closely related to the development of observation as an epistemic genre and its relation to the idea of experiment (Daston & Lunbeck 2011). Now, of course, the idea of facts or observations as neutral descriptions has long been criticized – in fact, for much longer than we might think. The interdependence of fact and theory is not some discovery of the post-positivism of the second half of twentieth century, but, as Mary Poovey has demonstrated in her *A History of the Modern Fact* (1998), something people have recognized since the concept of a fact in its modern sense was first developed in the seventeenth century. Although Poovey's book mostly explores the history of how the modern fact came to be, especially in its relation to numbers and statistics in the field of political economy, she makes the important point that the fact has always incorporated a tension between being a deracinated particular and being theory-laden. It is how this tension has been played out and changed its form that she devotes her study. Rehearsing the history of the fact is not my main concern here; rather it is to underline the point that just because facts or descriptions are theory-laden or interpretive does not mean the existence of facts or descriptions as autonomous texts is void. Archaeology is still replete with facts and textual descriptions, all of which still imply the basic characteristic of being deracinated. Calling a description interpretive may serve an argument, but it leaves us with a problem: if a description is interpretive, how can we still maintain a distinction between interpretation and description? Because we do.

Consider the example of the context sheet, a form for recording an excavated unit which Hodder used to illustrate the futility of separating description from interpretation (Hodder 1999: 68–69). We write a long, detailed description of a layer, noting its dimensions, colour, particle composition, compaction and so on. Then we write an interpretation – for example, floor layer. Such a format has an ancient pedigree and can be linked to the emergence of Renaissance styles of writing which separated observations (*curatio*) from a commentary (*scholion*; Pomata 2011). How should we characterize the distinction between these two texts? Hodder says we should not. The description is, of course, interpretive – it draws on soil science classifications and nomenclature, all of which are informed by theories of soil formation. So clearly it is theory-laden. But the relevant question is: is that theory in any way connected to the types of interpretation one writes on the context sheet? Not really – the interpretation of a floor layer will be based on its location vis-à-vis other features or layers on the site, as well as the properties described in the description which make it consistent with being a floor layer – for example, its degree of compaction. The issue here concerns the inferential independence of the two texts, and especially the independence of the description on the interpretation. To some extent, the interpretation necessarily depends on the description, because the description is deployed as evidence for the interpretation. We might even say the interpretation is description-laden, or fact-laden. Indeed, Hodder highlights this point. But the reverse is not the case – the compaction, for example, is not dependent on the interpretation of the layer being a floor layer and in fact the very variable compaction, whatever its value (i.e. compact or soft), was not selected as a descriptor based on the interpretation but in relation to general principles of soil classification.

This is not to suggest that one's interpretation of the deposit as a floor may not influence one's decision as to describing how compact the layer is; but there will always be a greater degree of autonomy than Hodder acknowledged.

To sum up: while in general all facts are theory-laden and vice versa, in any particular instance, while a theory or interpretation will be fact-/description-laden, the converse should not be the case, except in the most gross kinds of circular inference. What matters are the *specific* facts and the *specific* theories in question. It is in this sense that the separation of description and interpretation still holds (see the section on paradigm-dependence in Chapter 2 for a wider discussion of this issue). However, all of this is really only the prelude to the main question here, which concerns the epistemic criteria by which one evaluates a description. It is one thing to argue that a description is theoretically independent of a particular interpretation, but that only makes the epistemic issue one about the relationship between a descriptive text type and other text types. Indeed, this point touches on one of the peculiarities and unique features of descriptions as a text type, in contrast to the other three of narrative, argument and exposition. Description can rarely stand alone and carry a text for any length; it is almost always subservient to one of the other three, which is even why some textual linguists are hesitant to define it as a type at all. One of the reasons for this subservience is simply because a description, in itself, lacks any overt relevance. Of course, at a trivial level, its purpose is to describe some state of affairs – but why should the reader be interested in this? Description lacks the dynamic nature of narratives, arguments and expositions which engage the reader by being self-justifying. They contain the reason for being relevant in themselves. Descriptions carry no such connotation. A story, argument or exposition can be carried over pages and pages and keep the reader engaged, but how long can you suffer a description without getting bored? I am aware that some great works of literature contain such examples, but in such cases there is usually a literary or philosophical point being tacitly made, and there is a limit to how often this can be sustained or repeated. The thing about description is that its relevance is always external to it, unlike the other three text types.

Given that, how then should we assess the epistemic status of a description, internally? Since we have just raised the issue of a description's function, let us stay on this track and think about description in contrast to narrative in this regard. What does description do? A straightforward answer might be: it *represents*. But this will not suffice since this is also a function of historical/archaeological narrative insofar as such a narrative is about a set of events or state of affairs in a temporal register. There is nonetheless some symmetry with narrative; it could and has been suggested, as Alexander Bain did, that description is a form of representation of reality in its spatial register, as narrative is of the temporal register. However, I am not sure the distinction between narrative and description can so easily be mapped on to that between time and space. After all, description involves more than spatial aspects. It might be more appropriate to suggest that description involves the suspension of time from its representation of reality; description is fundamentally about the presence of things, held in a temporal vacuum, suspended in a moment where certainly the aspect of spatiality is enhanced, but more generally the concreteness of things.

We can return to my earlier example to illustrate this: describing a layer on an archaeological site. The process of description is, of course, temporally extended – we might note the colour of the soil, then pick up a piece and rub it between our fingers to note its texture; then examine the spatial extent of the layer, and so on. We may even write a description following this order. But nothing about the temporality of this description matters to the description itself. What matters is reproducing, in words, a sense of what this layer is and how it appears to our senses. This example brings to the fore two salient qualities of description. To describe requires that the person describing is co-present with the thing being described. Second, the description itself has to convey to the reader attributes of the thing in such a way that they also feel they are in the presence of this thing when they read it. This is quite different to narrative – the archaeologist is not co-present with the events they are telling (even if they are co-present with the sources used to tell this story); indeed, as we saw through the discussion of historical distance, this lack of co-presence is what defines to some extent the very epistemological challenge of narration. With description, the epistemic issues are precisely about how well co-presence has been articulated. But before I come to that, let me first address a potential objection to this portrayal of description.

We can, of course, use the word 'description' to cover a representation of rather abstract ideas – we can, for example, 'describe' Marx's theory of alienation – but I want to deliberately reserve such a usage for the term 'exposition', which I discuss in more detail below. Indeed, an important line separates narration and description on the one hand from argument and exposition on the other – namely the division between the abstract and the concrete. This is not to suggest that narratives cannot employ abstract concepts or that arguments cannot make use of concrete facts; rather that the dominant ontological register for narration/description is concrete, whereas that for argument/exposition is abstract. With that said, let me move on to consider the epistemological implications of description previously defined as the representation of presence.

Description implies co-presence – in effect it is a form of testimony, of witnessing; it implies 'I was there' or 'I saw, felt, experienced this'. This side of description has roots in the seventeenth-century emergence of experimental science and has been well researched (Dear 1985; Shapin 1984). Indeed the concept of autopsy (*autopsia*) was originally used to underline the role of co-presence as a key aspect of the new genre of observation, only later being reduced to its more modern definition associated with post-mortem examination (Pomata 2011). At the same time, our scientific conventions of such witnessing have developed since the seventeenth century, most notably the parameters and criteria of what counts as reliable descriptions have changed greatly, with perhaps the most important shift occurring in the nineteenth century. This too is a story that has been traced, primarily in the work of Lorraine Daston and Peter Galison, in relation to the concept of objectivity and is bound up with the formation and cultivation of the self or subject as scientist (Daston 1992; Daston & Galison 1992, 1997). Beginning in the seventeenth century when reliable descriptions were those performed by 'gentleman' witnesses, objectivity gradually became redefined so that by the nineteenth century reliable descriptions were those where the human witness was replaced as far as possible by non-human instruments or where the human involvement was disciplined to make itself as anonymous and effacing as possible – in short, to become an instrument herself. As Daston and Galison point out, objectivity is not so much about being faithful to the object (which is, after all, the problem to be solved) but the cultivation and later diminution or removal of subjectivity from our accounts of objects as a means of attaining such fidelity. The original association between observation and observance also underlines this, insofar as the science of observation was bound up with a rule-bound way of life (Daston 2011). When William Stukeley recorded Stonehenge in the eighteenth century, the veracity of his account was only accentuated by his presence in the description itself; to be credible, the description *needed* to imply him (e.g. see Stukeley 1740). When Mike Parker Pearson led a team to record Stonehenge in the early twenty-first century, although his and his colleagues' renown as leading archaeologists doubtless puts some extra shine on the account, what lends the descriptions credibility is their conventionality and the fact the descriptions actually bear no connection to him or any of his team; they are de-personalized, anonymous and conform to a widespread standard (e.g. Darvill et al. 2012). We have already seen how Hodder observed this shift in his study of archaeological site reports (Hodder 1989), but putting it in this broader context gives it a different twist to that raised by Hodder.

This emphasis on the cultivation of an archaeological detachment is now largely implicit in the whole system of training and pedagogy which essentially moulds the archaeological subject. But as archaeology was still being constituted as an academic discipline within universities, one can see more explicit vestiges of this operation in the earliest fieldwork manuals. Droop's manual of archaeological excavation from 1915 is a brilliant example, with chapters on the personal character requirements of an archaeologist and on the morality of excavation. Typical of the demands for detachment – iteratively masculine, of course – is this quotation: "He should be very patient, able to hold in check any natural human desire for undue haste to seize his spoil until his sober judgement tells him that the right moment has come" (Droop 1915: 34). Similar injunctions to character traits can be found in other early twentieth-century field manuals (e.g. Petrie 1904) which gradually shift towards an emphasis on training (Atkinson 1946: 13–15; Kenyon 1953: 54–67; Wheeler 1954: 153–177). But by the 1960s and 1970s, all such discussions disappear from field manuals which focus solely on methods and techniques (Webster 1963; Coles 1972; Barker 1982). The only trace of this earlier concern is an occasional reference to the status of amateurs, which has all but disappeared in the more recent textbooks (Drewitt 1999; Collis 2001; Carver 2009).

However, although of great interest and importance, the historical aspects of description are not my prime focus here; my main purpose in giving this brief sketch has been to prepare the ground for a discussion of the key epistemic tension in description as a form of textual composition. To recap: description implies copresence; that is, it is ultimately a form of testimony or witnessing. In philosophical discussions of testimony, one of the big issues is whether testimony – which has a fundamentally social or inter-subjective basis – can be assessed by appeals to non-social factors (i.e. principles of individual reasoning or inference; e.g. see Kusch & Lipton 2002). The debates here are partly caught up in the broader divisions between science studies and traditional epistemologies, one which situates testimony in relation to the social construction of truth (e.g. Shapin 1994; but also see the recent work by Miranda Fricker (2007) on epistemic injustice) and another which tries to reduce testimonial knowledge to conventional forms of inference (e.g. Lipton 1998; Fricker 1987). Not all philosophers on testimony fall neatly into these camps – Coady, for example, maintains a non-reductionist approach to testimony yet eschews the constructivism of Shapin (Coady 1992). My route, however, will largely follow Shapin, but links the discussion of testimony to a specific textual form: description.

The term 'virtual witness' coined by Shapin conveys very succinctly this idea of written descriptions; even in the seventeenth century when the scientific community was tiny compared with today, not everyone could be present at scientific experiments (Shapin 1984). Written reports of these experiments were essential but they also acted as proxies for the experiment themselves; readers needed to feel they were there, in the presence of the experiment too, albeit virtually. The same applies to early forms of scientific illustration, where three-dimensional, 'realistic' depictions tried to convey a sense of co-presence (Daston & Galison 1997). However, over time description also required objectivity, the training of the witness, to ensure that the object being described is as close to itself as possible, and not distorted by the bias of the scientist. Objectivity is what lends credibility to the description, but objectivity, at least in the sense discussed here, seems to imply the effacement or removal of the witness as author or subject, which is somewhat contradictory. It is as if to say: I was there but it should appear as if I wasn't. Somehow, being-there and not-being-there are both pre-requisites for a credible description. How is this possible? This contradiction can be brought into focus with a very simple example.

You pick up an archaeological site report and read about a description of a feature or artefact. Typically, the text itself bears no mark of an author, a subject who wrote the description. At the same time, there is a name appended to the text – the author – who may or may not be known to the reader. The name is crucial because, whoever they are, they guarantee the fact that this description is of a real feature or object and not a fictitious one. When we read a site report, we implicitly assume the site was real; of course, we can question the attribution of specific descriptions – maybe this feature described as a posthole was just an animal burrow, but whatever it was, *it was there*. It has not been made up. All science works on this most basic level of trust: that the data reported or described in texts are based on the experiences of the author of the text and not made up. This is how the idea of description as virtual witnesses still remains a core part of science, even if it has now become deeply sedimented and taken for granted. Given that, how do we square the contradiction between this trust we put in the author of a description as a witness and the contemporary conventions whereby such witnessing strives for self-effacement?

The political origins of this idea of a disembodied language stretch back to the seventeenth century as related by Bauman and Briggs in their important study *Voices of Modernity* (Bauman & Briggs 2003). They trace the emergence of a new discourse around language in the work of the philosopher Locke and his attempt to purge language from its associations with both Society and Nature. Against contemporary views which portrayed words as mirrors of nature, referring to things, Locke argued that language was not connected to things but to ideas. But in linking them to the human mind, Locke was equally concerned to disconnect language from society; as with Bacon and many other contemporaries, Locke shared a distrust of language in science insofar as it was prone to corrupt our knowledge because of its social connections – a quality most evident in the realm of rhetoric. Locke's vision was thus of language as a system of pure signs, purged of their prior association with both Nature and Society, and one solely linked to ideas. Only in this way could knowledge be guaranteed.

As Bauman and Briggs argue, such a vision only reconfigured the impurity of language; it did not abolish it. Connecting this to the work of Shapin, the new language of science that emerged in the seventeenth century was anything but pure: it was constructed on a political ideology that associated white, middle-class Englishmen with an exclusive access to this supposed, purified discourse. In the rest of their work, Bauman and Briggs track how this new hybrid operated in various scientific and disciplinary contexts over the next three centuries to mark distinctions between Nature and Society and facilitate the very project of modernity that Latour characterized as one defined by such acts of purification (Latour 1993). For Bauman and Briggs, language is the key, missing third term in Latour's narrative. While I do not wish to downplay the political ideology behind this notion of a disembodied language, the point I want to stress here is the very paradoxical idea of an autonomous language. This is, fundamentally, what I think description tries to achieve in its extreme forms.

Of course, not all description does aspire to self-effacement, especially in the humanities; indeed, today there is often the demand to write ourselves back into texts, to not hesitate to use the first person singular, to draw on emotion and affect – all these are pushing against the developments towards objectivity as detachment that crystallized in the nineteenth century. But here we need to remember that such developments may well apply to some text types more than others. While some archaeological text types (or images) have always borne the mark of a recognizable author, description is the one which is arguably most anonymous and remains so. Although perhaps most obvious in conventional cases such as soil descriptions, even phenomenological descriptions impart this sense of anonymity. Compare these two quotes:

> Structure III (F. 21): With a projected diameter of 7.50m, this 'C'-shaped gully was open to the northeast. Its shallow concave profile was 0.4–0.6m wide and 0.07–0.15m deep.
>
> *(Evans 2003: 44)*

> The Partridge section of the Cursus ... begins in the north-east in a relatively flat area of Martin Down. The terminal of the left bank is almost exactly 2km due north of the highest point of Penbury Knoll. From the vantage point of Penbury Knoll the entire stretch of the first section of the Cursus is visible, including both the terminals on Martin Down and Bottlebush Down.
>
> *(Tilley 1994: 173)*

Of course, the human perspective or presence is more evident in the phenomenological description, but it is still an impersonal presence. In many ways, the contradiction between being-there and yet absent is mediated and kept in check by a delicate operation. In short, while the presence of a witness has remained a constant in any descriptive account, it is the nature of the witness that has changed. As suggested by Daston and Galison, the witness needs to be detached from their normal self, either through the increased use of non-human devices (e.g. cameras) or by making herself as much like an instrument as possible through training and pedagogy. However, such operations of detachment are in many ways the pre-textual background to description; indeed, much of the literature on objectivity I have been drawing on, although it discusses texts and images, has mostly been concerned with objectivity in relation to practices of observation and its relation to forms of inscription – whether textual or graphic (also see Daston & Lunbeck 2011). But if we are to think about texts in terms of composition, the issues become somewhat different. When it comes to composing a descriptive text, what is it about its compositional structure that is epistemologically salient?

If I may be permitted a rather disrespectful analogy, one can think of a description as similar to an incantation or spell in terms of its performative or illocutionary force; just using the correct words in the correct manner guarantees success; it is not who utters the spell but the spell itself which is the agent here. Now aficionados of the dark arts might find fault with this, but I am just using a lay understanding to make a point: incantations rely on stylized, formulaic text strings. Archaeological descriptions do the same. Descriptions have enhanced epistemic credibility insofar as they rely on conventional language or standardized terminology – far more than any other text type. In this sense, the text register (i.e. 'language' or dialect) is far more relevant and constitutive of descriptions than most other text types. The efficacy of such conventionalized and stylized texts works only, of course, on those who have been trained to write the same kind of texts themselves; a soil description using specialized terminology only creates the effect of co-presence for a reader who can relate to such terminology.

## Argument: a sense of reason

The idea of an argument has two main meanings. One refers to a contentious discussion between two or more people who are disagreeing over an issue – in short, a dispute or quarrel – and has no particular connotations about how that dispute is conducted, except verbally. The other meaning relates to a form of inference or explanation, one where a set of reasons is offered in support of a claim. The latter sense is generally that used by philosophers when talking about argument, and while it can occur within a dispute, its general context of use is usually bracketed out in terms of a purely formal analysis of the structure of argument. Indeed, the philosophical sense of an argument usually carries the opposite connotation of the first sense: a cool, detached, logical investigation of an issue in contrast to the often heated and emotional aura surrounding a quarrel. It is also the second sense of an argument that tends to be implied when archaeologists and other scholars refer to arguments in the context of knowledge. However, I want to suggest that we need to hold both of these meanings together for reasons that will be become clear shortly. To that end, I will focus my discussion initially on critiques of the formal approach to argument, of which the philosopher Stephen Toulmin has been perhaps the most influential.

The formal analysis of arguments in philosophy, and related fields such as critical thinking, typically involve identifying two elements: premises and conclusions, where the premises effectively act to justify the conclusion. Conventionally, they can do this in two ways: deductively, where the conclusions *necessarily* follow from the premises (e.g. syllogisms), and inductively, where they *probably* do. Often a third way has also been cited, such as *abduction* or inference to the best explanation. On the whole, much of twentieth-century philosophy was geared towards increasing formalization of the logical structure of arguments such that it has developed into an esoteric branch of philosophy which requires grappling with specialized notation. One important figure who swam against this current was Stephen Toulmin, whose now classic book *The Uses of Argument* (1958) advocated reinstating argument back into the wild – that is, back into its context of use. He opposed what he called *analytical* arguments to *substantial* arguments, where the former referred to the idealized and rarefied systems of logic being developed by his contemporaries, and the latter, a situated account of logic-in-use. Toulmin was not interested in deduction or induction as ideal forms of reasoning; rather he wanted to understand the general structure of arguments as they were actually practised. Where analytical approaches drew on mathematics as their inspiration (hence the use of notation), a substantial approach sought parallels with jurisprudence and legal argumentation.

The bare bones of Toulmin's approach to argument is laid out in the third essay of his book. Here he provides a basic tripartite structure to an argument composed of a claim and data (i.e. evidence) which are bridged or connected through warrants. Warrants may themselves need support in the form of backing. Toulmin also used diagrams to help expose this structure. Since Chapman and Wylie use Toulmin's model to map several archaeological examples in their book, I will summarize one of their cases here: lead isotope analysis (Chapman & Wylie 2016: 164–184). During the 1990s, lead isotopes had been used to map the sources of copper during the Bronze Age in order to shed light on Mediterranean trade networks, although subsequently the results have been questioned. Chapman and Wylie map out one of the arguments at the centre of this debate – the movement of Cyprian copper across the

Mediterranean to Sardinia. This claim was evidenced by copper ingots found in Sardinia with lead isotope profiles that matched those from Cyprus. The critical warrant linking the claim to the evidence was the theory behind lead isotope chemistry. The important rebuttals focused on neither the evidence nor the claim, but on this warrant, which rested on a failure to consider other factors causing similar profiles, such as similar geologies but, most importantly, past practices of mixing and re-smelting copper.

I have greatly simplified Chapman and Wylie's account, but it nonetheless illustrates the key elements of Toulmin's model. Toulmin's work has aroused new interest in recent years, not least because of a reappraisal of the concepts of evidential reasoning and critical thinking within academia and pedagogy. For example, new work on inference networks, some of which is inspired by a similar informal approach to argument developed by the legal scholar John Henry Wigmore in the early twentieth century, has clear affinities with Toulmin's approach (Dawid et al. 2011; see Thomas 2015 for an archaeological application of Wigmore's method). Such interests can be linked to increasing concerns over the perceived declining standards of education during the 1970s and 1980s, when many higher education institutions started to place renewed emphasis on critical thinking in courses and programmes, so that by the 1990s what has been called a second wave of critical thinking had washed across the humanities (Walters 1994b). In reaction to what was seen as the reduction of critical thinking to logical thinking or logicism in the first wave, which began in the 1940s, this second wave of writing has tried to expand the concept of critical thinking to include aspects such as imagination and intuition and to critique the way first-wave, logicist approaches de-subjectified and de-contextualized critical thinking (e.g. see papers in Walters 1994a). It is in this context that Toulmin's work clearly comes to be seen as prescient – although in many ways, of course, even Toulmin's approach remains somewhat logicist in terms of its focus on structure, albeit using an informal rather than formal logic. Nonetheless, contemporary popular texts on critical thinking and argument are notable for the way in which Toulmin's model is reproduced, either directly or indirectly, albeit usually blended with more conventional concepts such as deduction and induction (e.g. Weston 2000; Walton 2006).

I have already mentioned Bob Chapman and Alison Wylie who adopted Toulmin's model quite closely, albeit extended and updated with the work of others in the philosophy of science (Chapman & Wylie 2016). But other archaeologists have more generally drawn on the resurgence in critical thinking to address similar concerns. Chuck Orser's book *Archaeological Thinking* (2015) draws on another 'oldie philosopher', Susan Stebbing, whose 1939 work *Thinking to Some Purpose* provided a role model for Orser (Orser 2015; Stebbing 1939). Orser's book is, in part, intended as a primer for students on how to reason and was motivated by a desire to develop critical thinking skills among students so they could distinguish the good from the bad and the downright crazy (i.e. pseudo-archaeology). It is a very readable book and very clearly modelled – intentionally or not – on general textbooks on critical thinking. A similar book – but with more of a textbook structure – has been written by Guy Gibbon called *Critically Reading the Theory and Methods of Archaeology* (Gibbon 2014). It very much has the same motivations and inspirations as Orser's, although it is an obviously different book.

However, one of the problems with all of these recent books is that they employ the notion of an argument as a broad concept, almost synonymous with critical thinking or reasoning. The same position underlies a similar approach by William Rehg to situate argument as a means to plug the gap between social constructivists and the more traditional logical formalists (Rehg 2009). Given the prime focus in this book on linking knowledge production to textual composition, I think the concept of argument needs to be given a tighter focus. In the first place, verbal arguments are very different from textual arguments, especially in academic papers where, in a sense, one is really only getting one side of the argument presented in an extended manner. Arguments in academic texts tend to be more like a lawyer's closing statement than a real-time dialogue. Nonetheless, I would still endorse the idea that an argument has a dialogic structure insofar as it is a form of engagement, one specifically related to a disputed or contentious issue. Here is where the second and perhaps more problematic aspect of many texts on argument falls short; argument reduced to critical reasoning remains still somewhat abstract and is thus partly why logicism remains a hard model to shake off. Arguments are always embedded in specific speech or text acts and it is important distinguish an argument from, for example, an explanation (e.g. see Walton 2006). I would like to preserve the sense that an argument is not simply 'a set of reasons offered in support of a conclusion', but, more specifically, one such in the context of a dispute. This makes the structure of an argument co-dependent with its function, which is to resolve an issue of doubt or contention and furthermore reunites the two senses of argument I outlined at the start of this discussion.

Defining an argument in this way may be too restrictive for some, especially as it seems to exclude explanation from its remit. Indeed, arguments have often been divided into two main kinds based on their function: advocacy and inquiry (Toulmin et al. 1984). Yet the structure of an argument does differ from the structure of an explanation, because they have different functions. An argument is advocating a position, making a claim; an explanation is simply attempting to inquire into or clarify a state of affairs. Both may use evidence and evidential reasoning, but in different ways. This will become clearer in the next section on exposition, where I discuss inquiry and explanation in more detail. But in emphasizing the disputatious nature of an argument, one also gives its epistemic properties (i.e. robustness or strength of warrants) an ontological and indeed political dimension. If we think about an argument in terms of a dialogue over a matter of doubt or dispute, then clearly – in advocating a position on this matter – it is also simultaneously inviting agreement or disagreement. Of course, one can agree or disagree with other text types – with a narrative or description, for example – but these forms do not inherently invite this response in the way an argument does. If I disagree with a description, then I am *initiating* an argument, not responding to one that has already started. In this sense, a critique can be the start of an argument. Indeed, of all the four text types I am discussing in this book, argument is the most mobile insofar as its dialogical structure allows it to latch on to the other text types whose focus is turned more inward.

Given that the intention of an argument is usually to seek agreement – even if disagreement might equally be the outcome – then it clearly has an ontological and political dimension in terms of achieving consensus among the people involved. This aspect of argumentation was central to Habermas's early work on communicative rationality and his famous notion of an ideal speech situation (Habermas 1984). In his *Theory of Communicative Action*, Habermas developed a theory of argumentation that was central to his pragmatic concept of rationality: argumentation is what enables a society to achieve and maintain consensus in the context of disagreement where routine practice fails us and where the resort to force or violence is undesirable (ibid. 17–18; for an archaeological appeal to Habermas, see Wilkie & Bartoy 2000). In developing his theory of argumentation, Habermas drew heavily on Toulmin's work because it broke away from the reductionist approaches of formal logic and initiated a more pragmatic approach to argumentation. However, for Habermas, Toulmin did not take the pragmatic nature of argumentation far enough. In disconnecting argument from the strictures of formal logic, he felt Toulmin's model was open to charges of relativism; what is a good argument in one context may not be so in another, an issue underlined by Toulmin's suggestion that different fields (e.g. legal or scientific) had different criteria of validation. For Habermas, the only way to rescue Toulmin's scheme was to embed it in a broader theory of communicative action. Ultimately, this was about stressing the fact that argument is a dialectical procedure as much as a logical structure, but especially about grounding argument on a consensus theory of truth, facilitated by ideal speech situations. That is, what ultimately guarantees the validity of an argument is general assent to its claim, though an assent gained not by convention or social norms, but rather through the establishment of a context which guarantees impartiality: an ideal speech situation.

Habermas's theory has, of course, been subject to much critique (e.g. Hesse 1978) and he himself subsequently abandoned some of these ideas, not least the consensus theory of truth. No one has explored the political dimension of consensus more forcefully than Jacques Rancière whose concept of disagreement and dissensus lies at the heart of his political philosophy (Rancière 2013). For Rancière, consensus and consensual politics is about the ordered construction of social life – about what he calls, more generally, the distribution of the sensible. If we translate this into epistemological terms, it broadly resembles Kuhn's notion of normal science: this is the way we do things. For Rancière, this is not politics but the actual eclipse of the political. Rather, politics involves the disruption of consensus – hence his concept of dissensus, which is more than simply disagreement or dispute, but a disruption of the very order of the sensible. Politics is not the battle of the Left and Right, but a disruption of the order which underpins their existence. Now, I do not want to push the relevance (or merit) of Rancière's philosophy here, but there is a very general point at which it touches with my discussion. In both cases, what is at stake is the nature of agreement and disagreement and the way we valorize these terms. Almost instinctively, we tend to favour consensus as a political and epistemic ideal, whereas Rancière throws a big question mark over this assumption.

What it also does, though, is raise the question of whether the topic of arguments are inherently unsusceptible to agreement. This evokes Gallie's notion of essentially contested concepts – concepts such as 'art' or 'democracy' which Gallie suggests are inherently irreducible to any form of consensual definition (Gallie 1956; also see Collier et al. 2006). Now, whether all arguments have such concepts as their subject is questionable; archaeological arguments are certainly not all about conceptual definitions! But the bigger issue here is that if some arguments are inherently unsusceptible to agreement, what then is their purpose? My slight digression into Habermas and Rancière does have a point, namely the critical connections between argument and consensus and the function that impartiality or bias plays here. In offering an argument, we stake a claim, take a position on an issue of dispute, as I have already mentioned. Some see this as the very foundation of archaeological research. Mark Leone, whose own career has been built on a very specific standpoint influenced by Marxism, makes this very explicit:

> I argue that we all lead scholarly lives based on making interventions in a pre-existing dialogue over something that concerns us. In my case it is usually an intervention based on something that annoys me or that I believe to be an intellectual error. … I get involved if I think I have something to say.
>
> *(Leone 2010; also see Dalglish 2007)*

In a way, though, this immediately raises a question about whether impartiality is ever possible in an argument; at the same time, the very nature of an argument as a form of rational discourse is surely about maintaining an air of impartiality, following the evidence no matter where it leads. This paradox of argumentation is perhaps most evident in a legal setting where two lawyers, both adopting opposed positions, nonetheless also attempt to portray their position as impartial and simply following the evidence. This paradox is, in many ways, analogous to what is known as the bias paradox in feminist epistemology and standpoint theory (Rolin 2006), where adopting a specific position actually leads to greater objectivity. In other words and turning Habermas upside down, what guarantees the validity of an argument is not some ideal speech situation and state of impartiality but the very opposite: a situated perspective where partiality actually engenders the cancellation of bias.

Let's examine this carefully. The bias paradox emerged from feminist epistemology, specifically standpoint theory. Standpoint theory, initially coined by Mary Hartsock (1983), is most associated with the work of philosopher Sandra Harding (1991). Common to other approaches espousing the social nature of scientific knowledge such as Haraway's situated knowledges (Haraway 1991) and the largely Edinburgh-based strong programme of the sociology of science (e.g. Bloor 1976), it assumes that all knowledge is embedded in social relations. However, its distinctive characteristic is that it regards knowledge production as still objective, the issue being about how one defines objectivity. For Harding, objectivity does not imply neutrality or a value-free stance as it conventionally is assumed to mean – in Nagel's pithy phrase, the view from nowhere (Nagel 1986). Rather, objectivity is about the contestation of bias on the part of the scientist (see Harding 1991). The problem of achieving objectivity, then, is not 'How do I attain a neutral stance?' but rather 'How do I best ensure my bias is brought to the surface and thus controlled?'

In some ways there are parallels here with Gaston Bachelard's notion of scientific knowledge as the removal of epistemic obstacles (Bachelard 2002), although one should be cautious in overstating the similarities. Harding and standpoint theory generally argue that the only way to achieve this is to listen to and engage with socially marginalized groups – such as women – because they have privileged access to the bias present among the dominant groups. It is hard for the dominant group – or indeed any group – to recognize its own prejudices, at least those that run deep and structure our everyday discourse and behaviour at an unconscious and implicit level. On the other hand, someone excluded or outside that group will have a much better chance of doing so. Harding likens this to the ethnographer or stranger visiting an alien culture; they can often see things about that culture that the 'native' cannot. But it is more than simple perspectivism at stake here; the political foundation of bias means that such a viewpoint becomes a moral imperative. For Harding, adopting this strategy means *strengthening* objectivity, not weakening it – hence her notion of strong objectivity (Harding 1991). Alison Wylie, of course, made this a key part of her discussion of feminist archaeology (Wylie 2002, 2003).

The idea is extremely compelling, but it has been also the subject of some concern and critique by other feminist thinkers (e.g. Hekman 1997). One of the key issues appears to be a paradox around the role of bias. Essentially, some see a contradiction between the assumption that all knowledge is socially situated and the assertion that some situations or standpoints nonetheless produce better knowledge (Rolin 2006), the problem being: how do we decide which positions these are? From what standpoint do we make the claim that these are marginal positions? Helen Longino has addressed this problem with perhaps the most finesse and arguably reconfigured standpoint theory by suggesting that it is not so much a case of one position being better than others, as many positions are better than one (Longino 1993: 113). As she so aptly puts it, objectivity is defined not as the view from nowhere (conventional theory) or even somewhere (standpoint theory) but rather the view from 'many wheres'. In other words, the more diverse positions or perspectives involved, the greater the chances of each standpoint acting as a check on other standpoints and exposing bias. Diversity of bias will thus, ironically, enhance objectivity. To use a physics metaphor, we might describe this as *bias interference*; just as the superposition of two waves of light or water can cancel each other out, leaving 'calm' spots, so two standpoints, when they meet, can mitigate their individual bias.

Longino, I think, offers a really important modification to standpoint theory yet one which still preserves its essential feature: using the inherent bias in any standpoint to act as a counterweight to bias in other standpoints. Such mobilization of bias thus actually increases objectivity rather than the opposite – so long as pluralism is maintained. Ironically, Longino's four strategies for ensuring such pluralism (e.g. Longino 1992:

76–79) are vaguely reminiscent of Habermas's criteria for ideal speech situations, despite her criticism of Habermas (Longino 1992: 197–202). Also like Habermas, Longino stresses the community-based structure and dialogical nature of science. But unlike Habermas, Longino dispenses with the idea that consensus is what ultimately frames such situations. For Longino, although restricted forms of consensus are necessary for science to work, there is no need for this to be a universal or global feature as Habermas claimed. All of which brings me back to the topic of argument.

Is the point of argument, then, ultimately to seek agreement, as I initially suggested? Or is it perhaps a means of mobilizing bias – that is, to use the situated nature of knowledge production as a means to draw out implicit bias within any given field? In other words, an argument not only seeks to support a claim with good reasons, but to do so in such a way that it exposes the flaws and blind spots of other positions or claims on the same issue. I think this articulation captures that head slapping moment of a good argument, where one side not just acquiesces to the other's point but actually realizes that their own claim was founded on some premises they simply had not questioned. It recalls – albeit only obliquely – Deleuze's distinction between a conversation and a discussion, where the latter is described as an act of narcissism, showing off your own viewpoint in contrast to the learning process of a conversation (Deleuze 2007: 380). This distinction can also be linked to Eve Sedgwick's opposition between paranoid and reparative readings (Sedgwick 2003). These are epistemic practices or positions, one of which develops what Ricoeur coined the hermeneutics of suspicion (Ricoeur 1970), or, more simply, critique; the other is more about mending rifts, building bridges, creating consensus. I think arguments are best seen as involving both components, although, quite commonly, one element might dominate. Some arguments are pure critiques. This is almost the inverse of Deleuze's definition of a discussion where, instead of being narcissistic and showing off your own point of view, your chief goal is to downgrade your interlocutor's position. Any good argument (or conversation) will probably always find itself dancing a fine line between the paranoia of critique (Sedgwick) and the narcissism of discussion (Deleuze).

## Exposition: a sense of order

In the last section, I defined argument somewhat narrowly in terms of advocacy of a claim in the context of dispute. I deliberately excluded the idea of argument as the more general idea of 'giving reasons in support of a claim', under which other concepts such as explanation might fall. In this final section on exposition, I want to tackle these other cases of 'argument' and explore the particular epistemic issues they involve. But to begin, let me define what I mean by exposition in more detail. Exposition is, like the concept of argument, often used very broadly to refer to almost any type of academic or scholarly text: science, defined generally as a project whose purpose is to explain and enquire, is therefore obviously defined by a literature which has similar features. From student essays to peer-reviewed articles, the basic scientific text is often regarded as expository. However, I do not think one can so easily map a general function of an activity on to its texts in such a simple way, not to mention the fact that defining science in such a general way is itself problematic. Furthermore, real scholarly texts actually exhibit much more diversity than the label 'exposition' implies, as I hope previous sections of this book have amply demonstrated.

Nevertheless, the definition of exposition as a form of inquiry and explanation can still be retained. Only following my approach with the other text types, we do not need to employ it in such a way as if it defined whole texts, but merely text sections – even if, as with other text types, it can dominate a whole text, thereby lending it the flavour of an exposition. Given these caveats, how can we approach the topic of exposition, especially in terms of its epistemology and role in knowledge production? Most of the work on expository texts has been from within composition studies or discourse analysis where the aim has been largely about how an expository text is structured An empirical research essay is an obvious example with its format of introduction, methods, results and conclusion/discussion; the typical student essay is another, with its tripartite organization of introduction, body and conclusion. In discourse analysis, the structure is typically related to issues of communication and the functional properties of its individual sections vis-à-vis the whole (e.g. Lewin et al. 2001). In composition studies, the structure is usually explained in terms of the logic of an argument, as discussed in the previous section: stating a claim in the introduction and then supporting the claim with evidence in the main body. This latter makes a distinction between expository essays and argumentative essays on the grounds that an exposition offers an 'argument' as a way of providing information, whereas an argumentative essay presents its 'argument' with the intention to persuade or convince.

On the whole, I have adopted this latter distinction, but unlike the convention in composition studies, I find that that logical structure of an argument imputed to exposition is not really fitting. Specifically, I find it hard to see that an exposition necessarily has a claim or thesis which it seeks to support through evidence; rather it has a topic or problem which it seeks to elucidate through analysis. Part of the problem derives, I think, from a confusion over different meanings of an explanation (and indeed argument, as discussed in the previous section). Thus one sense of explanation involves giving reasons or causes for why something happened or is the way it is; this is the typical sense in which we use it in archaeology and indeed more broadly in the philosophy of science. Whether we argue that such causes operate at a level of generalization (i.e. law-like) is another matter and one that is not directly relevant to the matter at hand. But another sense of explanation refers simply to acts of clarification. The difference emerges very clearly in the two questions 'Can you explain why you did this?' and 'Can you explain how this works?' The first question is prompting an answer which gives reasons or causes; the second question is prompting an answer which makes comprehensible a confusing or unfamiliar state of affairs. In many ways, the first sense of explanation could be defined as one particular form of the second; that is, to make something comprehensible can sometimes involve a causal explanation. But there are other ways such as using analogy or making distinctions through simple classifications or enumerations. My explanation of the concept 'explanation' invokes just such a strategy, distinguishing between two different senses. Given that the broader sense of explanation is more inclusive, it is this sense I shall employ in the rest of my discussion of exposition.

If we thereby understand exposition as a mode of clarification, obviously the primary epistemological criteria for evaluating an exposition is the notion of clarity. But what is clarity? Ironically, it would seem like a rather vague and slippery concept to define. But more than that, it is also a somewhat contested concept and nowhere more so than in the field of social theory and philosophy. Thus, one of the common criticisms of some theory is its lack of clarity, specifically the use of what is perceived as an obfuscatory style of language: the use of jargon, of neologisms, of a manner of exposition which is simply hard to follow. This is an old refrain which often carries implications of intellectual posturing and superficial cleverness masking lack of substance (e.g. see Orwell 1968 for an early and very antagonistic view on unclear exposition; also Stebbing 1939). The usual comeback is that complex and difficult ideas cannot always be reduced to simple, clear language, and new ideas especially might require a new language. I do not want to get entangled in this debate, which had its most recent outing in the wake of the Sokal affair/hoax where a physics professor published a made-up article in a humanities journal to prove his point: the shallowness and laziness of contemporary social thinking (Sokal 1996; Sokal & Bricmont 1998). The Sokal affair, however, can be seen simply as part of a related set of wider divisions that emerged in the second half of the twentieth century, such as that between the two 'cultures' of the science and the humanities (Snow 1959) or between analytic and continental philosophy (Glock 2008), where one side of this divide has routinely criticized the other of obscurantism.

Given that the concept of clarity is then immediately caught up in this history, one has to manoeuvre a course very carefully through it. Indeed, despite the long list of insults cast at various scholars and discourses over the years for their obscurantism, few people have ever taken the trouble to actually reflect on what is involved in issues of clarity or obscurity, epistemologically speaking. The philosopher McGee is a recent exception and although his approach to the issue is clearly coloured by his analytical background, he does attempt to distinguish different levels of clarity (McGee 2014). Thus he argues that we need to separate clarity at the sentence level from the whole textual level: Wittgenstein wrote very clear sentences but the overall meaning of his texts can be very obscure. In contrast, Kant penned truly awful sentences but his works display an extremely lucid structure. However, at the level of the whole text, McGee makes a further distinction, after the philosopher Suzanne Langer (1957), between the discursive and presentational structure. The discursive structure is how the text is actually organized and flows, whereas the presentational structure refers to the underlying ideas and the final sense of comprehension one has at the end of reading a text. I am not so sure this latter distinction is actually that helpful and in fact ultimately makes clarity synonymous with comprehensibility.

Of course, the two are intimately related, but comprehensibility is something all the text types I have been discussing strive for; it is how they achieve it that differs. And yes, surely all also strive for a certain clarity too, but I would suggest that clarity is much more central to exposition than narrative, description or argument, the reason being exposition is premised on the need to clarify a confused or unfamiliar subject. Here, there is a close connection between exposition and ignorance. Ironically, ignorance as a topic has generally been itself ignored although there have been attempts recently to develop a field of agnotology – that is, the study of ignorance (Proctor & Schiebinger 2008). In Proctor's introductory chapter to a recent edited volume, he usefully distinguished between three forms or dimensions of ignorance (Proctor 2008). The first is what he calls a native state or given condition and is characterized by a deficit, or lack, of knowledge. It is the most conventional epistemological view insofar as the development of knowledge acts to fill this deficit or gap. The second form of ignorance is more subtle and acknowledges that because every enquiry has a focus, it is necessarily selective. This means it excludes as much as includes, and in directing attention towards some things, it also leads to ignorance about others. Where, under the first dimension, ignorance is slowly reduced with the advance of knowledge, under the second dimension, ignorance develops with (and potentially faster than) knowledge. For every question answered, several new questions emerge. Finally, while under the first two forms, ignorance is largely unintended or uncontrolled, in the third form is it actively cultivated as part of a strategy to deceive: spreading fake news, withholding information or otherwise deliberately conducting a campaign to misdirect and block knowledge.

Proctor recognizes that the distinctions between these three forms are not necessarily that sharp, especially the second and third, since bias clearly plays a role in both. The interests of the tobacco industry in concealing research on the harmful effects of smoking (Proctor 2008; Oreskes & Conway 2010) and the interests of European explorers of the sixteenth and seventeenth centuries ignoring knowledge and practices related to abortifacients (Schiebinger 2008) both pertain to bias and involved intentional selection. The complexities of such selectivity in relation to archaeology were very neatly explored in Alison Wylie's contribution to the agnotology volume which outlined a slightly different typology of ignorance: epistemological, ontological and political (Wylie 2008b). Epistemological ignorance is similar to Proctor's first form and describes a lack or deficit of knowledge, which can be related either to a lack of data or a lack of a theoretical framework. Both can be remedied, either by fieldwork or imagination. Ontological ignorance, however, refers to an intrinsic limit to knowledge; no amount of fieldwork can bring to light evidence which has not survived, and no amount of imagination can resolve anomalies or confusions if our conceptualization of the data is inadequate. Regarding the latter, one of the most common reasons for this inadequacy relates to the political context and bias which informs that conceptualization. Wylie uses the history of archaeological research on the Moundbuilders to illustrate this, drawing on Trouillet's forms of silencing in relation to history to enhance her analysis.

There is a lot to be gained by considering this work on ignorance in relation to my focus on exposition. At a general level, one can argue that exposition is premised on a condition of ignorance in a way that is not intrinsically the case for narrative, description or argument. But drawing on studies like the above, one cannot simply equate ignorance with a lack of knowledge. It is possible to see an exposition in this way – as a basic presentation of information. But most expository texts are far more sophisticated insofar as they might address a topic with which we are familiar but either in a very vague way or a misguided way. What we know is selective and/or muddled. In a sense, exposition is a form of ignorance correction. That is, some expository texts might grapple with a topic whose lack of clarity is acknowledged, while some will take a topic that we think we know, but through exposition reveal its hidden complexities and nuances, making us see things in a different way to before. One extreme example of this is Ordinary Language Philosophy whose claim was that many philosophical problems could be dissolved once language misuse was taken into consideration. But even in routine exposition in the sciences, one of the driving forces is the desire to draw out different facets or dimensions of a topic or phenomenon and provide a conceptual road map as a means of comprehending it better. Thus an exposition of the concept of 'agency' or 'materiality', for example, might review different approaches, different meanings of the terms, and typically is informed by a literature review. A really successful exposition does this in a novel way and one which, moreover, makes us see the topic in a new way.

The philosopher Peirce (famous for his theory of signs) more than a century ago wrote one of the few other texts to deal with idea of clarity (Peirce 1966). There, he identified three different grades or dimensions of clarity. The first was unreflective familiarity – something is clear simply by virtue of being familiar and therefore usually not even requiring elucidation. Once I understand and know how to use the concept of *terminus post quem* (TPQ) in archaeology, it never occurs to me that it requires any further exposition. The second grade refers to the formulation of explicit definitions, which are usually done in cases where there is confusion or unfamiliarity with something. A first-year archaeology student will be very glad of an explicit definition of *terminus post quem* when they are starting to get their heads around archaeological methodology, even if their professor knows it instinctively. However, it is the third grade of clarity which Peirce considered the most important and this was the pragmatic value of clarity – what consequences it has or entails and whether these continue to make sense. Thus it is only when our student finally gets to use the concept of TPQ with actual data, that its meaning becomes clearest.

There is something in Peirce's pragmatism here that is worth underlining; in putting a concept to use, you may well gain a deeper enlightenment about it. But the converse is also true: you may expose what has been called a sense of false clarity, which is more prevalent than we might think (van Deemter 2010; Varzi 2003). If I say this artefact dates to the late second century BC, that sounds perfectly clear and comprehensible; but if we were to ask what do you mean by 'dates to', darkness starts to descend: was the pot *made* in the late second century or *deposited* then? What is at stake here is the degree or quality of clarity which we can refer to in terms of vagueness or its opposite, crispness/sharpness. For philosophers, vagueness has received much more attention than clarity, perhaps because vagueness is largely perceived as a measure of clarity. Philosophers generally mean something very specific by vagueness: the admission of borderline cases (see van Deemter 2010 for an extended and engaging discussion of the concept). Many everyday terms exhibit this property – 'grey' being almost a paradigmatic example insofar as it shades between black and white. Qualitative measures are another – how many times have you read a description of an artefact as 'small' or a quantity as 'many' and been somewhat unsure what actually counts as being small or many?

Such vagueness is, of course, something we try to avoid, and a typical response might be that we just need to be more precise. Instead of saying we found a lot of pottery, we should say we found 546 sherds, which may indeed be a lot – or not, depending on the context: 546 sherds is a lot for a twelfth-century farm in Iceland, but not so much for a site in London of the same date. At least having the numbers now gives us better scope to appreciate this. Problem solved. Or is it? Let's say that of these 546 sherds, 300 are of type A and 246 of type B. Still clear enough? Maybe, but it rather depends on how clear the distinction is between type A and type B pottery. Someone else might come along and sort the pottery and find there are only 280 of type A and 266 of type B. Of course we can question the competence of one of the people (or both), but the relevant issue here is whether a portion of the sherds (e.g. 20 or 3–4%) have an inherently unclear attribution. That is, the typology admits of borderline cases. Anyone who has ever worked with typologies will know this is almost universally the case. They have an intrinsic vagueness.

What this means is that while clarity may be possible, it also depends on the level of crispness you desire – or the level of vagueness you are willing to accept. Tim Flohr Sørensen is one of the few archaeologists to have taken up this concept of vagueness and suggested that we embrace it, given that it is an inherent quality of human experience (Sørensen 2016; also see Marila 2017). He also makes an important distinction between vagueness and ambiguity; ambiguity is a concept promoted especially within feminist archaeology and is about keeping interpretation open, allowing for multiple narratives and accepting that our accounts of the past or the archaeological record will always be characterized by a degree of uncertainty (see especially Gero 2007). This notion of ambiguity in many ways resonates with Gallie's suggestion of essentially contested concepts and thus relates more to arguments (Gallie 1956; see above). But vagueness is different – it is about the fuzziness of things or concepts. With ambiguity, what is at stake is the certainty of a claim; with vagueness, it is clarity.

Accepting vagueness into our accounts, however, does not mean we have to abandon clarity, which is what Sørensen seems to be implying – indeed, he explicitly concludes with a call for archaeology to develop a "methodology capable of embracing the erosion of clarity" (Sørensen 2016: 19). The sociologist John Law has taken this even further, arguing for a disciplined lack of clarity in the social sciences or a 'knowing confusion'. His claim is that because the world is inherently messy and unruly, we need a messy methodology – or, better, a method which can do justice to this mess rather than one which always tries to straightjacket it and tidy it up. More specifically, he espouses the need for different types of text which can address such mess – ones that take inspiration from poetry and allegory (Law 2004). While I can accept that our sciences may not capture fully or even partially the messy and confused nature of reality, and that other means of representation are necessary – I also feel his position is unnecessarily extreme. I think one of the mistakes that both Law and Sørensen make is to equate lack of clarity with vagueness. Vagueness is a gradational term, a sliding scale if you like and a measure (not necessarily quantitative) of clarity. Of course, if we increase vagueness, we decrease clarity, but I do not see that clarity has to be abandoned here – and especially in the context of exposition. Another, perhaps clearer way to express the difference between vagueness and clarity is that while vagueness is about the fuzziness of boundaries (whether of objects, concepts or whatever – hence the notion of borderline cases), clarity is more about existence of any boundaries at all. Clarity, in other words, is about the making of distinctions.

It is helpful at this point to return to Peirce. At the very start of his paper, he makes a distinction between two kinds of clarity as conventionally implied in philosophy: familiarity and distinctness. The first he dismisses quickly and as ultimately derivative of the second, so I will begin with the latter. Distinction is a very important concept for exposition and arguably lies at the heart of its operation; indeed, it has even been claimed as the fundamental method of philosophy (Sokolowski 1998). But what is it? To make something distinct is to create edges where none previously existed. In very simple terms, distinction is about creating identity by marking difference, specifically relevant difference. Whether we enumerate a list of different meanings around a concept, draw an opposition between competing viewpoints or even develop a classification, all of these are forms of distinction. These distinctions may turn out to be vague, but they are still there. They are also classic strategies of exposition. Any good definition does the same and in some ways a definition is simply an exposition writ small (or vice versa). Distinguishing is a way of bringing order, sorting out a mess, resolving a confusion. Sokolowski even suggests than in making distinctions one is also essentially creating an ontology (ibid.). I am not sure I would venture that far, but the connection is surely there nonetheless. More relevant for my discussion is how this characterization of distinction relates to the other quality of clarity that Peirce so easily dismissed – familiarity. I think it was too quick of Peirce to simply say that familiarity presupposes distinction.

If we recall my earlier discussion on ignorance, then exposition as clarification involves the correction of ignorance, but of an ignorance about something we know – not ignorance as the absence of knowledge. Clarification thus works on the familiar, not the unfamiliar, contra Peirce. In this sense, we are conducting a kind of reverse engineering on Peirce's grades of clarity. Exposition is ultimately a process of de-familiarization – at least when it is done well. In this sense, it has something in common with the pedagogic principle of unlearning (Cirnu 2015).

We make the familiar unfamiliar as a platform upon which to build an exposition. Why? Simply because if we don't, we have not really learned anything. For an exposition to count as knowledge-producing, it has to do this; otherwise it is just a synopsis. Another way to phrase this is in terms of problematization; we make something that seems obvious or taken for granted appear problematic. Making the familiar unfamiliar has been a common way to characterize archaeology practised on the recent or contemporary past (Buchli & Lucas 2001). Rodney Harrison has critiqued this idea for sustaining a sense of self-doubt and a need to justify the expansion of the archaeological into new territory (Harrison 2011), and while he may have a point with regard to these sub-disciplines, there is also a sense in which such archaeology was also underlining the fact that it can inform us about things which we think we already knew. More specifically, de-familiarization becomes a strategy of detachment: a way of trying to imagine a concept or phenomenon as alien to us, permitting us to see it as if for the first time.

Of course, this is a fiction – of a kind. But what is really involved in de-familiarization is akin to going off the beaten track through a territory; there may be plenty of guidebooks and maps out there about a phenomenon, concept or subject, but they surely do not exhaust it. No map is equivalent to what it represents. There is always another way, another route through it; another way of marking distinctions. Of course, risks always come with making new maps – that we lose our way. In an attempt to clarify through exposition, we may actually risk obscuring matters further. Indeed, during first forays into any such endeavour, that is often how one feels – that is how I felt writing this book at times. My desire to try to look at knowledge production in a different way in archaeology has led me down many dead-ends and into periods of confusion. In the end, though, I hope I have produced not just a different way of seeing, but one that is also relatively clear.

## Conclusion: detachment as an epistemic virtue

I think it would be useful to pause now and recap my preceding discussion of the epistemological aspects of the four text types I have examined. My basic argument has been that different text types embody different epistemic values and criteria, and that we should not evaluate a text on the basis of some presumed, primordial structure of knowledge. This is not to suggest that there are not continuities between texts or values; I am certainly not suggesting that each text is locked into its own epistemic world, like Kuhn's incommensurable paradigms. Indeed, this is something I will address in detail in the following chapter. For now, though, and as a way of closing this chapter, I want to make the strategic claim that different texts have different epistemologies.

In brief, each text type has a different epistemic register which defines the criteria upon which one can evaluate the strength and quality of its knowledge production (Table 4.1). Narratives are basically texts which tell stories, relate actions and/or events in time: the virtue of historical distance conceived as hindsight is its primary epistemic register. The essential tension this register/virtue has to mediate is between the narrator being both after and yet part of the events they relate – both inside and outside of time. If time is too alienated from the events, the events become reduced to a meaningless sequence, as in annals; if, however, the distinction between events and time collapses altogether, then meaning and emplotment dominate and a sense of futurity, of openness is eclipsed. Descriptions are texts which report what was experienced or witnessed; they are essentially testimonies, implying 'I was there' and thus presence is its epistemic register. The core dilemma for descriptive knowledge is mediating the demand for such presence with an equal imperative to remove oneself from the description so as to not stand in between the object of description and the reader of the description. Your co-presence must somehow translate into the reader's co-presence. The third text type, argument, involves advocacy – hence adopting a standpoint or point of view as its epistemic register. Such positions have to construct robust warrants to invite agreement, but their very positionality also carries the problem of partiality. Yet impartiality can actually be nurtured insofar as the very existence of a standpoint serves to expose hidden and unacknowledged bias in an opponent's position. Finally, exposition as an enquiry assumes a register of ignorance in the face of a confused or vague state of affairs. The mitigation of ignorance is effected through a process of clarification defined as the marking of distinctions (and connections). Such distinctions typically have to either sharpen or reconfigure pre-existing distinctions, which means de-familiarizing the familiar.

Despite these differences, though, I think one can still discern a common thread running through all of them: detachment. In narrative, detachment takes the form of historical distance, by which I primarily mean hindsight – coming after the event. As we saw, this is not a simple matter of chronology, since defining what counts as 'after' invokes the whole notion of an end and, therefore, of emplotment. But the distance is nonetheless crucial and involves an active temporal detachment – putting oneself after the fact, or, rather, outside the story. In description, detachment takes the more familiar shape of removing oneself from the frame – creating a sense that a description

**TABLE 4.1** Text types and their epistemic features

| Text type | Epistemic function | Epistemic strategy | Epistemic register | Epistemic virtue (Mode of Detachment) |
|---|---|---|---|---|
| Narration | Story | Endings | Hindsight | Historical distance: being both 'after' and 'part of' the event |
| Description | Testimony | Conventions | Presence | Objectivity: being both 'there' and 'not there' |
| Argument | Advocacy | Warrants | Standpoint | Impartiality/neutrality: being the view from 'somewhere' and 'nowhere/everywhere' |
| Exposition | Enquiry | Distinctions | Ignorance | Clarity: being both 'familiar' and 'unfamiliar' |

lacks an author, as if the object of the description merely presented itself, in words. It is the illusion of things that talk. But this illusion – like any good illusion – is simply misdirection and masks the real action, which is not about objectivity so much as the removal of subjectivity. Again, detachment is an active process. Arguments embody yet another species of detachment: the mobilization of bias in order to create what I have called bias interference – where the superposition of bias acts to create a contingent space of impartiality. To distance ourselves from our own prejudices, we need to be exposed to the standpoint of others. Finally, with exposition, detachment becomes a process of de-familiarization, of unlearning – of alienating ourselves from what we already know in order to expose the ignorance embedded in knowledge.

But if the epistemic registers of all four text types incorporate different versions of detachment or distancing, is this something to make a virtue out of? After decades of postmodern critique, surely detachment has become a dirty word? The short answer is no, as a recent volume, exploring the multiple dimensions and manifestations of detachment make clear (Candea et al. 2015). In particular, the editors highlight the problematic way in which not only detachment, but its celebrated opposite, engagement, has been conceptualized. They argue that the elevation of engagement, which they see as connected to a rise in relational thinking and a privileging of relations over entities, has gone too far in the other direction, creating its own set of problems. Their call for a reconsideration of detachment is not, however, a return to the old, conventional view but rather an emphasis on seeing detachment and engagement as intimately related processes and something which is negotiated depending on the context (Candea et al. 2015). In this regard, their distinction between detachment as a process and detachment as a completed state is critical. The papers in their volume address some of the diversity and complexity of this concept and I will not attempt to summarize them here. However, it is worth working backwards and looking at some of the pioneering work which also addressed the idea of detachment, most of which was influential to this volume.

Among the first studies which avoided the knee-jerk response that detachment was automatically suspect were those of Lorraine Daston on scientific detachment (Daston 1992, 1995) and Amanda Anderson in literary studies (Anderson 2001). I have already discussed Daston's work in the section on description, but it is worth stressing the key connection she draws between detachment and what she calls a moral economy. Anderson's work, however, expands this moral economy of detachment to encompass a broader field within European culture, including literature. Her studies of writers such as George Eliot, Charles Dickens and Oscar Wilde attempted to underscore the idea that detachment was ambivalent in Victorian culture – that there were desirable as well as undesirable aspects of it, but that it was nonetheless fundamentally embedded in practices of self-cultivation. In short, detachment comes to be seen as morally enabling as much as morally dangerous. Mill's utilitarianism illustrates this nicely, where 'the greatest good for the greatest number' requires a moral resolve which mediates between sympathy for the whole and a detachment towards those individuals who might suffer in its name. Similarly in Eliot's fiction, balancing between sympathy and distance was seen as comparable to the ethnographic mediation of participant observation – being involved yet being detached.

Where Anderson's work shows the wider role detachment played in Victorian literary culture, the German philosopher Peter Sloterdijk has considered its function within the long tradition of Western philosophy, tracing it back to Socrates and Plato (Sloterdijk 2012). Sloterdijk is especially concerned to stress the long-standing association between detachment and scholarship epitomized in the secluded spaces of academia, from Plato's eponymous academy to the modern university. Moreover, in the development of modern science it is not only subjects who become detached from the world, but objects do too, as in the paradigmatic case of deracinated particulars – facts. However, central to his analysis is the idea of detachment as a form of disembodiment, a pseudo-death or what he calls suspended animation. Such a characterization brings detachment close to a religious state of being, and indeed for Sloterdijk this is the ultimate issue; detachment involves not only the idea of withdrawal from the world and a cultivation of an 'inner witness' but, through this, the attainment of a higher level of existence or state of being. Although Sloterdijk's analysis is sweeping and broad-brushed, the connections he draws between scientific detachment and religious ecstasy reveal yet another dimension to this concept, one which nonetheless preserves the association between detachment and knowledge, but where knowledge becomes a state of being rather than simply a mental state.

The ontological nature of 'knowing' is, of course, nothing especially new – it is a hallmark of Heidegger and, after him, hermeneutic philosophers such as Gadamer and Ricoeur. Ricoeur is particularly relevant, given my earlier discussion of his work on narrative, as many of his ideas can be traced to a very simple and singular tension which characterizes all human understanding: that between distanciation and belonging (Clark 1990; Ricoeur 1973). Recurrent through so much of his writing, whether explicit or not, this couplet mirrors that raised by Candea *et al.* between detachment and engagement, as discussed above. I find it a very useful way to think through the various epistemic tensions that play out in the four text types I have been discussing in this chapter, albeit refracted through different compositional structures. On narrative and historical distance, it is about mediating the problem of being both inside and outside the events being told; in description it is about both being there, as a witness, and yet effacing your presence and letting the object speak for itself; in argument it is about remaining impartial while yet holding fast to a position; and finally in exposition it concerns the imperative to de-familiarize something in order to actually make it more comprehensible.

Arguing that all the text types exhibit variations on the same theme – detachment – does go some way to holding together what could be viewed as an over-fragmented portrayal of knowledge. For the danger in describing archaeological knowledge through four different text types is that one is almost implying there are four different types of archaeological knowledge, each locked into its own world. How do we ensure there is communication between these four types? Which clearly there is. Somehow, the fact that all types can be viewed as variations on the theme of detachment is not really enough; it is simply a recognition of similarity. In order to make the connections more concrete, we need to turn to the issue of how ideas and concepts travel between text types and epistemic strategies. This is the issue I take up in the next and final chapter.

# 5

# MOBILE KNOWLEDGE

## Introduction

At the end of the last chapter, I argued that while my discussion of text types allows for a more diverse characterization of knowledge, there is the danger that such pluralism might lead to fragmentation, where knowledge produced in one mode, such as narrative, could never be squared with knowledge produced in another, such as exposition. The fact that this does not happen in practice suggests there must be ways in which these modes 'talk to each other'. This is essentially the same issue raised by those arguing for the irreducible pluralism of the sciences; given the epistemic fractures between different scientists, theories, laboratories, not to mention different sub-disciplines and disciplines, how is communication still possible between them? Peter Galison developed the idea of trading zones to deal with just such an issue, and much of his work has explored this in the context of the material culture of particle physics (Galison 1997; also see Collins et al. 2007; Gorman 2010 for extensions of Galison's idea). Wylie and Chapman have drawn on Galison in their recent work, shedding important light on the practices involved at the intersection of archaeology and other sciences (Chapman & Wylie 2016). Archaeometry or the archaeological sciences in general are surely fertile trading zones which warrant much further exploration. However, my focus is somewhat different; it deals more with the issue of communication between writing practices in archaeology – what one might call the issue of inter-textuality.

To address this topic, let me return to the discussion which concluded the last chapter where I suggested that all four text types could be viewed as variations of the same basic ontological position: detachment. On its own, this is not sufficient to account for this communication. However, there is a sense in which detachment still nevertheless serves as the starting point or condition for such communication. Detachment as a condition of mobilization. Think back to this idea of facts as 'deracinated particulars' (Daston 1991; Poovey 1998), information stripped of its context of production. To make facts work as evidence, they need to be detached from such contexts and enter new contexts as 'given', or what Latour would call black-boxed (Latour 1987). For example, the generation of a radiocarbon date is based on a whole set of processes and theories, but as that 'date' travels from the lab report to the site report and then into secondary literature, it has shed all these processes and theories to become a deracinated particular, employed as evidence in another context. The ability to detach or uproot information, ideas and concepts from their context is the precondition of their being able to travel or move. It is this basic idea which I want to expand on in this final chapter and explore how the mobility of knowledge is the essential counterpoint to its composition in textual forms.

This task, however, is by no means straightforward. A radiocarbon date is one thing, a complex idea, such as agency, quite another, yet both clearly travel between texts albeit in different ways. The case of a radiocarbon date is in some ways most complex at the point of its initial construction; indeed, this is what the work of Latour and others has demonstrated so well in science studies, and what I tried to do with archaeological facts generated through fieldwork in an earlier book (Lucas 2012). The difficult part is that of 'semantic ascent' – turning things into words or signs, as I also discussed in Chapter 1. Once created, the hard work appears to be done and such facts then circulate relatively freely between texts. However, more recent work on how facts travel has suggested that even for facts it is not that simple. Mary Morgan in particular has been at the forefront of research on this topic, which grew out of her recognition that knowledge always starts locally, situated in specific contexts and generated in small chunks. From this, the problem then becomes how to move it from one context to another (Morgan 2014b).

Morgan suggested three broad strategies for engendering mobility or what she calls resituating knowledge. The first is a simple direct transfer, metaphorically labelled as stepping stones or bridges; her examples include transferring laboratories or set-ups from one site to another or modelling the analysis of one organism on another. All archaeological excavations are mobile laboratories in this sense. The second is 'ladders' which involve processes of abstraction such as in classification schemes that allow comparison between different datasets or computer modelling which similarly works in multiple contexts. The third is representative cases – either as a result of statistical/averaged functions that characterize the norm, or because they exemplify a broad category concept. Morgan's typology of mobilizing strategies is interesting, and will have some echoes in my discussion that follows, which worked off another source of inspiration. But Morgan's later reflections on how facts travel offers another dimension to the issue: how *well* does a fact travel? (Morgan 2011).

She suggests there are two key aspects to this; one concerns the question of how far a fact will travel, the other, how fruitful it will be. These two features can be related; for example, a single radiocarbon may circulate in endless papers and texts because it has major implications for the origin or timing of some event in the past (e.g. adoption of pottery and its implications for wider issues such as sedentism or agriculture). However, these two aspects need not go together; if that same date is subject to scrutiny and doubt, even though it has spread like wildfire through the discipline its fertility is severely curtailed if does not hold water. For Morgan, for a fact to travel well, it needs to remain steadfast and solid as well as have important ramifications beyond its immediate context of generation (Morgan 2011: 25). But defining how well a fact travels is one thing; another is what processes or conditions act to facilitate this. Morgan suggests two things a fact needs: good companions and a good personality. A fact that is well accompanied, whether with an attractive image or graph or eloquent text, is certainly going to be well received. It is critical, though, that these 'companions' can be immediately shed and the fact repackaged or reused; otherwise its mobility will be weighed down by all those clingy companions. But a fact also has to be inherently appealing, headline-grabbing, to be effectively mobile. A radiocarbon date comes with all kinds of packaging (calibration curves, probability measures, etc.) but at the end of the day, it can be reduced to a simple date.

Morgan makes some valuable points although her metaphors sometime may over-reach themselves. For me, the most important point she makes is that for facts to travel, they have to be modular – discrete chunks of information – and these need to retain their integrity as they move across contexts. Certainly packaging facts well will enhance mobility and here the work of Sabina Leonelli on bio-informatics is especially insightful (Leonelli 2011, 2015, 2016). Like Morgan, Leonelli's interests lie in how facts circulate as fungible objects: what makes them portable. She also stresses the importance of understanding how facts become decontextualized from their context of production but also need packaging to allow subsequent recontextualization in another locale. Part of her work is a critique of some of the more naïve views on the potential of big data and machine epistemology to automatically generate knowledge without any prior 'theory' (e.g. see Wheeler 2017). In fact, a lot of work goes into the coding of big data and it is the ontologies generated by database curators that are packaging and thus channelling the ways in which such data can be recontextualized. Leonelli's work on bio-ontologies and biological databases shows how these processes are operating in one scientific field, but the implications are no less relevant to archaeology, especially in the current work on cyberinfrastructures I discussed in Chapter 3.

In her discussion, Leonelli is mostly focusing on what she calls small facts – bits of data that, on their own, are fairly meaningless but only have power in numbers. This is exactly the kind of fact that fits well into databases and travels best as part of a team or group. She contrasts small facts with big facts – whether those are headline statements in the media or simply the conclusions of a journal article where the basic results can be summed in a few simple statements or propositions (e.g. 'earliest pottery in X now dated to Y'). Big facts are more likely to travel alone and the nature of their packaging is sure to be different (here Morgan's discussion would seem to be more relevant). Big facts, however, are also in many ways far more complex – simply because they congeal and condense a whole string of reasoning and argumentation that also makes their integrity far more unstable. In many ways, I think we can think about the distinction between small and big facts as one which overlaps with that between Gardin's concepts of compilations and explanations or Manovich's distinction of database and narratives discussed in Chapter 3. Thinking about how big facts travel is, arguably, also connected to thinking about how theory travels.

For it is one thing to discuss the mobility or portability of something like a radiocarbon date and quite another with something like the concept of 'agency' or even theories such as 'structuralism'. You can surely recall any number of instances where an archaeologist outlines some concept or theory developed in another context and then tries to apply it to their own data set; you have probably tried it yourself and know how difficult it is. Deracinated facts are one thing, deracinated concepts and theories quite another. Indeed, arguably concepts never become completely detached from their context of origin, as will become clearer in the course of my discussion. However, I do not want to necessarily overstate the distinction here or create a rigid dichotomy. If my following discussion is focused mainly on the mobility of concepts and theories, this is simply because I feel these are more closely connected to the textual forms in which they are packaged, as discussed in the last section.

To address the more specific question of how concepts – and theories – travel, I think it is helpful to begin by taking the rather more easy and familiar case of methods. In Morgan's threefold strategies of relocating knowledge, many of her examples pertain to what one might characterize as methods – the almost tacit knowledge or know-how of science rather than more conventional propositional, know-that knowledge. At the same time, this distinction is rendered superfluous when thinking about how knowledge moves. Archaeological methods are something we learn at the start of our undergraduate training, whether it is how to excavate a trench or sort out pottery into types, plan an earthwork or draw a stone tool. Methods are really important vehicles for understanding how knowledge is mobilized because this is what they are designed to do: to move – that is, to be applicable to a diverse set of real-world contexts. When you learn how to sort potsherds on one set of material, you can take that technique and apply it on another assemblage, and another, and so on. Of course, if you are taught how to sort Roman pottery into types, the specifics may not help you when faced with a collection of Neolithic ceramics. At the same time, you can still adapt and modify what you know to the new material and the method is not completely useless. If you cut your teeth on Romano-British ceramics but then you are yourself faced with a collection of Roman period ceramics from Turkey, you ought to have better luck. Methods will always have different levels of applicability which means they will always need adapting, the further removed they are from their original context of development or learning. Yet the basic premise of methods is that they will at least have wide applicability to multiple real-world situations and that they can adapt – within limits – to the differences these situations throw up.

Take a method like excavation; every archaeological textbook will discuss this and may even present more than one technique. Carver's textbook on field methods, for example, discusses three different methods of excavation, illustrated with both hypothetical and real exemplars of how it works (Carver 2009: 117–124). They can and do work on any real-world site, although, as Carver suggests, some might be better suited to certain conditions than others. Indeed, textbooks are the *locus classicus* of method in any discipline. What they all do is describe a performative sequence, like any manual or how-to book; and like any method or technique, the best way to fully understand it is to do it yourself. Simply because it is a performance, not just an abstract idea.

The same ultimately applies to the use of theories and concepts; they are, of course, almost by definition abstract ideas, but to fully understand them, you have to use them. Now although the performative aspect is extremely important and has particular relevance when it comes to teaching theory in the classroom – or the field (e.g. Cobb & Croucher 2014, 2016; Hamilakis 2004; Rainbird & Hamilakis 2001; Conkey & Tringham 1996), it is the ability of theory to travel that is my focus here. Which means theory is really just like method in principle – it is all about applicability. The only difference is that where a method has essentially been codified and conventionalized as part of the disciplinary matrix – what one might call 'normalized' in the sense of Kuhn's concept of normal science – theory remains contentious and lacks the broader consensus of method. For the same reason, one might invoke the rather traditional idea of method as being concerned with fact collection or data retrieval and theory as interpretation, but only because facts, by definition, are the product of codified or conventionalized practices, whereas interpretation, by definition, is not (Lucas 2015b).

## Paradigms and exemplars

This idea of applicability goes to the heart of Kuhn's attempt to resolve some of the confusion around his concept of a paradigm. This concept, as discussed in Chapter 2, had a major influence on archaeology and indeed the humanities during the 1970s and 1980s. However, a paradigm was generally understood as a short-hand for some kind of metaphysical worldview or, at least, theoretical framework; thus processualism or postprocessualism were often called paradigms, but so was Marxism or Cultural Ecology (see Lucas 2017). Kuhn later argued that what he largely meant by paradigm – at least retrospectively – was more like an exemplar: a model solution to a problem, accepted as exemplary or 'paradigmatic' by the community (Kuhn 1977). Now Kuhn was, of course, largely discussing physics, and physics textbooks are somewhat different to archaeological textbooks. If you take an archaeological textbook, such as Renfrew and Bahn's widely used *Archaeology: Theories, Methods and Practice*, which is currently in its seventh edition, numerous exemplars are given, especially in its boxed sections (Renfrew & Bahn 2016). Some of these, of course, have slightly changed or been modified over the editions, reflecting new research and new problems; moreover, other textbooks would no doubt use other exemplars. Certainly in a discipline like archaeology, then, model solutions are not as stable or consensual – that is, paradigmatic, as in physics – but this is only a matter of degree. But for me, this is not the important point of Kuhn's reappraisal of the paradigm concept. The important point is that as a paradigm or exemplar, it is there to be copied or imitated.

This is a point also stressed by David Turnbull, a science studies scholar who argues for the critical role paradigms play in mobilizing knowledge:

*Exemplars* ... are shared examples of puzzle solutions and are based essentially on agreements about which kinds of problems are sufficiently similar as to be treated in the same way. These 'learned similarity relations' provide the ability to perceive otherwise disparate problem situations as alike and thence to apply known techniques and solutions.

(Turnbull 2000: 8; italics in original)

In archaeology, our methods perform this function all the time, but one also sees the same strategy adopted in more 'theoretical' cases. For example, in North American historical archaeology, George Miller wrote a famous paper on the pricing of nineteenth-century ceramics which he used to develop value indices for different vessel and decorative types; these indices were then used to compare the 'value' of ceramics found at six different sites, suggesting a link between ceramic investment and the wealth/status of the household (Miller 1980). Miller's work became widely imitated and thus served as a clear case of an exemplar (e.g. papers in Spencer-Wood 1987). The study of socio-economic status in North American historical archaeology had a paradigm or role model which could be widely imitated because Miller provided a detailed list of indices (which he later updated; Miller 1991) and a set of how-to instructions which were very easy to copy. Needless to say, the model was not without its problems, many forewarned by Miller himself, and today it is rarely, or at least more cautiously, used (Mullins 2011).

Miller's paper, although short-lived as a paradigm, nonetheless is a great example of how theory and method are hard to separate. Yes, the paper was methodological in many ways in offering a technique for scaling ceramics found on excavated sites, but it was also deeply theoretical in the assumptions it carried regarding the association between socio-economic status and ceramic investment. Yet there is another layer of mobility in Miller's article that I want to draw our attention to: that which underwrote his value indices. These were based on the wholesale price lists recorded by various potteries among other documents. These documents attach monetary values to ceramics but, importantly, it was the detailed description of the ceramics in the documents that allowed the link to physical, archaeological specimens to be made. Information about one set of objects – 'textual pots' – could be converted into information for another set of objects – 'archaeological pots' – an equivalence being established between the two. This kind of work has, indeed, often been described as a form of middle-range theory, but one using texts instead of ethnography (Leone 1988; Potter 1992). This kind of travelling is also one that crosses domains or fields – in this case, from historical to archaeological material. As such, it leads us to perhaps the most important facet of how theories or concepts travel: not within a field or discipline but across them.

Let me take a different example of cross-domain travelling – this time, Ian Hodder's use of Hayden White's rhetorical tropes to interpret prehistoric material culture sequences (Hodder 1993, 1995; White 1973). White's scheme was discussed in Chapter 3 along with its influence on archaeology. But Hodder took it in a very novel direction in the early 1990s by suggesting that prehistoric people may have conceived of their own history in terms of White's four tropes; as he put it, "narratives and rhetorics are not only in the domain of the observer" (Hodder 1995: 167). With White, his four tropes served to characterize changing regimes of historiography or historical writing over the nineteenth century, with each trope linked to a specific form of emplotment, argument structure and ideology (White 1973). Hodder took this conceptual structure or classification and applied it to European Neolithic periodizations, suggesting these rhetorical strategies were readable in the material culture sequences. Thus, in one of his examples, the early Neolithic in southern Scandinavia is characterized by a romantic narrative of human conquest of nature through agriculture, later replaced by a tragedy of internal schisms and social hierarchies, then through the comedy of ritual in the middle Neolithic, culminating in the irony of social stasis.

Of course, Hodder was somewhat sceptical of his own experiment, especially the periodic or cyclical nature of these four tropes, and as a 'potential paradigm' it never really took and consequently is not so well known today. Yet, like the previous examples, I have discussed it because it illustrates in a clear way the manner in which theories travel: a very concrete conceptual framework, which applies to one set of material, is moved and applied to another. For my last example, let me take the case of structuralism – a high-level theory if there ever was one. Structuralism, as is well known, was a theory developed in relation to language and, as every textbook on theory will tell you, is closely linked to the linguist Ferdinand de Saussure. It was Roland Barthes who provided one of the clearest expositions on how material culture could be viewed as a sign system like language along the lines of Saussurean linguistics (see especially his compact book, *Elements of Sociology*; Barthes 1967; also Olsen 1990). As archaeologists, however, we perhaps associate structuralism mostly with the work of Claude Lévi-Strauss and his use of binary oppositions, which are a somewhat simplified version of the Saussurean system. In many ways, the key to translating linguistic structuralism into material culture structuralism involves a simple substitution; in the axiomatic couplet of signifier–signified, one simply replaces the form of the signifier – conventionally a word – with an object or image. Thus the words 'male' and 'female' get substituted by osteologically sexed skeletons, and from the chain of associations that run off these objects, one builds up a cosmological system that is, essentially, no different in structure from that derived purely from the analysis of words or narratives embodied in myth (see Tilley 1991 for what remains still one of the best examples of this genre).

Pettit, in a small book on structuralism from the 1970s, drew out the paradigmatic function of structuralism very clearly, defining it as a paramorphic model which operates metaphorically by translating one part of reality in terms of another (Pettit 1975). But it is not just a loose or general metaphor, but a very systematic one, which Pettit suggested operated through a three-tier ontological translation of elements (e.g. words, artefacts), strings (sentences, find contexts) and systems (languages, cosmologies/ideologies; ibid.: 109–110). Pettit's discussion is interesting in the way it discusses structuralism in terms of metaphors, models and archetypes, especially drawing on the work of Max Black, whom I discuss in the next section. Because while structuralism can work quite concretely in this way, it is also such a broad theory that I could have discussed it in either of the next two sections on analogies and concepts. The relevance of this will become clearer by the end of the chapter.

I have deliberately tried to describe the theory in all these examples as more like a method, simply because I think this captures best the aspect of theory I want to stress: their mobility. However, it also highlights the performative and practical nature of theory over its usual connotation of being abstract or purely conceptual. In some ways, all of these examples could be rendered as instances of a certain epistemic genre – the case study. I discussed Morgan's work on case studies in the last chapter, and, although instructive, it does tend to work on a rather common notion of what a case study is: namely as a typical or representative exemplar (Morgan 2014a, 2014b). But Galison's discussion of case studies, especially as they relate to their origin in legal studies and case law from the late nineteenth century, suggests a more 'Kuhnian' view, where case studies act as exemplars (Galison 1997: 55–58). The difference is crucial because it reflects on whether one sees a case study in representational terms (i.e. as a typical example) or in performative terms (as a role model). Examples like Miller's ceramic indices or Hodder tropological periodizations are, I suggest, better viewed as performative case studies than representational ones. At the same time, I recognize there is a lot of archaeological theory which works in a much vaguer way than in the examples I have given here, cases where the translation from one domain to another is much less transparent. Sometimes this is about how well the cases are written. But mostly I think it relates to a difference in the conceptual vehicle. To develop this discussion, I want to continue drawing on Kuhn's work.

## Analogies and metaphors

In his reappraisal of the paradigm concept, Thomas Kuhn suggested that paradigms – as exemplars – were just one of three elements which bound a scientific community together within a disciplinary matrix (Kuhn 1977: 297–298). The other two were what he called symbolic generalizations and models. By symbolic generalizations, he meant expressions typically cast in logical form (e.g. $E = MC^2$). In the field of physics, such generalizations, of course, frequently relate to mathematical equations and laws, but in the biological and social sciences, one might more commonly think of symbolic generalizations as taxonomies or typologies. Concepts like 'Neolithic' or 'shell-edged pearlware' refer to typologies, in this case of periods and pottery. By models, Kuhn refers to 'preferred analogies', metaphorical statements which help to comprehend the nature of phenomena – either heuristically or with implicit ontological commitment. Thus, when we think of gas behaving "like a collection of microscopic billiard balls", this analogy heuristically describes something we might only otherwise depict using mathematical formulae (Kuhn 1977: 298). In archaeology, models and analogies are often associated with specific exemplars, though not always; some classic instances would include analogies for culture such as when processualists likened culture to a 'system' or postprocessualists modelled it on a 'text'. Let me start with the issue of the model or analogue, and then, in the next section, end with that of symbolic generalization.

To begin, it may be judicious to define what I mean by model here, especially in relation to the concepts of analogy and metaphor. The concept of a model can be used to refer to something that is exemplary or paradigmatic as in the phrase 'model solution', as discussed in the previous section. It can also carry a connotation of something abstract or idealized, yet something which is still somehow representative of reality; when we talk about archaeological models, this is usually what we mean. David Clarke thus described models as "pieces of machinery that relate observations to theoretical ideas" (Clarke 1972a: 1), but in distinguishing between controlling models (theoretical frameworks which he referred to as 'paradigms' and methods) and operational models (consciously deployed constructs, like systems theory), one senses that, for Clarke, the term model was almost synonymous with theory – or at least a particular view of what theory should be. Alison Wylie's more recent discussion of archaeological models articulates this much better, suggesting that models are really forms which incorporate both theory and data equally (Wylie 2017). More importantly, in offering a taxonomy of archaeological models, Wylie essentially suggests that modelling is what archaeologists do most of the time in producing knowledge, with some models being more about ordering existing data (e.g. typologies, site formation processes) while others incorporate more explanatory and causal processes (e.g. agent-based models).

In presenting her taxonomy, Wylie explicitly acknowledges the key role analogy plays in modelling, drawing on earlier work such as Hesse (1966), which Clarke also mentions and which I discuss further below. The analogical aspect is crucial and so most of my discussion will focus on this. Analogy has always been a key feature of archaeological interpretation since its antiquarian beginnings, especially (if not almost exclusively) ethnographic and ethno-historic analogy. Between the 1950s and 1980s there was a peak of theoretical debate about its status in archaeological interpretation, which ties in to the epistemological issues surveyed in Chapter 2. There is no need to review this literature and, in many ways, Wylie's review which was published at the tail end of this debate summarizes this literature and the key issues beautifully (Wylie 1985). The drop-off in theoretical discussion, however, has not signalled any reduction in the actual use of analogy (see Spriggs 2008 for a recent and critical discussion of the use of analogy in post-1980s archaeology; for a more positive perspective, see Thomas 2004b: 238–241). One of the key issues today is whether analogies are simply heuristic – that is, good to think with – or carry ontological commitments, whether acknowledged or not. Julian Thomas argues the former, insofar as analogies offer an initial 'what if' scenario: what if Neolithic Wessex was like twentieth-century Melanesia? For Thomas, their ultimate point is not to set up a resemblance between archaeological and ethnographic cases but, through this, to disrupt our own sense of normality via a process of defamiliarization.

Matthew Spriggs, for his part, acknowledges this function, and in fact both he and Thomas recognize this has perhaps always been an important function of analogies – a kind of 'bedtime reading' for archaeologists (Spriggs 2008: 542). But Spriggs argues that this purely heuristic justification is disingenuous and that in fact archaeologists also continue to use analogies which do carry ontological commitments – that is, transferring Melanesian ontologies like those of personhood or Big Men social systems into European prehistory. He has a point; but at the same time I wonder if this distinction between a heuristic analogy and one with more specific ontological commitments is even a valid one to make. One of the seminal works to study the role of analogies in science was Max Black's paper on 'models and archetypes' from the late 1950s where he draws on this distinction, weighing up the gains and losses of each. Describing the heuristic versus existential interpretations of Maxwell's analogy for comprehending electrical fields as like an imaginary fluid, Black states:

> The difference is between thinking of the electrical field *as if* it were filled with a material medium, and thinking of it *as being* such a medium. One approach uses a detached comparison reminiscent of simile and argument from analogy; the other requires an identification typical of metaphor. In *as if* thinking there is a willing suspension of ontological unbelief, and the price paid, as Maxwell insists, is absence of explanatory power. Here we might speak of the use of models as *heuristic fictions*. In risking existential statements, however, we reap the advantages of an explanation but are exposed to the dangers of self-deception by myths (as the subsequent history of the ether sufficiently illustrates).
>
> *(Black 1962: 228; italics in original)*

In short, a heuristic view of such an analogy is safe, but ultimately unproductive, whereas one which carries ontological commitments, risky yet with explanatory potential. In other words, unless your analogy is going to carry some form of ontological commitment, it simply won't serve any purpose and so the distinction between heuristic and existential analogies in science is somewhat irrelevant.

This, essentially, is also the key point made in contemporary discussions of models in the philosophy of science. Morrison and Morgan, for example, discuss this in terms of the tension between models as autonomous agents and models as instruments (Morrison & Morgan 1999). Their discussion is framed more in terms of the opposition between theory and data, where they critique the idea of models as purely operational tools or instruments linking theory and data, and instead argue that models work more autonomously, integrating both data and theory. The value of rephrasing Black's heuristic versus existential views in this way underlines the point that fact and theory are never really separable. But whether we describe models as autonomous agents or as existential statements, the question remains the same: what is the nature of their ontological commitments?

Wylie's taxonomy, discussed above, suggests that some models have very limited ontological commitments, especially those she labels as homeomorphic – those where the ontology of the model corresponds with its target (Wylie 2017). Others, defined as paramorphic, incorporate entities and processes not present in the archaeological record. The distinction between homeomorphic and paramorphic models was coined by Ron Harré (1970), and we saw it also being used by Pettit to describe structuralism as a paramorphic model (see above). For Wylie, the distinction between these two roughly also coincides with the distinction between models which are largely descriptive and order existing data, and those which are explanatory and explain such data. To some extent, this distinction can be mapped on to earlier discussions, especially in the work by Mary Hesse on *Models and Analogies in Science* (1966). Hesse picks up Black's argument for the explanatory potential of analogies, recasting Black's distinction into two types of analogy: formal and material. Formal analogies simply draw a one-to-one correspondence between two things, whereas material analogies carry interpretive consequences beyond the immediate correspondence (Hesse 1966: 68). The reason being, that with material analogies, there is a causal dimension that is lacking in formal analogies. This is effectively the same distinction between formal and relational analogies used in archaeology by Hodder (1982d) and Wylie (1985), and it is material or relational analogies that are of most relevance. However, while archaeologists have tended to focus on the *problem* of how to strengthen such analogies in the face of their ampliative nature, here it is the interpretive *potential* of this amplification that I want to stress – and which was, in fact, the main stress of the philosophers Max Black and Mary Hesse. This potential is best elucidated by drawing out the links Black made between scientific models and literary metaphors (Black 1962).

Behind Black's argument for the productive or explanatory function of scientific models is the connection he draws between such models and metaphors. In another well-known paper on metaphor, Black argues for what he calls an interaction view of metaphors in opposition to the substitution view (Black 1962). The substitution view essentially suggests that a metaphor is simply a substitute for a literal term or phrase; thus, describing King Richard as a lion or lionheart is simply another way of saying he is brave. The problem with the substitute view is that it begs the question of why use a metaphor at all. Sometimes it may be because we lack a word for the quality; for example, if there was no English word for the colour orange, we might use the fruit metaphorically to describe this colour. Etymologically, the use of the word 'orange' for the fruit certainly seems to have preceded its usage as a colour by three centuries. But, in most cases, this is not really what impels the use of metaphor; for example, we have the word 'brave' so why call Richard a lion? Invoking an appeal to aesthetic or poetic licence does not really explain anything. What does the term 'lion' do that 'brave' does not? Black argues that when we use the term 'lion', even if we want to mainly evoke the quality of bravery, we also invoke all the other associations that the word 'lion' conjures up. Metaphors enchain not just one specific similarity but a whole chain or system of qualities. This is the interactionist view, which stresses the function of a metaphor in generally connecting two things together, not substituting one term for another. This is why one can describe metaphors as meaningfully rich and why Black regards scientific models as metaphorical.

Mary Hesse elaborates on this by suggesting that in scientific analogies or models one distinguishes between positive, negative and neutral analogies (Hesse 1966: 8; also see Wylie 1985: 94). Positive analogies refer to the particular features of correspondence, such as that two societies both subsist by hunting and gathering.

Negative analogies refer to features they don't share – such as one society lives in a desert, another in a forest. Neutral analogies refer those aspects of the two societies which we don't know if they share or not – and therefore are those aspects of the analogy that carry the most potential and, in a way, make the difference between a formal and material (or relational) analogy. It is the unknown or unintended aspects of an analogy that are also those most productive and generative of new ideas and new interpretations. Let me explore this with some archaeological examples so as to make my point clearer.

The Folkton Drums are a set of three chalk objects with ornate carvings found in a Neolithic burial in the north of England. An earlier archaeologist described these objects as looking like Melton Mowbray pork pies (Figure 5.1). This analogy is interesting; at one level it is quite amusing, though I think the intention of making the comparison was not to elicit a laugh but to give some indication to the reader about the general size and shape of the objects, using a contemporary object they would have been familiar with. Obviously, the positive analogy here lies in its dimensions and form; the negative analogy in the material they are made from and the lack of decoration on pork pies. But if the analogy is going to be productive, interpretively speaking, it is the neutral analogy that matters – and in this case, there almost certainly are not any. As an analogy, this has very little potential. More productive are the similarities that have been observed between the decoration of the chalk drums and other, broadly contemporary objects.

The similarity of the decorative style to other Neolithic objects from Britain such as Grooved Ware pottery, maceheads and carvings on tombs has been

**FIGURE 5.1** A reproduction of one of the Folkton Drums next to a Melton Mowbray pork pie (photo: author)

often observed (e.g. Longworth 1999), and this too is a form of analogy; the positive analogy is the decorative motifs, the negative analogy, the material or objects on which the decoration is applied. But, in this case, one immediately feels the neutral analogy may hold out more potential than the pork pie case. Unfortunately, however, beyond recognizing the similarities in decoration, most archaeologists have usually been stumped to venture any further interpretation of these objects. Indeed when I looked at them as part of my own doctoral research in the early 1990s, I felt incapable of drawing them into my narrative in any useful way. However, one exception to this interpretive impasse comes from Andrew Jones who, besides reflecting on aspects of their size and inter-referentiality as a 'set', stresses their citationality to other objects as part of their performance (Jones 2012: 174–180). This performative function is linked to the fact that the decoration on each drum includes motifs resembling eyes and eyebrows which serve to animate the objects, to make the objects like/as people. The juxtaposition of two analogies – stylistic similarity to other Neolithic finds and a stylistic resemblance to the human face – work together to stress a performative-citational interpretation of the objects. How much more insight we have into the objects because of this is debatable, but it does focus our attention away from how they look to how they acted. In that sense, we have gained from these analogies. The analogy between people and things is also a predominant feature of my next example.

John Chapman's fragmentation thesis argues that – a least in his context of study in the Balkan Neolithic and Chalcolithic – broken fragments of objects such as pots can be viewed as part of deliberate practices of fragmentation as a way of creating social relations. Just like two lovers or friends might take the halves of an object to symbolize their connection, so fragmented objects like pottery served to enchain people together (Chapman 2000). Now, the basis for this idea derived not directly from ethnography but indirectly from the juxtaposition of two topics in ethnography: personhood and exchange. Drawing on ethnographies of the partible or fractal person on the one hand (e.g. Strathern 1988; Wagner 1991) and ethnographies of gift exchange on the other, which stressed the intimate relationship and blurred boundaries between people and things (Strathern 1988; Weiner 1992), Chapman argues that if people are partible and people and things are also inextricably linked, then things ought to be partible too in a way that relates to partible personhood. In other words, Chapman is drawing some novel possibilities from ethnographic analogies to help interpret fragmentation in the archaeological record. Such object fragmentation is not present in the ethnographic analogies he draws on – at least not in the sense he uses it; it is rather the ontological implications about personhood and social relations and gift exchange from these analogies that are applied to Balkan prehistory.

This is a much more complex example that the Folkton Drums, because the analogy between Balkan prehistoric societies and modern Melanesian societies is almost purely neutral; no initial positive analogies were being posited by Chapman, although they might have been assumed in their use (e.g. both small-scale, agricultural societies) and the negative ones are obvious (different environments, different historical and cultural contexts). Now, Spriggs might define this as disingenuous – and maybe it is. But the facts is that an analogy is being used here to make a novel interpretation about the past which is not given in the initial analogy. And just like the case with the Folkton Drums, it is the juxtaposition of two analogies (fractal persons and person/object hybrids) in relation to archaeological data that really engenders the novelty.

Both of these examples show how analogies in archaeology have the capacity to be productive; they are heuristic but they are also existential, to use Black's terms: they carry ontological commitments. One can argue about how strong they are, especially in the example of the Folkton Drums, but as the fragmentation example shows, it is the interpretive potential such analogies opened up that is perhaps their most important feature. In that sense, analogies might work best where they provide a broad, conceptual space of possibilities rather than any close model or representation. Here, I would turn to Black again and his concept of the conceptual archetype which he proposes as a very broad type of analogy, one that frames one's thinking: "By an *archetype* I mean a systematic repertoire of ideas by means of which a given thinker describes, by *analogical extension*, some domain to which those ideas do not immediately and literally apply" (Black 1962: 241). It is also conceptual archetypes that Georges Canguilhem was mostly thinking about in his discussion of models and analogies in the life sciences, especially the mechanical analogues used to represent organisms such as Harvey's characterization of the blood system in terms of valves and pumps (Canguilhem 1963).

I would suggest that, in archaeology, conceptual archetypes include the idea of culture as a physical system or as a language or text. Unlike ethnographic type analogies, these analogies provide a general framework for thinking about a whole range of phenomena, but at a very general level. This is not to say that such analogies cannot be spelt out in some detail, but their value lies primarily in the interpretive possibilities they open up. Conceptual archetypes even arguably define the way we think about even more basic concepts such as time, although here the basis for such analogies goes beyond the disciplinary confines of archaeology or even academia. Black's conceptual archetypes in many ways prefigured the development of conceptual metaphor theory (CMT) as originally proposed by George Lakoff and Mark Johnson (1980). Compare this 'standard' definition of CMT with Black's definition of conceptual archetypes, quoted above: "A conceptual metaphor is understanding one domain of experience (that is typically abstract) in terms of another (that is typically concrete)" (Kövecses 2017).

CMT captures the fact that, especially with abstract concepts, we often invoke concrete metaphors as a way of articulating them. Indeed, one of the important though by no means universal functions of metaphor is to provide a vocabulary and terminology for talking about new concepts and ideas where none exist. With CMT, however, it is the abstract–concrete relation that is most salient. For example, the emotion of anger is often mapped on to the phenomenon of fire so that various different expressions of anger might all use the same analogy with fire (e.g. inflammatory remarks, burning with anger, flaring up) and where the intensity of the fire analogy corresponds with the intensity of anger. In archaeology, Cris Simonetti (2018) has explored the function of conceptual metaphors, especially in relation to how our understanding of archaeological time through stratigraphy and periodization is articulated by embodied metaphors of movement and orientation (e.g. the past as 'below' or 'behind' us). Although Simonetti is concerned to distinguish his notion of sentient conceptualization from CMT, these differences are not so important to my discussion.

There are also interesting parallels between Black's conceptual archetypes, CMT and the work by linguist Halliday on the generation of grammatical metaphors in scientific language (Halliday & Martin 1993). Halliday argues that the operation of nominalization – converting adjectives and verbs into nouns – is a key feature of how scientific language developed. Acting as a kind of objectification or reification – that is, turning relations into things – concepts such as weight, motion or refraction all subtly developed from an original verb or adjectival form. Once nominalized, though, they then become subject to analysis and qualification – or recursive modification; motion thus can be described as linear or uniform, and so on. This discussion of conceptual archetypes and conceptual and grammatical metaphors in many ways crosses over into the next and final type of conceptual vehicle I want to discuss, alongside exemplars and analogies: that of concepts.

## Concepts and generalizations

Concepts are in many ways one of the most obvious and common vehicles for connecting different texts together as, like facts, they are far more compact that exemplars or even analogies, and thus move fairly easily; usually a concept is manifest through a single word or short phrase. Concepts such as 'agency', 'materiality' or even 'Neolithic' can be deployed in narratives, descriptions, expositions and arguments with equal ease. And yet concepts are not really like facts at all. Exploring this distinction will help to elucidate the nature of concepts and how they mobilize knowledge. The best place to start is with some of the older debates on concept formation in the social sciences.

Concept formation is a topic that received a fair amount of attention in the mid-twentieth century but has substantially waned since then. The debate largely revolved around the concept of 'ideal types' in the work of Max Weber, who argued for their fundamental role in social science (Weber 1949). Weber considered concept formation in the sciences as one of its most basic operations since it involved bringing a selective focus on to the 'flux of events' through abstraction. He broadly distinguished two forms of abstraction: generalization and individualization, one focusing on commonalities between phenomena, the other on their unique qualities. Such a distinction, of course, largely replayed the hermeneutic division of nomothetic and idiographic science and underlines Weber's intellectual genealogy in hermeneutics. For example, when archaeologists talk about the 'Wessex culture' to refer to a particular suite of sites and material culture in southern England during the Early Bronze Age, this is a concept which refers to an individual 'entity'. However, when archaeologists use the word 'culture', this has a much more general reference which expresses certain commonalities across all human societies.

But does the term 'culture' refer to anything real or is it simply a useful abstraction? Does 'culture' have the same status as, say, 'gravity'? Weber thought not. Although Weber did not hold to any rigid division between the sciences, and saw the importance of generalization to the social sciences, he argues that the form of generalization used in the social sciences was not the same as that in the natural sciences. 'Gravity' in expressing something common between apples falling from trees and the earth revolving around sun, pointed to an underlying common cause that could be expressed in the form of a law. 'Culture' on the other hand in expressing something both the English and the Icelander has, pointed to something more fictive and more fluid. Weber coined a third species of concept besides generalizations and individuals to refer to this: the ideal type.

An ideal type is an abstraction and resembles a generalization insofar as one could point to numerous instances of it (e.g. the Wessex culture as an instance of 'culture'). Examples of Weber's own ideal types include 'Capitalism' and 'Christianity'. At the same time, Weber wanted to acknowledge the fact that none of the instances one could point to perfectly matched the type. The type was an idealization, a concept which had no perfect incarnations or instantiations but only approximate or imperfect examples. Indeed, it was the very discrepancy between the instances and the ideal type that acted as a motor for developing knowledge about society, which is why Weber considered ideal types as heuristic rather than descriptive or even explanatory. Ideal types were not generalizations akin to laws, but tools for thinking about society (Drysdale 1996).

Weber's concept of the ideal type was subject to lengthy discussion between the 1960s and 1980s. To a large extent, the issue got caught up in the question of whether ideal types were simply conceptual abstractions or referred to real entities in some way. Outhwaite's book on concept formation was largely an extended meditation on concepts as nominal (i.e. ideal) or real, he favouring the latter via Bhaskar's theory of transcendental realism (Outhwaite 1983). For others, however, the issues were more epistemological than ontological; one of the key points was whether a generalization that only had a vague or imperfect link to empirical reality had any value; most thought it did, but differed as to how to express that value (e.g. Schutz 1954; Hempel 1965; Nagel 1963; Papineau 1976). Ultimately, though, because similar questions around the nature of theoretical entities in the natural sciences were being raised, Weber's notion of ideal types as distinct from generalizations has become somewhat moot. Indeed, the dichotomous nature of generalizations/ideal types versus individuals needs to be regarded as somewhat forced. Nancy Cartwright in exploring the function of measurement in the sciences, offers a more considered view on this, especially in terms of her discussion of abstraction (Cartwright 1989).

For Cartwright, abstraction is fundamental to how science is practised but she argues that we have no really good idea of how scientists go about making and using them. She suggests that generalizations, such as laws, presuppose abstraction and should not be conflated with it. Abstraction, she argues, is essentially a subtractive process; to get to the concept of 'culture', we abstract properties from concrete objects or situations, and the more properties we subtract, the more abstract our concept becomes. In her rather simple example of a right-angled triangle drawn with chalk on a blackboard, if we remove the chalk and slate embodiment of the triangle, we are left with the more abstract, geometrical figure of a right-angled triangle. If we go further and remove the right angle, we are left with the even more abstract concept of a 'triangle'. In other words, there are degrees of abstraction and concreteness. But the important bit comes next; to develop a successful abstraction, it needs to be able to fit back into the real world and in such a way that it enhances our understanding of the world. A successful abstraction is also an explanatory one. To achieve this entails now *adding* properties to the abstraction. In a way, this is a kind of reversal, but it is a reversal that draws in different properties to those originally subtracted, which is why she calls this second stage *material abstraction*. But what a material abstraction ultimately does is also make a concept more concrete.

Cartwright has elaborated upon the performative nature of concept formation in a recent co-authored paper exploring the nature of measurement in the social science. Cartwright takes a classic example of a Weberian ideal type – 'civil war' – and examines how the concept is formed and operationalized in terms of specific sets of practices (Cartwright & Runhardt 2014). Three key moments or stages are identified: concept definition, representation and operationalization. If we take an archaeological example such as the concept of 'chiefdom', then its definition will involve characterizing its attributes, such as the permanent pre-sence of a central authority based on kinship, whose key political function involves either the control or the redistribution of strategic goods or services. Such definitions typically involve the first stage of abstraction discussed above, examining actual societies or communities and removing features from them which are deemed irrelevant to the concept. From that definition, we then need to develop ways in which such a definition is represented in the data: what variables, for example, does an archaeologist need to identify a chiefdom? This might include evidence of settlement morphology indicative of centralized authority and funnelling of goods through such centres. Finally, to actually investigate this, one needs to decide on the best procedures that will make this concept work in the context of real data. Again, this might encompass anything from reviewing previously excavated settlement plans to instigating a provenan-cing study on material recovered from such sites. During these latter two stages, one is now trying to make the abstraction more concrete again, and in the pro-cess, new aspects will be brought into play.

Obviously, this is a very simplified sketch and some archaeologists who work with the chiefdom concept may be horrified by my crude outline; I am only too aware of the ink spilt over competing definitions of what a chiefdom is (see Earle

1987 for an early review). Indeed, in many ways, concept definition is the most sensitive and critical stage of the process. Although Cartwright and Runhardt mention various issues around definition such as the inherently fuzzy nature of most social science concepts (often known as *Ballung* concepts), the most important issue that emerges in their paper concerns the intersection of fact and value in concept formation. In the same key text on objectivity in the social sciences where Weber discusses ideal types, he also discusses the ineluctable intersection of social values and scientific research. They summarize Weber's argument very succinctly:

> It is the job of social science to study the things that our societies care about – which in large part depends on what we value and disvalue. Second, there is the aim of finding concepts that aid in explanation, prediction, and control. As we've noted, it is not always easy to bring these aims into accordance.
>
> *(Cartwright & Runhardt 2014: 283)*

In their examples of the concepts of 'civil war' or 'poverty', these are issues we care about; but, as concepts, how much explanatory power do they really have? Fundamentally, this goes to the heart of the idea of social science as a critical science – that is, a science which seeks to not simply understand society but change it. It is about the role of science in altering the terms of debate, of changing how we think about the world. In my archaeological example of chiefdoms, Pauketat, for example, has questioned the social values implicit in the concept of chiefdom (i.e. links to nineteenth-century evolutionism) and, by association, its explanatory potential (Pauketat 2007).

Cartwright's discussions on measurement and abstraction have certainly moved the debate about concept formation in science in a more fruitful direction, away from issues of realism, such as whether chiefdoms really exist, or indeed away from any polarized distinctions about generalization in the natural and social sciences. The focus on how concepts work in terms of the mediation of abstraction and the concrete is an important development. However, I think there is another dimension here that is still missing, not only one that deals with the relation between concepts and the world through abstraction, but also one that considers the relation of concepts to each other. There is a lateral or horizontal dimension to concept formation that we need to consider, alongside its vertical dimension manifest in the abstract–concrete relation.

Here I think we can draw connections to the last joint work of Deleuze and Guattari in their book *What is Philosophy?* which is partly devoted to an analysis of what concepts are (Deleuze & Guattari 1994; Gane 2009). They, of course, were masters in the development of new concepts and/or a conceptual reworking of familiar words – that is, *catachresis*. It is precisely the creative function of concepts that they highlight in their book, although in doing so they distinguish between different motivations or approaches. A traditional philosophical one is characterized as encyclopaedic – one where concepts classify the world, which in the sciences is typically related to the construction of taxonomic and typological concepts. The second is commercial and relates to the commodification of ideas and the annexation of concept creation by the market place through designers, advertisers and companies who sell ideas as their stock in trade. For Deleuze and Guattari, neither of these approaches is acceptable; the first because of its totalizing ambition, the latter because of the debasement it brings by reducing concept creation to capital accumulation. If one is too lofty, the other is too vulgar. There is, of course, a middle way which is what they offer in their book: a pedagogical approach to concept creation.

Nicholas Gane, who has argued for several parallels between their pedagogical view and Weber's concept of ideal types, describes it well:

> [T]hey argue that concepts are about *creation*: the creation of precarious and unstable bridges between the empirical world and its presentation in thought. Concepts are not fixed but are what they call *becomings*: devices that draw on the complexities of the empirical world in order to open our theoretical imagination to things as they might be, rather than to represent or capture these complexities in knowledge. Concepts deal with possibilities.
>
> *(Gane 2009: 87)*

I take this to mean that pedagogical concepts, like ideal types, function as virtual entities, acting not so much to describe or explain actual instances but creating a conceptual space in which actual instances can be comprehended in new ways.

In some ways, one can tie this in with the first stage of Cartwright's analysis of abstraction. But I would like to draw on Deleuze and Guattari's typology of concept formation to think about how concepts actually work along two axes. One is that between a concept and its concrete instances, as I have largely been discussing in this section so far. The other, which has only been implied but not explicitly drawn out, is that between a concept and other concepts. The concept of 'Roman pottery', for example, not only has a relation to its instances, but also to other concepts – most immediately, either pottery from other time periods or cultural traditions (if the 'Roman' part is being stressed) or other artefacts of Roman attribution (if the 'pottery' part is being stressed). This trans-conceptual axis is what Deleuze and Guattari are largely referring to in the encyclopaedic function of concepts; concepts are providing a totalizing framework which, at its most systematic, constitutes a taxonomy or typology. The 'Roman' in 'Roman pottery' is a concept which, for example, forms part of a wider conceptual system of periodization. Its use is connected to its difference from other, yet related concepts which in England would include 'Anglo-Saxon', 'Iron Age' and so on. But even non-typological concepts still invoke other concepts; 'agency' commonly invokes the concept 'structure', while 'materiality' might invoke the concept of 'immateriality'. The difference is that these concepts are less bound to others, or rather the associations are looser, less prescribed.

But what does this entail? Simply this: concepts are most free to move when they are also most detached from other concepts. Deracinated concepts, like deracinated particulars, travel much more easily. I think one can view Deleuze and Guattari's commercial and pedagogic concepts as both deracinated in this sense, though, of course, made to then move for very different purposes. This also resonates somewhat with the idea of travelling concepts which has been the focus of some attention recently. The phrase was coined by the cultural theorist Mieke Bal as a way to foster interdisciplinary and transnational dialogue in the humanities (Bal 2002). She argued that concepts, although they look like words, are really miniature or shorthand theories, an idea which I think is important – although which needs some qualification. Of particular salience here is the role of concept-metaphors as discussed by Henrietta Moore in anthropology (Moore 2004). By concept-metaphors she means terms like gender, identity, agency or the self; Moore argues they work because they have a weak ontological commitment and can thus be developed by any number of different disciplines in different ways. They provide a domain within which to think – like a mini-theory. The problem with them, though, as she also points out, is that their meaning can be constantly shifting and changing. For Moore, this is a positive trait as they maintain ambiguity between universal claims and specific contexts; they keep debate open and keep knowledge moving – gender being a good exemplar. The danger, however, with concept-metaphors is that of overreach; in becoming so elastic, they lose any real analytical potential. The concept of 'landscape' in archaeology is a good example of a term that was applied so widely in the 1990s and early 2000s that it has now arguably lost its productive capacity.

In some ways, concept-metaphors dominate archaeological theory today, and indeed have done so for the past thirty years if not longer. They are the postmodern response to the grand theories of the late nineteenth and early twentieth century – Marxism, structuralism, evolutionism. They also are a vital way of keeping the social sciences and humanities connected without reducing them to within a total system. Similarly for Bal, travelling concepts do not just describe the objects they apply to but transform them: they are performative. Concepts such as 'gender' or 'materiality' subtly change as they move across disciplinary contexts, but this does not so much hinder cross-disciplinary communication as enhance it, establishing contact zones.

Bal's notion of travelling concepts was in many ways prefigured by Edward Said's earlier evocation of travelling theories (Said 1983) which draws out many of the same issues; the shift, however, from 'theory' to 'concept' is important. It signals a lighter way to move, like travelling with one small piece of hand luggage instead of a set of trunks; being less encumbered, they detach and travel more easily. Yet Said's notion of travelling theories reminds us that just because some concepts are more bundled up with others, as in typologies, this does not mean they cannot travel at all. Think back to my example of Hodder's use of White's tropological scheme: here, a set of concepts did move from one domain to another, but, of course, they moved as a set, as a schema, which is why I considered it more appropriate to discuss this under the notion of a paradigm or exemplar. Yet, arguably, single concepts still travel faster and further than bundles, which is the point of Bal's approach. Mieke Bal's work consequently also had a greater focus on the dynamics of such concept mobility, which more recent work has continued to develop (Neumann & Nünning 2012), exploring in greater depth why, for example, some concepts travel more easily than others.

Now, although, based on my earlier discussion, the idea of deracinated concepts seems to apply more to some concepts than others – for example, concepts not connected to specific taxonomies or typologies – this is not necessarily the case. Although the typical examples of travelling concepts are terms like 'culture' or 'materiality', more taxonomic concepts such as 'periodizations' also move. A good example is the concept 'Neolithic', which emerged as a purely taxonomic concept, being a refinement of the Three Age System; however, over the hundred and more years since its inception, its usage and meanings have changed quite substantially (Thomas 1993). This kind of mobility is not cross-disciplinary, certainly, but concepts move within a discipline too – by becoming disconnected from other concepts. Thus 'Neolithic' at the end of the nineteenth century referred primarily to a technological stage in prehistory with explicit evolutionary connotations; it was very tightly bound with other periods as part of a system or taxonomic ordering of technological development. Consider Lubbock's classic definition:

> The Later or Polished Stone Age; a period characterized by beautiful weapons and instruments made of flint and other kinds of stone; in which, however, we find no trace of the knowledge of any metal, excepting gold, which seems to have been sometimes used for ornament. This we may call the "Neolithic" period.
>
> *(Lubbock 187: 2–3)*

During the early twentieth century, however, the concept 'Neolithic' started to get loosened from its taxonomic straightjacket. Gordon Childe's functional-economic reinterpretation of the Three Age system was a critical turning point:

> Neolithic will mean 'food-producing' and will point to a contrast with the food-gathering economy of the Old Stone Age. Such a division will agree passably with classical definitions of the Neolithic; all authorities mention domestic animals and agriculture as well as polished stone axes, pottery and weaving.
>
> *(Childe 1935: 7)*

Although Childe tried to retain the old Thomsen–Lubbock technological view and make his new functional-economic interpretation simply a deeper and richer enhancement of the old taxonomy, by the mid-twentieth century it was clear that technological aspects and subsistence aspects could not be so neatly aligned. Piggott's discussion of this change to the conceptualization of the Neolithic makes it very clear, especially his discussion of pottery as no longer a defining trait of the Neolithic (Piggott 1965: 24–26). Indeed, as Julian Thomas points out in his analysis of the changing meanings of the concept, aspects which have later become very characteristic of the Neolithic in Britain, for example – such as monuments – were very marginalized in early twentieth-century discussions about the concept (Thomas 1993: 366).

I think Thomas's paper on the discourse about the Neolithic is a brilliant example of how a concept becomes deracinated. That is, how a concept like the 'Neolithic' gradually loosened its position within a taxonomic system to become a more free-floating idea. For Thomas, writing at the time when this deracination was almost complete, this was about dissolving the concept as a totality:

> Having noted the way in which the concept of the Neolithic has shifted from one meaning to another, one point of continuity which has been detected is that it has always been represented as a totality, an entity which can be analysed as a coherent whole. If not actually homogeneous, the Neolithic has always been seen as a something which possessed a stable set of defining characteristics. I would claim that if we now wish to maintain the term in any useful way, we should do away with any such totalising vision entirely. … If we want to talk about the Neolithic in the 1990s, we have to consider not a thing but a field composed of sometimes interlocking and sometimes unrelated social practices and traditions, elaborated by numerous relays and resistances.
>
> *(Thomas 1993: 389–390)*

True to his word, Thomas continues to conceptualize the Neolithic in these terms, as his recent book on Neolithic Britain makes clear: "'Neolithic' is a deeply protean term, which can refer to a particular subsistence economy, a level of technological development, a chronological interval, a specific set of cultural entities, to racial or ethnic identities, or to a specific type of society" (Thomas 2013: 1). I think this is how many other if not most prehistorians now think of the Neolithic too; although it still has traces of its taxonomic ancestry, its distinction from adjacent concepts (i.e. Mesolithic and Bronze Age) is far more blurred, exemplified in the focus on 'transitions'. More importantly, what characterizes the Neolithic is that it is much less characterized by its difference from other period concepts, and more on its own, internal set of attributes.

## Concluding remarks

I began this chapter by stressing the importance of detachment as a condition of mobility; the notion of facts as deracinated particulars meshes well with Latourian accounts of 'immutable mobiles' and how facts, once constituted in symbolic form (e. g. as words or numbers), can then move freely between texts. But this chapter has focused more on the mobility of concepts and theories than facts, and I adopted Kuhn's tripartite division of paradigms, analogies and symbolic generalizations as a general guide to explore this. However, I want to put my own gloss on these concepts. Paradigms or exemplars refer to ready-made model solutions and include a lot of what we might call methods or methodological concepts, although I prefer to see paradigms as instances where the theory/method distinction is the least helpful. All typologies and taxonomic systems are paradigms in this sense, but so too are more theoretical case studies which embody an easy-to-use/apply approach – whether Hodder's adoption of Hayden White's scheme or Miller's ceramic indices. Analogies and metaphors are somewhat looser, less ready-made, but nonetheless still offer all the parts for a mobile interpretation; all they require is some self-assembly. Ethnographic analogies or conceptual metaphors establish a system of resemblances which can then be exploited as one sees fit. Finally, we come to concepts and generalizations. These are the loosest conceptual vehicles we have; they exhibit very few constraints but require a lot of work to operationalize them.

Despite the way I have discussed these three conceptual vehicles, the distinctions between them is not a very rigid one. We have just seen how a term like 'Neolithic' has in fact changed over time from being taxonomic and thus closer to a paradigm or exemplar to more like a concept-metaphor. In fact, the important lesson from using Kuhn's scheme has been to highlight the property of deracination as a sliding scale or continuum in relation to concepts. At one end are conceptual vehicles which operate as part of a conceptual system, with several concepts working together to provide a ready-made theory or method, one which can move between data sets and texts with very little work. At the same time, because they are so pre-formed, their mobility is limited: they work better on some data than others, and they fit better within some text types more than others. At the other extreme are those conceptual vehicles which are more free-floating, the most deracinated, and they tend to travel alone or at least with only very weak links to other concepts. Because of this, they are lighter, can travel further – especially between disciplines, but also range over a greater diversity of data and text types. But also because of this, they are much less ready-made and require a lot more skill, effort and inventiveness to operationalize (Table 5.1).

The distinction between the two poles of this continuum in many ways resonates with Eve Sedgwick's distinction of strong and weak theory, especially as elaborated by Kathleen Stewart (Sedgwick 2003; Stewart 2008). According to Stewart, weak theory is:

> [t]heory that comes unstuck from its own line of thought to follow the objects it encounters, or becomes undone by its attention to things that don't just *add up* but take on a life of their own as problems for thought. She calls this "reparative" theory – a good thing – in contrast to "paranoid" or "strong" theory that defends itself against the puncturing of its dream of a perfect parallelism between the analytic concept, her subject, and the world – a kind of razed earth for academic conversation.
>
> *(Stewart 2008: 72)*

**TABLE 5.1** Strategies for mobilizing knowledge

| Strategy | Connectivity | Applicability |
|---|---|---|
| Paradigm/exemplar | Embedded ('strong' theory) | Ready-made but with restricted mobility |
| Model/analogy | Loose | Self-assembly needed but moderately mobile |
| Concept/concept-metaphor | Deracinated ('weak' theory) | Require work but highly mobile |

Rather than see strong and weak theory as oppositional, however, as Sedgwick and Stewart argue, I feel this difference works better as a relational scale.

Thinking of concepts and theory in terms of mobility has offered us a useful way to tie together the potentially fragmented characterization of knowledge that was given in Chapter 4, where different epistemic and ontological registers were linked to different text types. I am not claiming this now constitutes a new unity, or some kind of unified and homogeneous description of what archaeological knowledge is. There will always be fractures and differences in what counts as knowledge and in our ability to reconcile and evaluate different knowledge claims because of the different material forms these claims take. But, more importantly, the focus on mobility in this chapter draws out a more general tension in knowledge practices that has run throughout this book. On the one hand, the recognition that knowledge is always local, context specific, and yet, at the same time, has the potential to move and work in different contexts.

In terms of the main focus of this book – knowledge and literary production – I see these two aspects manifest in the way different text types act to situate knowledge, to fix it, make it stick, on the one hand, and, on the other, how exemplars, analogies and concepts allow knowledge to also move between texts or textual locations. To resurrect my horticultural metaphors, this is about how texts act to embed and yet also uproot knowledge. These processes have been already partially mapped out in the case of some text types like the database and some forms of knowledge like facts; but this book has aimed to extend these ideas into the realm of more complex text types such as narrative and more complex forms of knowledge such as concepts. But this broad distinction between text types which embed knowledge and conceptual vehicles which mobilize it is traversed by the fact that, in both, there is a tension between detachment and engagement. In all four text types, we saw how each embodied different epistemic virtues which expressed this tension in different ways: hindsight, impartiality, objectivity, unfamiliarity. Similarly, in the various conceptual vehicles, there was need for concepts or models to be contextualized with facts and yet not so attached that they could not move to work on other facts. Whether we are talking about the archaeologist showing the 'right' degree of detachment from/engagement to their subject, or concepts/facts exhibiting sufficient detachment from/engagement to other concepts/facts, the epistemic processes are the same.

# BIBLIOGRAPHY

Adam, J.-M. 1992. *Les Textes: Types et Prototypes*. Paris: Nathan.

Adams, R.McC. 1968. Archaeological Research Strategies: Past and Present. *Science* 160 (3833): 1187–1192.

Agrawal, A. 1995. Dismantling the Divide between Indigenous and Scientific Knowledge. *Development and Change* 26(3): 413–439.

Anderson, A. 2001. *The Powers of Distance: Cosmopolitanism and the Cultivation of Detachment*. Princeton: Princeton University Press.

Anderson, S. 2011. *Technologies of History: Visual Media and the Eccentricity of the Past*. Boston: Dartmouth College Press (UPNE).

Ankeney, R. & S. Leonelli. 2016. Repertoires: A post-Kuhnian perspective on scientific change and collaborative research. *Studies in History and Philosophy of Science* 60: 18–28.

Ankersmit, F.R. 1983. *Narrative Logic: A Semantic Analysis of the Historian's Language*. The Hague: Martinus Nijhoff Publishers.

Anscombe, E. 1957. *Intention*. Oxford: Basil Blackwell.

Arrington, P. 1986. The Traditions of the Writing Process. *Freshman English News* 14(3): 2–10.

Atalay, S. 2006. Indigenous Archaeology as Decolonozing Practice. *American Indian Quarterly* 30(3/4): 280–310.

Atalay, S. 2008. Multivocality and indigenous archaeologies. In J. Habu, C. Fawcett & J.M. Matsunaga (eds) *Evaluating Multiple Narratives: Beyond Nationalist, Colonialist, and Imperialist Archaeologies*. New York: Springer, pp. 29–44.

Atalay, S. 2012. *Community-Based Archaeology: Research with, by, and for Indigenous and Local Communities*. Berkeley: University of California Press.

Atalay, S., L.R. Clauss, R.H. McGuire & J. Welch (eds). 2014. *Transforming Archaeology: Activist Practices and Prospects*. Walnut Creek: Left Coast Press.

Atkinson, R.J.C. 1946. *Field Archaeology*. London: Methuen.

Austin, J.L. 1962. *How to Do Things with Words*. Oxford: Clarendon Press.

Babington, C. 1865. *Introductory Lecture on Archaeology*. Cambridge: Bell & Co.

Bachelard, G. 1984 [1934]. *The New Scientific Spirit*. Boston: Beacon Press.

Bachelard, G. 2002 [1938]. *The Formation of the Scientific Mind*. London: Clinamen Press.

Bacon, F. 2000. *The New Organon*. Cambridge: Cambridge University Press.

Bailey, D.W. 2014. Which ruins do we valorize? A new visual calibration for the Balkan past. In B. Olsen & Þ. Pétursdóttir (eds) *Ruin Memories: Materiality, Aesthetics and the Archaeology of the Recent Past*. London: Routledge, pp. 215–229.

Bailey, D.W. & M. Simpkin. 2015. Eleven minutes and forty seconds in the Neolithic: Underneath archaeological time. In R. Van Dyke & R. Berneck (eds) *Subjects and Narratives in Archaeology*. Boulder: University of Colorado Press, pp. 187–213.

Bailey, G.N. 2007. Time Perspectives, Palimpsests and the Archaeology of Time. *Journal of Anthropological Archaeology* 26: 198–223.

Bain, A. 1867. *English Composition and Rhetoric: A Manual*. New York: D. Appleton & Company.

Bakhtin, M. 1982. *The Dialogic Imagination*. Austin: University of Texas Press.

Bakhtin, M. 1986. Toward a methodology for the Human sciences. In M. Bakhtin, *Speech Genres and Other Late Essays*. Austin: University of Texas Press, pp. 159–172.

Bal, M. 2002. *Travelling Concepts in the Humanities: A Rough Guide*. Toronto: University of Toronto Press.

Ballard, C. 2003. Writing (Pre)History: Narrative and Archaeological Explanation in the New Guinea Highlands. *Archaeology in Oceania* 38(3): 135–148.

Bapty, I. & T. Yates (eds). 1990. *Archaeology after Structuralism*. London: Routledge.

Barceló, J. 2007. Automatic archaeology: Bridging the gap between virtual reality, artificial intelligence, and archaeology. In F. Cameron & S. Kenderdine (eds) *Theorizing Digital Cultural Heritage*. Cambridge, MA: MIT Press, pp. 437–456.

Barceló, J. 2009. *Computational Intelligence in Archaeology*. Hershey: Information Science Reference.

Barker, P. 1982. *Techniques of Archaeological Excavation* (2nd edition). London: Batsford.

Barthes, R. 1967. *Elements of Semiology*. New York: Hill and Wang.

Bauer, A. 2013. Multivocality and "Wikiality": The Epistemology and Ethics of a Pragmatic Archaeology. In G. Scarre & R. Conningham (eds) *Appropriating the Past: Philosophical Perspectives on the Practice of Archaeology*. Cambridge: Cambridge University Press, pp. 176–194.

Bauman, R. & C. Briggs. 2003. *Voices of Modernity: Language Ideologies and the Politics of Inequality*. Cambridge: Cambridge University Press.

Bayard, D.T. 1969. Science, Theory, and Reality in the "New Archaeology". *American Antiquity* 34: 376–384.

Bazerman, C. 1988. *Shaping Written Knowledge: The Genre and Activity of the Experimental Article in Science*. Madison: University of Wisconsin Press.

Bell, A., J. Swenson-Wright & K. Tyberg (eds). 2008. *Evidence*. Cambridge: Cambridge University Press.

Bell, J.A. 1991. Anarchy and Archaeology. In R. Preucel (ed.) *Processual and Postprocessual Archaeologies: Multiple Ways of Knowing the Past*. Carbondale: Southern Illinois University, pp. 71–80.

Bennett, J.W. 1943. Recent Developments in the Functional Interpretation of Archaeological Data. *American Antiquity* 9: 208–219.

Bennett, J.W. 1946. Empiricist and Experimentalist Trends in Eastern Archaeology. *American Antiquity* 11: 198–200.

Bevir, M. 2011. Why Historical Distance Is Not a Problem. *History and Theory* 50: 24–37.

Bhaskar, R. 1975. *A Realist Theory of Science*. Brighton: Harvester.

Bhaskar, R. 1979. *The Possibility of Naturalism: A Philosophical Critique of the Human Sciences*. New York: Humanities Press.

Biber, D. 1989. A Typology of English Texts. *Linguistics* 27: 3–43.

Binford, L. 1968. Archaeological Perspectives. In S.R. Binford & L.R. Binford(eds)*New Perspectives in Archaeology*. Chicago: Aldine Publishing Co., pp. 5–32.

Binford, L. 1972. Contemporary model building: Paradigms and the current state of Palaeolithic research. In D. Clarke (ed.) *Models in Archaeology*. London: Methuen, pp. 109–166.

Binford, L. 1977. General Introduction. In L. Binford (ed.) *For Theory Building in Archaeology: Essays on Faunal Remains, Aquatic Resources, Spatial Analysis, and Systematic Modelling*. New York: Academic Press, pp. 1–13.

Binford, L. 1980. Willow Smoke and Dog's Tails: Hunter-Gatherer Settlement Systems and Archaeological Site Formation. *American Antiquity* 45(1): 4–20.

Binford, L. 1982. Objectivity – Explanation – Archaeology 1981. In C. Renfrew, M.J. Rowlands & B. Segraves (eds) *Theory andExplanation in Archaeology*. New York: Academic Press, pp. 125–138.

Binford, L. 1983. *In Pursuit of the Past*. London: Thames & Hudson.

Binford, L. 1987. Data, Relativism and Archaeological Science. *Man* 22: 391–404.

Binford, L. 1989. Science to Seance, or Processual to "Post-Processual" Archaeology. In L. Binford, *Debating Archaeology*. New York: Academic Press, pp. 27–40.

Binford, L. & J. Sabloff. 1982. Paradigms, Systematics and Archaeology. *Journal of Anthropological Research* 38: 137–153.

Binford, S. & L. Binford (eds). 1968. *New Perspectives in Archaeology*. Chicago: Aldine Publishing Company.

Bintliff, J. 1988. A review of contemporary perspectives on the "meaning" of the past. In J. Binltiff (ed.) *Extracting Meaning from the Past*. Oxford: Oxbow Books, pp. 3–36.

Bintliff, J. 1989. Post-modernism, rhetoric and scholasticism at TAG: The current state of British archaeological theory. *Antiquity* 65: 274–278.

Bintliff, J. 2011. The death of archaeological theory? In J.L. Bintliff & M. Pearce (eds) *The Death of Archaeological Theory?*Oxford: Oxbow, pp. 7–22.

Black, M. 1962. *Models and Metaphors: Studies in Language and Philosophy*. Ithaca: Cornell University Press.

Bloor, D. 1976. *Knowledge and Social Imagery*. Chicago: University of Chicago Press.

Boast, R. & P. Biehl. 2011. Archaeological Knowledge Production and Dissemination in the Digital Age. In E. Kansa, S. Whitcher Kansa & E. Watrall (eds) *Archaeology 2.0: New Approaches to Communication and Collaboration*. Los Angeles: Cotsen Institute of Archaeology Press, pp. 119–156.

Bowden, M. 1991. *Pitt Rivers*. Cambridge: Cambridge University Press.

Bradley, F.H. 2011 [1874]. *The Presuppositions of Critical History*. Cambridge: Cambridge University Press.

Bradley, R. 2006. The Excavation Report as a Literary Genre: Traditional Practice in Britain. *World Archaeology* 38(4): 664–671.

Brown, H.D. 2000. *Teaching by Principles: An Interactive Approach to Language Pedagogy* (2nd edition). New York: Longman.

Brumfiel, E. 1996. The Quality of Tribute Cloth: The Place of Evidence in Archaeological Argument. *American Antiquity* 61(3): 453–462.

Buccellati, G. 2017. *A Critique of Archaeological Reason: Structural, Digital, and Philosophical Aspects of the Excavated Record*. Cambridge: Cambridge University Press.

Buchli, V. & G. Lucas (eds). 2001. *Archaeologies of the Contemporary Past*. London: Routledge.

Butler, B.R. 1965. The Structure and Function of the Old Cordilleran Culture Concept. *American Anthropologist* 67: 1120–1131.

Campbell, J. 1968. *The Hero with a Thousand Faces*. Princeton: Princeton University Press.

Candea, M., J. Cook, C. Trundle & T. Yarrow (eds). 2015. *Detachment. Essays on the Limits of Relational Thinking*. Manchester: Manchester University Press.

Canguilhem, G. 1963. The role of analogies and models in biological discovery. In A.C. Crombie (ed.) *Scientific Change: Historical Studies in the Intellectual, Social and Technical*

*Conditions for Scientific Discovery and Technical Invention, from Antiquity to the Present.* London: Heinemann, pp. 507–520.

Capurro, R. 2010. Digital hermeneutics: An outline. *AI & Society* 25: 35–42.

Carnap, R. 1967. *The Logical Structure of the World*. Berkeley: University of California Press.

Carr, D. 1986. Narrative and the Real World: An Argument for Continuity. *History and Theory* 25(2): 117–131.

Cartwright, N. 1989. *Nature's Capacities and Their Measurement*. Oxford: Clarendon Press.

Cartwright, N. & R. Runhardt. 2014. Measurement. In N. Cartwright & E. Montuschi (eds) *Philosophy of Social Science: A New Introduction*. Oxford: Oxford University Press, pp. 265–287.

Carver, M. 1989. Digging for Ideas. *Antiquity* 63: 666–674.

Carver, M. 1990. Digging for data: Archaeological approaches to data definition, acquistion and analysis. In R. Francovich & D. Manacorda (eds) *Lo scavo archeologico: Dalla diagnosi all'edizione*. Firenze: All'Insegna del Giglio SAS, pp. 45–120.

Carver, M. 2009. *Archaeological Investigation*. London: Routledge.

Chapman, J. 2000. *Fragmentation in Archaeology: People, Places and Broken Objects in the Prehistory of South Eastern Europe*. London: Routledge.

Chapman, R. 2003. *Archaeologies of Complexity*. London: Routledge.

Chapman, R. & A. Wylie (eds). 2015. *Material Evidence: Learning from Archaeological Practice*. London: Routledge.

Chapman, R. & A. Wylie. 2016. *Evidential Reasoning in Archaeology*. London: Bloomsbury.

Chatman, S. 1990. *Coming to Terms: The Rhetoric of Narrative in Fiction and Film*. Ithaca: Cornell University Press.

Chemla, K. & J. Virbel (eds). 2015. *Texts, Textual Acts and the History of Science*. New York: Springer.

Childe, V.G. 1935. Changing Methods and Aims in Prehistory. *Proceedings of the Prehistoric Society* 1: 1–15.

Childe, V.G. 1949. *Social Worlds of Knowledge*. L.T. Hobhouse Memorial Trust Lecture No. 19. Oxford: Oxford University Press.

Childe, V.G. 1950. *Magic, Craftsmanship and Science*. The Frazer Lecture, 1949. Liverpool: Liverpool University Press.

Childe, V.G. 1956. *Society and Knowledge*. London: George Allen & Unwin.

Cirnu, C.E. 2015. The Shifting Paradigm: Learning to Unlearn. *Internet Learning* 4(1), Article 8.

Clark, J.G.D. 1953. Archaeological Theories and Interpretation: Old World. In A.L. Kroeber (ed.) *Anthropology Today*. Chicago: University of Chicago Press, pp. 343–360.

Clark, J.G.D. 1957. *Archaeology and Society: Reconstructing the Prehistoric Past*. London: Methuen & Co.

Clarke, D.L. 1972a. Models and paradigms in contemporary archaeology. In D.L. Clarke (ed.) *Models in Archaeology*. London: Methuen & Co., pp. 1–60.

Clarke, D.L. 1972b. Review of "Explanation in Archaeology" by Watson, LeBlanc & Redman. *Antiquity* 46: 237–238.

Clarke, D.L. 1973. Archaeology: The loss of innocence. *Antiquity* 47: 6–18.

Clarke, D.L. 1978. *Analytical Archaeology*. London: Methuen & Co.

Clark, S.H. 1990. *Paul Ricoeur*. London: Routledge.

Clifford, J. & G. Marcus. 1986. *Writing Culture: The Poetics and Politics of Ethnography*. Berkeley: University of California Press.

Coady, C.A.J. 1992. *Testimony: A Philosophical Study*. Oxford: Clarendon Press.

Cobb, H. & K. Croucher. 2014. Assembling archaeological pedagogy: A theoretical framework for valuing pedagogy in archaeological interpretation and practice. *Archaeological Dialogues* 21(2): 197–216.

Cobb, H. & K. Croucher. 2016. Personal, Political, Pedagogic: Challenging the Binary Bind in Archaeological Teaching, Learning and Fieldwork. *Journal of Archaeological Method and Theory* 23(3): 949–969.

Cobb, H.L., O. Harris, C. Jones & P. Richardson (eds). 2012. *Reconsidering Fieldwork: Exploring on Site Relationships between Theory and Practice*. New York: Springer Verlag.

Cochrane, E. & A. Gardner (eds). 2011. *Evolutionary and Interpretive Archaeologies: A Dialogue*. New York: Routledge.

Cole, J.R. 1980. Cult Archaeology and Unscientific Method and Theory. *Advances in Archaeological Method and Theory* 3: 1–33.

Coles, J. 1972. *Field Archaeology in Britain*. London: Methuen & Co.

Collier, D., F.D. Hidalgo & A.O. Maciucenau. 2006. Essentially contested concepts: Debates and applications. *Journal of Political Ideologies* 11(3): 211–246.

Collingwood, R.G. 1944. *An Autobiography*. Harmondsworth: Penguin.

Collingwood, R.G. 1946. *The Idea of History*. Oxford: Clarendon Press.

Collingwood, R.G., A.E. Taylor & F.C.S. Schiller. 1922. Are History and Science Different Kinds of Knowledge? *Mind* 31(124): 443–466.

Collins, H., R. Evans & M. Gorman. 2007. Trading Zones and Interactional Expertise. *Studies in History and Philosophy of Science* 38: 657–666.

Collis, J. 2001. *Digging up the Past: An Introduction to Archaeological Excavation*. Stroud: Sutton Publishing.

Colt Hoare, R. 1812. *The History of Ancient Wiltshire* (Part 1). William Miller: London.

Colton, H.S. 1942. Archaeology and the Reconstruction of History, *American Antiquity* 7: 33–40.

Colwell-Chanthaphonh, C. & T.J. Ferguson (eds). 2008. *Collaboration in Archaeological Practice: Engaging Descendant Communities*. Lanham: AltaMira Press.

Colwell-Chanthaphonh, C., T.J. Ferguson, D. Lippert, R. McGuire, G.P. Nicholas, J.E. Watkins & L. Zimmerman. 2010. The Premise and Promise of Indigenous Archaeology. *American Antiquity* 75(2): 228–238.

Conkey, M. & J. Spector. 1984. Archaeology and the Study of Gender. *Advances in Archaeological Method and Theory* 7: 1–38.

Conkey, M.W. & R.E. Tringham. 1996. Cultivating thinking/challenging authority: Some experiments in feminist pedagogy in archaeology. In R.P. Wright (ed.) *Gender and Archaeology*. Philadelphia: University of Pennsylvania Press, pp. 224–225.

Connah, G. 2010. *Writing About Archaeology*. Cambridge: Cambridge University Press.

Connors, R.J. 1981. The Rise and Fall of the Modes of Discourse. *College Composition and Communication* 32(4): 444–455.

Crawford, O.G.S. 1932. The dialectical process in the history of science. *The Sociological Review* 24(2): 165–173.

Croker, D. 1849. Advantages of the Study of Archaeology. *Journal of the British Archaeological Association* 5: 288–289.

Crombie, A.C. 1988. Designed in the Mind: Western Visions of Science, Nature and Humankind. *History of Science* 24: 1–12.

Crombie, A.C. 1994. *Styles of Scientific Thinking in the European Tradition: The History of Argument and Explanation Especially in the Mathematical and Biomedical Sciences and Arts*. London: Duckworth.

Dalglish, C. 2007. Archaeology and democracy: An interview with Mark P. Leone. *Archaeological Dialogues* 14(1): 39–59.

Dallas, C. 2016. Jean-Claude Gardin on Archaeological Data, Representation and Knowledge: Implications for Digital Archaeology. *Journal of Archaeological Method and Theory* 23: 305–330.

Daniel, G. 1962. Comment. *Current Anthropology* 3: 504.

Daniel, G. 1973. Editorial. *Antiquity* 47: 174–175.

Daniel, G. 1975. *A Hundred and Fifty Years of Archaeology*. London: Methuen.

Darvill, T., P. Marshall, M. Parker Pearson & G. Wainwright. 2012. Stonehenge remodelled. *Antiquity* 86: 1021–1040.

Daston, L. 1991. Marvelous Facts and Miraculous Evidence in Early Modern Europe. *Critical Inquiry* 18(1): 93–124.

Daston, L. 1992. Objectivity and the Escape from Perspective. *Social Studies of Science* 22(4): 597–618.

Daston, L. 1995. The Moral Economy of Science. *Osiris* 10: 2–24.

Daston, L. 2011. The Empire of Observation, 1600–1800. In L. Daston & E. Lunbeck (eds) *Histories of Scientific Observation*. Chicago: Chicago University Press, pp. 81–113.

Daston, L. & P. Galison. 1992. The Image of Objectivity. *Representations* 40: 81–128.

Daston, L. & P. Galison. 1997. *Objectivity*. New York: Zone Books.

Daston, L. & E. Lunbeck (eds). 2011. *Histories of Scientific Observation*. Chicago: Chicago University Press.

Dawid, P., D. Schum & A. Hepler. 2011. Inference Networks: Bayes and Wigmore. In W. Twining, P. Dawid & D. Vasilaki (eds) *Evidence, Inference and Enquiry*. Oxford: Oxford University Press, pp. 119–150.

Dear, P. 1985. Totius in Verba: Rhetoric and Authority in the early Royal Society. *Isis* 76 (2): 145–161.

Dear, P. 1995. *Discipline and Experience: The Mathematical Way in the Scientific Revolution*. Chicago: Chicago University Press.

DeLanda, M. 2006. *A New Philosophy of Society: Assemblage Theory and Social Complexity*. London: Continuum.

DeLanda, M. 2016. *Assemblage Theory*. Edinburgh: Edinburgh University Press.

Deleuze, G. 2007. *Two Regimes of Madness: Texts and Interviews 1975–1995*. New York: Semiotext(e).

Deleuze, G. & F. Guattari. 1994. *What is Philosophy?* New York: Columbia University Press.

Dilthey, W. 1976. *Selected Writings*. Cambridge: Cambridge University Press.

Dixon, R.B. 1913. Some Aspects of North American Archaeology. *American Anthropologist* 15: 549–577.

Dorn, S. 2013. Is (Digital) History More than an Argument about the Past? In J. Dougherty & K. Nawrotzki (eds) *Writing History in the Digital Age*. Ann Arbor: University of Michigan Press, pp. 21–34.

Dougherty, J. & K. Nawrotzki (eds). 2013. *Writing History in the Digital Age*. Ann Arbor: University of Michigan Press.

Dougherty, J., K. Nawrotzki, C. Rochez & T. Burke. 2013. Conclusions: What We Learned from Writing History in the Digital Age. In J. Dougherty & K. Nawrotzki (eds) *Writing History in the Digital Age*. Ann Arbor: University of Michigan Press, pp. 259–277.

Drewitt, P. 1999. *Field Archaeology: An Introduction*. London: Routledge.

Droop, J. P. 1915. *Archaeological Excavation*. Cambridge: Cambridge University Press.

Droysen, J.G. 1897. *Outline of the Principles of History*. Boston: Ginn & Co.

Drysdale, J. 1996. How Are Social-Scientific Concepts Formed? A Reconstruction of Max Weber's Theory of Concept Formation. *Sociological Theory* 14(1): 71–88.

Earle, T.K. 1987. Chiefdoms in Archaeological and Ethnohistorical Perspective. *Annual Review of Anthropology* 16: 279–308.

Edgeworth, M. 2003. *Acts of Discovery: An Ethnography of Archaeological Practice*. Oxford: Archaeopress.

Edgeworth, M. (ed.). 2006. *Ethnographies of Archaeological Practice: Cultural Encounters, Material Transformations*. Lanham: AltaMira Press.

Edgeworth, M. 2016. Grounded Objects: Archaeology and Speculative Realism. *Archaeological Dialogues* 23(1): 93–113.

Edmonds, M. 1999. *Ancestral Geographies of the Neolithic: Landscapes, Monuments and Memory.* London: Routledge.

Ehrich, R.W. 1950. Some Reflections on Archaeological Interpretations. *American Anthropologist* 52: 468–482.

Evans, C. 1998. Historicism, Chronology and Straw Men: Situating Hawkes' Ladder of Inference. *Antiquity* 72: 398–404.

Evans, C. 2003. *Power and Island Communities: Excavations at the Wardy Hill Ringwork, Coveney, Ely.* Dereham: East Anglian Archaeology.

Fagan, B. 2006. *Writing Archaeology: Telling Stories about the Past.* Walnut Creek: Left Coast Press.

Fagan, G. (ed.). 2006. *Archaeological Fantasies: How Pseudoarchaeology Misrepresents and Misleads the Public.* London: Routledge.

Flannery, K. 1973. Archaeology with a Capital 'S', in C. Redman (ed.) *Research and Theory in Current Archaeology.* New York: Wiley, pp. 47–53.

Flannery, K. 1982. The Golden Marshalltown: A parable for the archaeology of the 1980s. *American Anthropologist* 84: 265–278.

Fleck, L. 1979. *Genesis and Development of a Scientific Fact.* Chicago: Chicago University Press.

Fludernik, M. 2000. Genres, text types, or discourse modes? *Style* 34(2): 274–292.

Fogelin, L. 2008. Inference to the Best Explanation: A Common and Effective Form of Archaeological Reasoning. *American Antiquity* 72(4): 603–625.

Foley, D. 2003. Indigenous Epistemology and Indigenous Standpoint Theory. *Social Alternatives* 22(1): 44–52.

Folsom, E. 2007. Database as Genre: The Epic Transformation of Archives. *Proceedings of the Modern Language Association/PMLA* 122(5): 1571–1612.

Forster, M. 2009. The Debate between Whewell and Mill on the Nature of Scientific Induction. In D. Gabbay, S. Hartmann & J. Woods (eds) *Handbook of the History of Logic. Volume 10: Inductive Logic.* Amsterdam: Elsevier, pp. 93–115.

Forte, M. & N. Dell'Unto. 2010. Embodied Communities, Second Life and Cyber Archaeology. In M. Ioannides, A. Addison, A. Georgepoulus, L. Kalisperis, A. Brown & D. Pitzalis (eds) *Heritage in the Digital Era.* Essex: Multi-Science Publishing, pp. 181–194.

Franklin, J. 1977. *Jean Bodin and the Sixteenth-Century Revolution in the Methodology of Law and History.* Westport: Greenwood Press.

Fricker, E. 1987. The Epistemology of Testimony. *Proceedings of the Aristotelian Society* 61: 57–83.

Fricker, M. 2007. *Epistemic Injustice: Power the Ethics of Knowing.* Oxford: Oxford University Press.

Fritz, J.M. & F.T. Plog. 1970. The Nature of Archaeological Explanation. *American Antiquity* 35(4): 405–412.

Frye, N. 1957. *Anatomy of Criticism.* Princeton: Princeton University Press.

Fuller, S. 2000. Why Science Studies Has Never Been Critical of Science: Some Recent Lessons on How to Be a Helpful Nuisance and a Harmless Radical. *Philosophy of the Social Sciences* 30(1): 5–32.

Fuller, S. 2003. *Kuhn vs. Popper: The Struggle for the Soul of Science.* Thriplow: Icon Books.

Fuller, S. & J. Collier. 2004. *Philosophy, Rhetoric and the End of Knowledge: A New Beginning for Science and Technology Studies* (2nd edition). Mahwah: Lawrence Erbaum Associates.

Gadamer, H.-G. 1975. *Truth and Method.* London: Sheed & Ward.

Gadamer, H.-G. 1977. *Philosophical Hermeneutics.* Berkeley: University of California Press.

Galison, P. 1997. *Image and Logic: A Material Culture of Microphysics.* Chicago: University of Chicago Press.

Galison, P. & D. Stump (eds). 1996. *The Disunity of Science: Boundaries, Contexts, and Power.* Stanford: Stanford University Press.

Gallay, A. 1989. Logicism: A French view of archaeological theory founded in computational perspective. *Antiquity* 63: 27–39.

Gallie, W.B. 1956. Essentially Contested Concepts. *Proceedings of the Aristotelian Society* 56: 167–198.

Gallie, W.B. 1964. *Philosophy and Historical Understanding*. London: Chatto & Windus.

Gane, N. 2009. Concepts and the 'New' Empiricism. *European Journal of Social Theory* 12(1): 83–97.

Garcia-Rovira, I. 2015. What about Us? On Archaeological Objects (or the Objects of Archaeology). *Current Swedish Archaeology* 23: 85–108.

Gardin, J.-C. 1980. *Archaeological Constructs: An Aspect of Theoretical Archaeology*. Cambridge: Cambridge University Press.

Gardin, J.-C. 1999. Calcul et Narrativité dans les Publications Archéologiques. *Archaeologia e Calcolatori* 10: 63–78.

Gardiner, P. (ed.). 1974. *The Philosophy of History*. Oxford: Oxford University Press.

Gellner, E. 1982. What is Structuralisme? In C. Renfrew, M.J. Rowlands & B. Segraves (eds) *Theory andExplanation in Archaeology*. New York: Academic Press, pp. 97–123.

Gero, J. 1985. Sociopolitics and the Woman-at-Home Ideology. *American Antiquity* 50(2): 342–350.

Gero, J. 1996. Archaeological practice and gendered encounters with field data. In R.P. Wright (ed.) *Gender and Archaeology*. Philadelphia: University of Pennsylvania Press, pp. 251–280.

Gero, J. 2007. Honoring Ambiguity/Problematizing Certitude. *Journal of Archaeological Method and Theory* 14: 311–327.

Gibbon, G. 1989. *Explanation in Archaeology*. Oxford: Blackwell.

Gibbon, G. 2014. *Critically Reading the Theory and Methods of Archaeology: An Introductory Guide*. Lanham: AltaMira Press.

Gibbs, J. 2000. Imaginary, But by No Means Unimaginable: Storytelling, Science and Historical Archaeology. *Historical Archaeology* 34(2): 1–6.

Ginzburg, C. 2001. *Wooden Eyes: Nine Reflections on Distance*. New York: Columbia University Press.

Gitelman, L. 2014. *Paper Knowledge: Toward a Media History of Documents*. Durham: Duke University Press.

Glock, H.-J. 2008. *What is Analytical Philosophy?*Cambridge: Cambridge University Press.

Gorman, M. (ed.). 2010. *Trading Zones and Interactional Expertise*. Cambridge: MIT Press.

Greenwell, W. 1890. Recent researches in barrows in Yorkshire, Wiltshire, Berkshire etc. *Archaeologia* 52: 1–71.

Guillory, J. 2008. How Scholars Read. *ADE Bulletin* 146: 8–17.

Guillory, J. 2010. Close Reading: Prologue and Epilogue. *ADE Bulletin* 149: 8–14.

Longworth, H. 1999. The Folkton Drums unpicked. In R. Cleal & A. McSween (eds) *Grooved Ware in Britain and Ireland* (Neolithic Studies Group Seminar Papers 3). Oxford: Oxbow Books, pp. 83–88.

Haber, A. & C. Gnecco. 2007. Virtual Forum: Archaeology and Decolonization. *Archaeologies* 3(3): 390–412.

Habermas, J. 1984. *Theory of Communicative Action (Vol. 1)*. Boston: Beacon Press.

Habu, J., C. Fawcett & J. Matsunaga (eds). 2008. *Evaluating Multiple Narratives: Beyond Nationalist, Colonialist, Imperialist Archaeologies*. New York: Springer.

Hacıgüzeller, P. 2017. Archaeological (Digital) Maps as Performances: Towards Alternative Mappings. *Norwegian Archaeological Review* 50(2): 149–171.

Hacking, I. 1990. *The Taming of Chance*. Cambridge: Cambridge University Press.

Hacking, I. 1992. 'Style' for Historians and Philosophers. *Studies in the History and Philosophy of Science* 23(1): 1–20.

Halliday, M.A.K. 1994. *An Introduction to Functional Grammar*. London: Edward Arnold.

Halliday, M.A.K.&R.Hassan. 1991. *Language, Context and Text: Aspects of Language in a Social-Semiotic Perspective*. Oxford: Oxford University Press.

Halliday, M.A.K. & J.R. Martin. 1993. *Writing Science: Literacy and Discursive Power*. London: Falmer Press.

Hamilakis, Y. 2004. Archaeology and the politics of pedagogy. *World Archaeology* 36(2): 287–309.

Hamilakis, Y. 2013. Enacted multi-temporality: The archaeological site as a shared, performative space. In A. Gonzáles-Ruibal (ed.), *Reclaiming Archaeology: Beyond the Tropes of Modernity*. London: Routledge, pp. 181–194.

Hamilakis, Y. 2017. Sensorial assemblages: Affect, memory and temporality in assemblage thinking. *Cambridge Archaeological Journal* 27(1): 169–182.

Hamilakis, Y., A. Anagnostopoulos & F. Ifantidis. 2009. Postcards from the edge of time: Archaeology, photography, archaeological ethnography. *Public Archaeology* 8(2–3): 283–309.

Hamilton, D.P. 1991. Research Papers: Who's Uncited Now? *Science* 251(4989): 25.

Hanen, M. & J. Kelley. 1989. Inference to the best explanation in archaeology. In V. Pinsky & A. Wylie (eds) *Critical Traditions in Contemporary Archaeology*. Cambridge: Cambridge University Press, pp. 14–17.

HarawayD. 1991. Situated knowledges: The science question in feminism and the privilege of partial perspective. In *Simians, Cyborgs, and Women: The Reinvention of Nature*. London: Free Association Books, pp. 183–201.

Harding, S. 1991. *Whose Science? Whose Knowledge? Thinking from Women's Lives*. Ithaca: Cornell University Press.

Hardy, T. 2005. *Tess of the D'Urbevilles*. Oxford: Oxford University Press.

Harman, G. 1965. The Inference to the Best Explanation. *Philosophical Review* 74: 88–95.

Harned, J. 1985. The Intellectual Background of Alexander Bain's "Modes of Discourse". *College Composition and Communication* 36(1): 42–50.

Harré, R. 1970. *The Principles of Scientific Thinking*. Chicago: University of Chicago Press.

Harrison, R. 2009. Excavating Second Life: Cyber-archaeologists, Heritage and Virtual Communities. *Journal of Material Culture* 14(1): 75–106.

Harrison, R. 2011. Surface assemblages: Towards an archaeology in and of the present. *Archaeological Dialogues* 18(2): 141–161.

Hartsock, M. 1983. The Feminist Standpoint: Developing the Ground for a Specifically Feminist Historical Materialism. In S. Harding & M.B. Hintikka (eds) *Discovering Reality: Feminist Perspectives of Epistemology, Metaphysics, Methodology and the Philosophy of Science*. Dordrecht: Reidel, pp. 283–310.

Hawkes, C. 1954. Archaeological Theory and Method: Some Suggestions from the Old World. *American Anthropologist* 56(2): 155–168.

Hawkes, C. 1973. Innocence retrieval in archaeology. *Antiquity* 47: 176–178.

Hawkes, J. 1951. *A Land*. New York: Random House.

Hawkes, J. 1968. The Proper Study of Mankind. *Antiquity* 42: 255–262.

Hayles, N.K. 2002. *Writing Machines*. Cambridge: MIT Press.

Hayles, N.K. 2003. Translating Media: Why We Should Rethink Textuality. *The Yale Journal of Criticism* 16(2): 263–290.

Hayles, N.K. 2012. *How We Think: Digital Media and Contemporary Technologies*. Chicago: University of Chicago Press.

Hegmon, M. 2003. Setting Theoretical Egos Aside: Issues and Theory in North American Archaeology. *American Antiquity* 68(2): 213–243.

Heidegger, M. 1962. *Being and Time*. Oxford: Blackwell.

Hekman, S. 1997. Truth and Method: Feminist Standpoint Theory Revisited. *Signs* 22(2): 341–365.

Hempel, C.G. 1945a. Studies in the Logic of Confirmation I. *Mind* 54(213): 1–26.

Hempel, C.G. 1945b. Studies in the Logic of Confirmation II. *Mind* 54(213): 97–121.

Hempel, C.G. 1965. *Aspects of Scientific Explanation, and Other Essays in the Philosophy of Science*. New York: The Free Press.

Hempel, C.G. & P. Oppenheim. 1948. Studies in the Logic of Explanation. *Philosophy of Science* 15(2): 135–175.

Hesse, M. 1966. *Models and Analogies in Science*. Notre Dame: Notre Dame University Press.

Hesse, M. 1974. *The Structure of Scientific Inference*. Berkeley: University of California Press.

Hesse, M. 1978. Habermas' Consensus Theory of Truth. *Proceedings of the Biennial Meeting of the Philosophy of Science Association* 1978: 373–396.

Hesse, M. 1995. Past Realities. In I. Hodder, M. Shanks, A. Alexandri, V. Buchli, J. Carman, J. Last & G. Lucas (eds) *Interpreting Archaeology: Finding Meaning in the Past*. London: Routledge, pp. 45–47.

Hill, J.N. 1972. The methodological debate in contemporary archaeology: a model. In D.L. Clarke (ed.) *Models in Archaeology*. London: Methuen & Co., pp. 61–107.

Hill, J.N. 1991. Archaeology and the accumulation of knowledge. In R. Preucel (ed.) *Processual and Postprocessual Archaeologies. Multiple Ways of Knowing the Past*. Carbondale: Southern Illinois University, pp. 42–53.

Hodder, I. (ed.). 1978. *The Spatial Organization of Culture*. London: Duckworth.

Hodder, I. 1982a. *Symbols in Action*. Cambridge: Cambridge University Press.

Hodder, I. (ed.). 1982b. *Symbolic and Structural Archaeology*. Cambridge: Cambridge University Press.

Hodder, I. 1982c. Theoretical Archaeology: A Reactionary View. In I. Hodder (ed.) *Symbolic and Structural Archaeology*. Cambridge: Cambridge University Press, pp. 1–16.

Hodder, I. 1982d. *The Present Past*, London: Batsford.

Hodder, I. 1984. Archaeology in 1984. *Antiquity* 58: 25–32.

Hodder, I. 1986. *Reading the Past: Current Approaches to Interpretation in Archaeology*. Cambridge: Cambridge University Press.

Hodder, I. 1989. Writing Archaeology: Site Reports in Context. *Antiquity* 63: 268–274.

Hodder, I. 1991. Interpretive Archaeology and Its Role. *American Antiquity* 56: 7–18.

Hodder, I. 1992. The Hasddenham Causewayed Enclosure – a Hermeneutic Circle. In I. Hodder. *Theory and Practice in Archaeology*. London: Routledge, pp. 184–207.

Hodder, I. 1993. The narrative and rhetoric of material culture sequences. *World Archaeology* 25: 268–282.

Hodder, I. 1995. Material Culture in Time. In I. Hodder, M. Shanks, A. Alexandri, V. Buchli, J. Carman, J. Last & G. Lucas (eds) *Interpreting Archaeology: Finding Meaning in the Past*. London: Routledge, pp. 164–168.

Hodder, I. 1999. *The Archaeological Process*. Oxford: Blackwell Publishers.

Hodder, I. 2008. 40 Years of Theoretical Engagement: A Conversation with Ian Hodder. *Norwegian Archaeological Review* 41(1): 26–42.

Hodder, I. & S. Hutson. 2003. *Reading the Past: Current Approaches to Interpretation in Archaeology*. Cambridge: Cambridge University Press.

Hodder, I., M. Shanks, A. Alexandri, V. Buchli, J. Carman, J. Last & G. Lucas (eds). 1995. *Interpreting Archaeology: Finding Meaning in the Past*. London: Routledge.

Hogarth, A.C. 1972. Common sense in archaeology. *Antiquity* 46: 301–304.

Hollander, J.den. 2011. Contemporary History and the Art of Self-Distancing. *History and Theory* 50: 51–67.

Hollander, J.den, H. Paul & R. Peters (eds). 2011. Introduction: The Metaphor of Historical Distance. *History and Theory* 50: 1–10.

Holtorf, C. 2005. Beyond crusades: How (not) to engage with alternative archaeologies. *World Archaeology* 37(4): 544–551.

Holtorf, C. & H. Karlsson (eds). 2000. *Philosophy and Archaeological Practice*. Göteborg: Bricoleur Press.

Horner, W.B. 1981. Speech-Act Theory and Writing. *FFORUM: A Newsletter of the English Composition Board* (University of Michigan) 3: 9–10.

Huggett, J. 2012. Lost in information? Ways of knowing and modes of representation in e-archaeology. *World Archaeology* 44(4): 538–552.

Humboldt, W. von. 1967. On the Historian's Task. *History and Theory* 6(1): 57–71.

Ihde, D. 1998. *Expanding Hermeneutics: Visualism in Science*. Evanston: Northwestern University Press.

Ihde, D. 2009. *Postphenomenology and Technoscience: The Peking University Lectures*. Albany: State University of New York Press.

Ion, A. 2017. How Interdisciplinary is Interdisciplinarity? Revisiting the Impact of aDNA Research for the Archaeology of Human Remains. *Current Swedish Archaeology* 25: 177–198.

Jakobson, R. 1960. Linguistics and Poetics. In T. Sebeok (ed.) *Style in Language*. Cambridge, MA: MIT Press, pp. 350–377.

Johnsen, H. & B. Olsen. 1992. Hermeneutics and Archaeology: On the Philosophy of Contextual Archaeology. *American Antiquity* 57(3): 419–436.

Johnson, L. 1972. Problems in "Avant-Garde" Archaeology. *American Anthropologist* 74: 366–377.

Johnson, M. 2010. *Archaeological Theory: An Introduction* (2nd edition). Oxford: Wiley-Blackwell.

Johnson, M. 2011. On the nature of empiricism in archaeology. *Journal of the Royal Anthropological Institute* 17: 764–787.

Johnson, M. & S. Coleman. 1990. Power and Passion in Archaeological Discourse. In F. Baker, S. Taylor & J. Thomas (eds) *Writing the Past in the Present*. Lampeter: St David's University College, pp. 13–17.

Jones, A. 2012. *Prehistoric Materialities: Becoming Material in Prehistoric Britain and Ireland*. Oxford: Oxford University Press.

Jones, T. & I. Levy (eds). 2018. *Cyber-Archaeology and Grand Narratives: Digital Technology and Deep-Time Perspectives on Culture Change in the Middle East*. New York: Springer.

Joyce, M. 1995. *Of Two Minds: Hypertext Pedagogy and Poetics*. Ann Arbor: University of Michigan Press.

Joyce, R. 2002. *The Languages of Archaeology: Dialogue, Narrative and Writing*. Oxford: Blackwell Publishers.

Joyce, R. 2006. Writing Historical Archaeology. In D. Hicks & M. Beaudry (eds) *The Cambridge Companion to Historical Archaeology*. Cambridge: Cambridge University Press, pp. 48–67.

Joyce, R. & R. Tringham. 2007. Feminist Adventures in Hypertext. *Journal of Archaeological Method and Theory* 14(3): 328–358.

Kansa, E. 2011. New Directions for the Digital Past. In E. Kansa, S. Whitcher Kansa & E. Watrall (eds) *Archaeology 2.0: New Approaches to Communication and Collaboration*. Los Angeles: Cotsen Institute of Archaeology Press, pp. 1–26.

Kansa, E., S. Whitcher Kansa & E. Watrall (eds). 2011. *Archaeology 2.0: New Approaches to Communication and Collaboration*. Los Angeles: Cotsen Institute of Archaeology Press.

Kelley, J. & M. Hanen. 1988. *Archaeology and the Methodology of Science*. Albuquerque: University of New Mexico Press.

Kenyon, K. 1953. *Beginning in Archaeology*. London: Phoenix House.

Kermode, F. 1967. *The Sense of an Ending: Studies in the Theory of Fiction*. Oxford: Oxford University Press.

Kinneavy, J. 1969. The Basic Aims of Discourse. *College Composition and Communication* 20 (5): 297–304.

Kinneavy, J.L. 1971. *A Theory of Discourse: The Aims of Discourse*. Englewood Cliffs: Prentice-Hall.

Kintigh, K. 2006. The Promise and Challenge of Archaeological Data Integration. *American Antiquity* 71(3): 567–578.

Kittler, F. 1990. *Discourse Networks 1800/1900*. Stanford: Stanford University Press.

Kittler, F. 1999. *Gramophone, Film, Typewriter*. Stanford: Stanford University Press.

Kluckhohn, C. 1939. The Place of Theory in Anthropological Studies. *Philosophy of Science* 6: 328–344.

Kluckhohn, C. 1940. The Conceptual Structure of Middle American Studies. In C.L. Hay, R. Linton, S.K. Lothrop, J. Shapiro & G.C. Vaillant (eds) *The Maya and their Neighbours*. New York: Dover, pp. 41–51.

Knorr-Cetina, K. 1999. *Epistemic Cultures: How the Sciences Make Knowledge*. Cambridge, MA: Harvard University Press.

Koehler, A. 2017. *Composition, Creative Writing Studies and the Digital Humanities*. London: Bloomsbury.

Kohl, P. 1993. Limits to a Post-Processual Archaeology (or, The Dangers of a New Scholasticism). In N. Yoffee & A. Sherratt (eds) *Archaeological Theory: Who Sets the Agenda?* Cambridge: Cambridge University Press, pp. 13–19.

Kosso, P. 1991. Method in Archaeology: Middle Range Theory as Hermeneutics. *American Antiquity* 56(4): 621–627.

Kosso, P. 2001. *Knowing the Past: Philosophical Issues of History and Archaeology*. New York: Humanity Books.

Kövecses, Z. 2017. Conceptual metaphor theory. In E. Semino & Z. Demjén (eds) *The Routledge Handbook of Metaphor and Language*. London: Routledge, pp. 13–27.

Kristensen, T. & R. Davis. 2015. The Legacies of Indigenous History in Archaeological Thought. *Journal of Archaeological Method and Theory* 22(2): 512–542.

Kristiansen, K. 2014. Towards a New Paradigm? The Third Science Revolution and Its Possible Consequences in Archaeology. *Current Swedish Archaeology* 22: 11–34.

Kuhn, T. 1970. *The Structure of Scientific Revolutions* (2nd edition). Chicago: Chicago University Press.

Kuhn, T. 1977. Second Thoughts on Paradigms. In T. Kuhn, *The Essential Tension: Selected Studies in Scientific Tradition and Change*. Chicago: Chicago University Press, pp. 293–319.

Kusch, M. & P. Lipton. 2002. Testimony: A Primer. *Studies in the History and Philosophy of Science* 33: 209–217.

Lakoff, G. & M. Johnson. 1980. *Metaphors We Live By*. Chicago: Chicago University Press.

Lamarque, P. 1990. Narrative and Invention: The Limits of Fictionality. In C. Nash (ed.) *Narrative in Culture: The Uses of Storytelling in the Sciences, Philosophy and Literature*. London: Routlegde, pp. 133–155.

Lampeter Archaeology Workshop. 1997. Relativism, objectivity and the politics of the past. *Archaeological Dialogues* 4(2): 164–198.

Lampeter Archaeology Workshop. 1998. Relativism, objectivity and the politics of the past. *Archaeological Dialogues* 5(1): 30–53.

Landau, M. 1984. Human Evolution as Narrative. *American Scientist* 72: 262–268.

Landau, M. 1991. *Narratives of Human Evolution: The Hero Story*. New Haven: Yale University Press.

Landow, G. 1992. *Hypertext: The Convergence of Contemporary Critical Theory and Technology*. Baltimore: Johns Hopkins University Press.

Langer, S. 1957. *Philosophy in a New Key*. Cambridge, MA: Harvard University Press.

Latour, B. 1987. *Science in Action*. Cambridge, MA: Harvard University Press.

Latour, B. 1993. *We Have Never Been Modern*. Cambridge, MA: Harvard University Press.

Latour, B. 1999. Circulating Reference: Sampling the Soil in the Amazon Forest. In *Pandora's Hope: Essays on the Reality of Science Studies*. Cambridge, MA: Harvard University Press, pp. 24–79.

Latour, B. 2004a. Why Has Critique Run out of Steam? From Matters of Fact to Matters of Concern. *Critical Inquiry* 30: 225–248.

Latour, B. 2004b. How to Talk about the Body? The Normative Dimension of Science Studies. *Body and Society* 10(2–3): 205–229.

Laufer, B. 1913. Remarks. *American Anthropologist* 15: 573–577.

Law, J. 2004. *After Method: Mess in Social Science Research.* London: Routledge.

LeBlanc, S. 1973. Two Points of Logic Concerning Data, Hypotheses, General Laws and Systems. In C.L. Redman (ed.) *Research and Theory in Current Archaeology.* New York: John Wiley & Sons, pp. 199–214.

Lecourt, D. 1975. *Marxism and Epistemology: Bachelard, Canguilhem, Foucault.* London: NLB.

Lee, D. 2001. Genres, Registers, Text Types, Domains and Styles: Clarifying the Concepts and Navigating a Path through the BNC Jungle. *Language, Learning and Technology* 5(3): 37–72.

Lenoir, T. (ed.). 1998. *Inscribing Science: Scientific Texts and the Materiality of Communication.* Stanford: Stanford University Press.

Leone, M. 1972. Issues in Anthropological Archaeology. In M. Leone (ed.) *Contemporary Archaeology.* Carbondale: Southern Illinois University Press, pp. 14–27.

Leone, M. 1988. The Relationship between Archaeological Data and the Documentary Record: 18th Century Gardens in Annapolis, Maryland. *Historical Archaeology* 22(1): 29–35.

Leone, M. 2010. Walter Taylor and the Production of Anger in American Archaeology. In A. Maca, J. Reyman & W. Folan (eds) *Prophet, Pariah, and Pioneer: Walter W. Taylor and Dissension in American Archaeology.* Boulder: University of Colorado Press, pp. 315–330.

Leonelli, S. 2011. Packaging Small Facts for Re-Use: Databases in Model Organism Biology. In P. Howlett & M. Morgan (eds) *How Well Do Facts Travel? The Dissemination of Reliable Knowledge.* Cambridge: Cambridge University Press, pp. 325–348.

Leonelli, S. 2015. What Counts as Scientific Data? A Relational Framework. *Philosophy of Science* 82: 810–821.

Leonelli, S. 2016. *Data-Centric Biology: A Philosophical Study.* Chicago: University of Chicago Press.

Lepore, J. 2001. Historians Who Love Too Much: Reflections on Microhistory and Biography. *The Journal of American History* 88(1): 129–144.

Lesure, R. 2015. Emplotment as Epic in Archaeological Writing: The Site Monograph as Narrative. *Norwegian Archaeological Review* 48(2): 57–74.

Levin, M.E. 1973. On Explanation in Archaeology: A Rebuttal to Fritz and Plog. *American Antiquity* 38: 387–395.

Levine, P. 1986. *The Amateur and the Professional: Antiquarians, Historians and Archaeologists in Victorian England 1838–1886.* Cambridge: Cambridge University Press.

Lewin, B., J. Fine & L. Young. 2001. *Expository Discourse: A Genre-based Approach to Social Research Text.* London: Continuum.

Lidén, K. & G. Eriksson. 2013. Archaeology vs. Archaeological Science. Do we have a case? *Current Swedish Archaeology* 21: 11–20.

Lipton, P. 1991. *Inference to the Best Explanation.* London: Routledge.

Lipton, P. 1998. The Epistemology of Testimony. *Studies in the History and Philosophy of Science* 29(1): 1–31.

Llobera, M. 2011. Archaeological visualization: Towards an archaeological information science (AISc). *Journal of Archaeological Method and Theory* 18: 193–223.

Longacre, R.E. 1983. *The Grammar of Discourse.* New York: Plenum Press.

Longino, H. 1992. *Science as Social Knowledge: Values and Objectivity in Scientific Inquiry.* Princeton: Princeton University Press.

Longino, H. 1993. Subjects, Power and Knowledge: Description and Prescription in Feminist Philosophies of Science. In L. Alcoff & E. Potter (eds) *Feminist Epistemologies.* London: Routledge, pp. 101–120.

Lopes, D. 2009. Drawing in a social science: Lithic illustration. *Perspectives on Science* 17: 5–25.

Love, J. & M. Meng. 2016. Histories of the dead? *Time and Mind* 9(3): 223–244.

Lowther, G.R. 1962. Epistemology and Archaeological Theory. *Current Anthropology* 3: 495–503.

Lubbock, J. 1872. *Pre-historic times, as illustrated by ancient remains and the manners and customs of modern savages.* New York: D. Appleton and Company.

Lucas, G. 2001a. *Critical Approaches to Fieldwork.* London: Routledge.

Lucas, G. 2001b. Destruction and the Rhetoric of Excavation. *Norwegian Archaeological Review* 34(1): 35–46.

Lucas, G. 2012. *Understanding the Archaeological Record.* Cambridge: Cambridge University Press.

Lucas, G. 2015a. Debating Archaeological Empiricism: Some Closing Comments. In J. Siapkas & C. Hillerdal (eds) *Debating Archaeological Empiricism.* London: Routledge, pp. 188–192.

Lucas, G. 2015b. The Mobility of Theory. *Current Swedish Archaeology* 23: 13–82.

Lucas, G. 2017. The Paradigm Concept in Archaeology. *World Archaeology* 49(2): 260–270.

Lynch, M. 2014. From Normative to Descriptive and Back: Science and Technology Studies and the Practice Turn. In L. Soler, S. Zwart, M. Lynch & V. Israel-Jost (eds) *Science after the Practice Turn in the Philosophy, History, and Social Studies of Science.* London: Routledge, pp. 93–113.

McCarthy, J.P. 2003. More than just "Telling the Story": Interpretive Narrative Archaeology. In J. Jameson, J. Ehrenhard & C. Finn (eds) *Ancient Muses: Archaeology and the Arts.* Tuscaloosa: University of Alabama Press, pp. 15–24.

McGee, P. 2014. Clarity in Philosophy. *Philosophy* 89(3): 451–462.

McGhee, R. 2008. Aboriginalism and the Problems of Indigenous Archaeology. *American Antiquity* 73: 579–597.

McGuire, R. 2008. *Archaeology as Political Action.* Berkeley: University of California Press.

McTaggart, J. 1908. The Unreality of Time. *Mind* XVII: 457–474.

Malone, C. & S. Stoddart (eds). 1998. Special Section. David Clarke's 'Archaeology: the loss of innocence' (1973) 25 years after. *Antiquity* 72(277): 676–702.

Manovich, L. 2001. *The Language of New Media.* Cambridge, MA: MIT Press.

Mantel, H. 2017. The BBC Reith Lectures for 2017. Transcripts downloaded from www.bbc.co.uk/radio4 on 13.06.2017.

Marila, M. 2017. Vagueness and Archaeological Interpretation: A Sensuous Approach to Archaeological Knowledge Formation through Finds Analysis. *Norwegian Archaeological Review* 50(1): 66–88.

Martin, P. 1971. The Revolution in Archaeology. *American Antiquity* 36(1): 1–8.

Martin, J.R. 1989. *Factual Writing: Exploring and Challenging Social Reality.* Oxford: Oxford University Press.

Martin, J.R. 1997. Analysing genre: Functional parameters. In F. Christie & J.R. Martin (eds) *Genre and Institutions: Social Processes in the Workplace and School.* London: Cassell, pp. 3–39.

Matsagouras, E. & S. Tsipilako. 2008. Who's Afraid of Genre? Genres, Functions, Text Types and their Implications for a Pedagogy of Critical Literacy. *Scientia Paedagogica Experimentalis* 45(1): 71–90.

Maxwell, N. 1984. *From Knowledge to Wisdom: A Revolution in the Aims and Methods of Science.* Oxford: Blackwell Publishers.

Meretoja, H. 2014. Narrative and Human Existence: Ontology, Epistemology and Ethics. *New Literary History* 45(1): 89–109.

Meskell, L. (ed.). 2009. *Cosmopolitan Archaeologies.* Durham: Duke University Press.

Mickel, A. 2013. Excavation, Narration, and the Wild Man: Montage and Linearity in Representing Archaeology. *Anthropology & Humanism* 38(2): 177–186.

Mickel, A. 2015. Reasons for Redundancy in Reflexivity: The Role of Diaries in Archae-ological Epistemology. *Journal of Field Archaeology* 40(3): 300–309.

Miller, C. 1984. Genre as Social Action. *Quarterly Journal of Speech* 70: 151–167.

Miller, G. 1980. Classification and Scaling of 19th Century Ceramics. *Historical Archaeology* 14: 1–40.

Miller, G. 1991. A revised set of CC index values for classification and economic scaling of English ceramics 1787–1880. *Historical Archaeology* 25(1): 1–25.

Mink, L.O. 1966. The Autonomy of Historical Understanding. *History & Theory* 5(1): 24–47.

Mink, L.O. 1970. History and Fiction as Modes of Comprehension. *New Literary History* 1 (3): 541–558.

Mink, L.O. 1987. *Historical Understanding*. New York: Cornell University Press.

Moessner, L. 2001. Genre, text type, style, register: A terminological maze? *European Journal of English Studies* 5: 131–138.

Moore, A.Z. 1943. Extensive reading versus intensive reading in the study of modern for-eign languages. *The Modern Language Journal* 27(1): 3–12.

Moore, H. 2004. Global Anxieties, Concept-metaphors and Pre-theoretical Commitments in Anthropology. *Anthropological Theory* 4(1): 71–88.

Moretti, F. 2007. *Graphs, Maps, Trees: Abstract Models for a Literary History*. New York: Verso.

Morgan, C. 1973. Archaeology and Explanation. *World Archaeology* 4: 259–276.

Morgan, C. 1974. Explanation and Scientific Archaeology. *World Archaeology* 6: 133–137.

Morgan, M. 2011. Travelling Facts. In P. Howlett & M. Morgan (eds) *How Well Do Facts Travel? The Dissemination of Reliable Knowledge*. Cambridge: Cambridge University Press, pp. 3–42.

Morgan, M. 2014a. Case Studies. In N. Cartwright & E. Montuschi (eds) *Philosophy of Social Science: A New Introduction*. Oxford: Oxford University Press, pp. 288–307.

Morgan, M. 2014b. Resituating Knowledge: Generic Strategies and Case Studies. *Philosophy of Science* 81: 1012–1024.

Morrison, M. & M.S. Morgan. 1999. Models as mediating instruments. In M.S. Morgan & M. Morrison (eds) *Models as Mediators: Perspectives on Natural and Social Science*. Cambridge: Cambridge University Press, pp. 10–38.

Morgan, M. & M. Wise (eds). 2017. Special Issue on Narrative Science. *Studies in History and Philosophy of Science* 62.

Moser, S. 2014. Making expert knowledge through the image: connections between anti-quarian and early modern scientific illustration. *Isis* 105(1): 58–99.

Moshenka, G. 2008. 'The Bible in Stone': Pyramids, Lost Tribes and Alternative Archae-ologies. *Public Archaeology* 7(1): 5–16.

Mullins, P. 2011. *The Archaeology of Consumer Culture*. Gainesville: University Press of Florida.

Mytum, H. 2010. Ways of Writing in Post-Medieval and Historical Archaeology: Introdu-cing Biography. *Post-Medieval Archaeology* 44(2): 237–254.

Nagel, E. 1963. Assumptions in Economic Theory. *American Economic Review* 53(1): 211–219.

Nagel, T. 1986. *The View from Nowhere*. Oxford: Oxford University Press.

Neumann, B. & A. Nünning (eds). 2012. *Travelling Concepts for the Study of Culture*. Berlin: De Gruyter.

Newton, C. 1851. On the Study of Archaeology. *The Archaeological Journal* 8: 1–26.

Niccolucci, F. & J.D. Richards. 2013. ARIADNE: Advanced Research Infrastructure for Archaeological Dataset Networking in Europe. *International Journal of Humanities and Arts Computing* 7(1–2): 70–88.

Noël Hume, I. 1991. *Martin's Hundred*. Charlottesville: University of Virginia Press.

Olivier, L. 2011. *The Dark Abyss of Time: Archaeology and Memory*. Lanham: AltaMira Press.

Olsen, B. 1990. Roland Barthes: From sign to text. In C. Tilley (ed.) *Reading Material Culture*. Oxford: Basil Backwell, pp. 163–206.

Olsen, B., M. Shanks, T. Webmoor & C. Witmore 2012. *Archaeology: The Discipline of Things*. Berkeley: University of California Press.

Oreskes, N. & E. Conway 2010. *Merchants of Doubt*. New York: Bloomsbury.

Orser, C. 2015. *Archaeological Thinking: How to Make Sense of the Past*. Lanham: Rowman & Littlefield.

Orwell, G. 1968. Politics and the English Language. In S. Orwell & I. Angos (eds) *The Collected Essays, Journalism and Letters of George Orwell* (Vol. 4). New York: Harcourt, Brace, Javanovich, pp. 127–140.

Osborne, P. 2011. *The Politics of Time: Modernity and Avante-Garde*. London: Verso.

Outhwaite, W. 1983. *Concept Formation in Social Science*. London: Routledge & Kegan Paul.

Papineau, D. 1976. Ideal Types and Empirical Theories. *The British Journal for the Philosophy of Science* 27(2): 137–146.

Pauketat, T. 2007. *Chiefdoms and Other Archaeological Delusions*. Lanham: AltaMira Press.

Paul, H. 2011. Distance and self-distanciation: Intellectual virtue and historical method around 1900. *History and Theory* 50: 104–116.

Pearson, M. & M. Shanks. 2001. *Theatre/Archaeology*. London: Routledge.

Peirce, C.S. 1966. How to Make Our Ideas Clear. In C.S. Peirce, *Selected Writings*. New York: Dover.

Perry, S. 2015. Crafting knowledge with (digital) visual media in archaeology. In R. Chapman & A. Wylie (eds) *Material Evidence: Learning from Archaeological Practice*. London: Routledge, pp. 189–210.

Petrie, F. 1904. *Methods and Aims in Archaeology*. London: Macmillan & Co.

Petrie, F. 1906. Archaeological Evidence. In *Lectures on the Methods of Science*, ed. T.B. Strong. Oxford: Clarendon Press, pp. 218–230.

Pettigrew, T.J. 1850. On the Study of Archaeology, and the Objects of the British Archaeological Association. *Journal of the British Archaeological Association* 6: 163–177.

Pettit, P. 1975. *The Concept of Structuralism: A Critical Analysis*. Berkeley: University of California Press.

Pétursdóttir, Þ. & B. Olsen. 2018. Theory adrift: The matter of archaeological thinking. *Journal of Social Archaeology* 18(1): 97–117.

Phillips, M.S. 2004. Distance and Historical Representation. *History Workshop Journal* 57: 123–141.

Phillips, M.S. 2011. Rethinking Historical Distance: From Doctrine to Heuristic. *History and Theory* 50: 11–23.

Phillips, M.S. 2013. *On Historical Distance*. New Haven: Yale University Press.

Phillips, P. & G. Willey. 1953. Method and Theory in American Archeology: An Operational Basis for Culture-Historical Integration. *American Anthropologist* 55(1): 615–633.

Pickering, A. (ed.). 1992. *Science as Practice and Culture*. Chicago: University of Chicago Press.

Piggott, S. 1965. *Ancient Europe*. Edinburgh: Edinburgh University Press.

Piggott, S. 1966. *Approach to Archaeology*. Harmondsworth: Penguin.

Pitt Rivers, A.H.L.F. 1906. *The Evolution of Culture and Other Essays*. Oxford: Clarendon Press.

Pluciennik, M. 1999. Archaeological Narratives and Other Ways of Telling. *Current Anthropology* 40: 653–678.

Pomata, G. 2011. Observation Rising: Birth of an Epistemic Genre, 1500–1650. In L. Daston & E. Lunbeck (eds) *Histories of Scientific Observation*. Chicago: Chicago University Press, pp. 45–80.

Poovey, M. 1998. *A History of the Modern Fact: Problems of Knowledge in the Sciences of Wealth and Society*. Chicago: University of Chicago Press.

Potter, Parker B. 1992. Middle-Range Theory, Ceramics, and Capitalism in 19th-Century Rockbridge County, Virginia. In B. Little (ed.) *Text-Aided Archaeology*. Boca Raton: CRC Press, pp. 9–23.

Praetzellis, A. 1998. Introduction: Why every archaeologist should tell stories once in a while. *Historical Archaeology* 32(1): 1–3.

Praetzellis, A. 2000. *Death by Theory: A Tale of Mystery and Archaeological Theory*. Lanham: AltaMira Press.

Praetzellis, A. 2015. *Archaeological Theory in a Nutshell*. Walnut Creek: Left Coast Press.

Praetzellis, M. 1998. Archaeologists as Storytellers. *Historical Archaeology* 32(1).

Preucel, R. (ed.). 1991. *Processual and Postprocessual Archaeologies: Multiple Ways of Knowing the Past*. Carbondale: Southern Illinois University.

Proctor, R. 2008. Agntology: A Missing Term to Describe the Cultural Production of Ignorance (and Its Study). In R. Proctor & L. Schiebinger (eds) *Agnotology: The Making and Unmaking of Ignorance*. Stanford: Stanford University Press, pp. 1–36.

Proctor, R. & L. Schiebinger (eds). 2008. *Agnotology: The Making and Unmaking of Ignorance*. Stanford: Stanford University Press.

Propp, V. 1968: *Morphology of the Folktale*. Austin: University of Texas Press.

Quine, W.O. 1960. *Word and Object*. Cambridge, MA: MIT Press.

Rainbird, P. & Y. Hamilakis (eds). 2001. *Interrogating Pedagogies: Archaeology in Higher Education*. Oxford: Archaeopress.

Rancière, J. 2013. *Dissensus: On Politics and Aesthetics*. London: Bloomsbury.

Randall-MacIver, D. 1933. Archaeology as a Science. *Antiquity* 7: 5–20.

Read, D.W. & S.A. LeBlanc. 1978. Descriptive Statements, Covering Laws, and Theories in Archaeology. *Current Anthropology* 19(2): 307–317.

Read, D.W. & S.A. LeBlanc. 1979. More on Covering Laws and Theory in Archaeology. *Current Anthropology* 20(1): 181–184.

Rehg, W. 2009. *Cogent Science in Context: The Science Wars, Argumentation Theory, and Habermas*. Cambridge, MA: MIT Press.

Reinard, J.C. 1991. *Foundations of Argument: Effective Communication for Critical Thinking*. Dubuque: William C Brown.

Renfrew, C. 1982a. Explanation Revisited. In C. Renfrew, M.J. Rowlands & B. Segraves (eds) *Theory andExplanation in Archaeology*. New York: Academic Press, pp. 5–23.

Renfrew, C. 1982b. Discussion: Contrasting paradigms. In C. Renfrew & S. Shennan (eds) *Ranking, Resource and Exchange*. Cambridge: Cambridge University Press, pp. 141–143.

Renfrew, C. 1989. Comments on archaeology into the 1990s. *Norwegian Archaeological Review* 22: 33–41.

Renfrew, C. & P. Bahn. 2016. *Archaeology: Theories, Methods and Practice* (7th edition). London: Thames & Hudson.

Renfrew, C., M.J. Rowlands & B. Segraves (eds). 1982. *Theory andExplanation in Archaeology*. New York: Academic Press.

Richards, J.D. 2002. Digital Preservation and Access. *European Journal of Archaeology* 5(3): 343–366.

Richards, J.D. 2006. Archaeology, e-publication and the Semantic Web. *Antiquity* 80: 970–979.

Richards, J.D., D. Tudhope & A. Vlachidis. 2015. Text Mining in Archaeology: Extracting Information from Archaeological Reports. In J. Barcelo & I. Bogdanovic (eds) *Mathematics in Archaeology*. Florida: CRC Press, pp. 240–254.

Ricoeur, P. 1970. *Freud and Philosophy: An Essay on Interpretation*. New Haven: Yale University Press.

Ricoeur, P. 1973. The Hermeneutical Function of Distanciation. *Philosophy Today* 17(2): 129–141.

Ricoeur, P. 1984. *Time and Narrative (Vol. 1)*. Chicago: University of Chicago Press.

Ricoeur, P. 1985. *Time and Narrative (Vol. 2)*. Chicago: University of Chicago Press.

Ricoeur, P. 1988. *Time and Narrative (Vol. 3)*. Chicago: University of Chicago Press.

Rolin, K. 2006. The Bias Paradox in Feminist Standpoint Epistemology. *Episteme* 3(1–2): 125–136.

Rouse, J. 1996. *Engaging Science: How to Understand Its Practices Philosophically*. Ithaca: Cornell University Press.

Rowley-Conwy, P. 2007. *From Genesis to Prehistory: The Archaeological Three Age System and Its Contested Reception in Denmark, Britain and Ireland*. Oxford: Oxford University Press.

Rudebeck, E. 1996. Heroes and tragic figures in the transition to the Neolithic: Exploring images of the human being in archaeological texts. *Journal of European Archaeology* 4:55–86.

Rudebeck, E. 2000. *Tilling Nature, Harvesting Culture: Exploring Images of the Human Being in the Transition to Agriculture*. (Acta Archaeologica Lundensia Series, No. 32). Stockholm: Almqvist & Wiksell International.

Ryan, M.-L. 2002. Beyond Myth and Metaphor: Narrative in Digital Media. *Poetics Today* 23(4): 581–609.

Said, E. 1983. Travelling Theory. In E. Said, *The World, the Text, and the Critic*. Cambridge, MA: Harvard University Press, pp. 226–247.

Salmon, M.H. 1975. Confirmation and Explanation in Archaeology. *American Antiquity* 40 (4): 459–464.

Salmon, M.H. 1976. "Deductive" versus "Inductive" Archaeology. *American Antiquity* 41(3): 376–380.

Salmon, M.H. 1982a. *Philosophy and Archaeology*. New York: Academic Press.

Salmon, M.H. 1982b. Models of Explanation: Two Views. In C. Renfrew, M.J. Rowlands & B. Segraves (eds) *Theory and Explanation in Archaeology*. New York: Academic Press, pp. 35–44.

Salmon, M.H. 1992. Philosophical Models for Postprocessual Archaeology. In L. Embree (ed.) *Metaarchaeology*. Dordecht: Kluwer Academic, pp. 227–242.

Salmon, M.H. 1993. Philosophy of Archaeology: Current Issues. *Journal of Archaeological Research* 1(4): 323–343.

Salmon, M.H. & W.C. Salmon. 1979. Alternative Models of Scientific Explanation. *American Anthropologist* 81: 61–74.

Salmon, W.H. 1982. Causality in Archaeological Explanation. In C. Renfrew, M.J. Rowlands & B. Segraves (eds) *Theory and Explanation in Archaeology*. New York: Academic Press, pp. 44–55.

Schiebinger, L. 2008. West Indian Abortifacients and the Making of Ignorance. In R. Proctor & L. Schiebinger (eds) *Agnotology: The Making and Unmaking of Ignorance*. Stanford: Stanford University Press, pp. 149–162.

Schrire, C. 1995. *Digging through Darkness: Chronicles of an Archaeologist*. Charlottesville: University Press of Virginia.

Schutz, A. 1954. Concept and Theory Formation in the Social Sciences. *The Journal of Philosophy* 51(9): 257–273.

Scott, R. 1967. On Viewing Rhetoric as Epistemic. *Central States Speech Journal* 18(1): 9–17.

Searle, J. 1969. *Speech Acts: An Essay in the Philosophy of Language*. Cambridge: Cambridge University Press.

Sedgwick, E. 2003. Paranoid Reading and Reparative Reading, Or, You're So Paranoid, You Probably Think This Essay Is About You. In E. Sedgwick. *Touching Feeling: Affect, Pedagogy, Performativity*. Durham: Duke University Press, pp. 123–151.

Shanks, M. 1992. *Experiencing the Past: On the Character of Archaeology*. Routledge: London.

Shanks, M. & I. Hodder. 1995. Processual, postprocessual and interpretive archaeologies. In I. Hodder, M. Shanks, A. Alexandri, V. Buchli, J. Carman, J. Last & G. Lucas (eds) *Interpreting Archaeology: Finding Meaning in the Past*. London: Routledge, pp. 3–29.

Shanks, M. & C. Tilley. 1987. *Re-Constructing Archaeology*. Cambridge: Cambridge University Press.

Shanks, M. & C. Tilley. 1989. Archaeology into the 1990s: Questions rather than answers. *Norwegian Archaeological Review* 22: 1–14.

Shanks, M. & C. Tilley. 1992. *Re-Constructing Archaeology* (2nd edition). London: Routledge.

Shanks, M. & T. Webmoor. 2010. A Political Economy of Visual Media in Archaeology. In S. Bonde & S. Houston (eds) *Re-Presenting the Past: Archaeology through Image and Text*. Providence, RI: Brown University Press, pp. 87–110.

Shapin, S. 1984. Pump and Circumstance: Robert Boyle's Literary Technology. *Social Studies of Science* 14(4): 481–520.

Shapin, S. 1994. *A Social History of Truth: Civility and Science in Seventeenth-Century England*. Chicago: University of Chicago Press.

Shepherd, N. 2007. Archaeology dreaming: Post-apartheid urban imaginaries and the bones of the Prestwich Street dead. *Journal of Social Archaeology* 7(1): 3–28.

Shott, M. 2014. Digitizing archaeology: A subtle revolution in analysis. *World Archaeology* 46 (1): 1–9.

Siapkas, J. & C. Hillerdal (eds). 2015. *Debating Archaeological Empiricism: The Ambiguity of Material Evidence*. London: Routledge.

Sillitoe, P. 1998. The Development of Indigenous Knowledge: A New Applied Anthropology. *Current Anthropology* 39(2): 223–252.

Sillitoe, P. 2002. Globalizing indigenous knowledge. In P. Sillitoe, A. Bicker & J. Pottier (eds) *Participating in Development: Approaches to Indigenous Knowledge*. London: Routledge, pp. 108–138.

Simonetti, C. 2018. *Sentient Conceptualizations: Feeling and Thinking in the Scientific Understanding of Time*. London: Routledge.

Skibo, J. & M. Schiffer. 2008. *People and Things: A Behavioural Approach to Material Culture*. New York: Springer.

Sloterdijk, P. 2012. *The Art of Philosophy: Wisdom as a Practice*. New York: Columbia University Press.

Smith, B.D. 1977. Archaeological Inference and Inductive Confirmation. *American Anthropologist* 97: 598–617.

Smith, C. & H. Burke. 2005. Becoming Binford: Fun ways of teaching archaeological theory and method. *Public Archaeology* 4(1): 35–49.

Smith, C. & M. Wobst (eds). 2005. *Indigenous Archaeologies: Decolonizing Theory and Practice*. London: Routledge.

Smith, H. 1911. Archaeological Evidence as Determined by Method and Selection. *American Anthropologist* 13(3): 445–448.

Smith, M. 1955. The Limitations of Inference in Archaeology. *The Archaeological Newsletter* 6 (1): 3–7.

Snow, C.P. 1959. *The Two Cultures and the Scientific Revolution*. Cambridge: Cambridge University Press.

Sokal, A. 1996. Transgressing the Boundaries: Toward a Transformative Hermeneutics of Quantum Gravity. *Social Text* 46–47: 217–252.

Sokal, A. & J. Bricmont. 1998. *Intellectual Impostures*. London: Profile Books.

Sokolowski, R. 1998. The Method of Philosophy: Making Distinctions. *The Review of Metaphysics* 51(3): 515–532.

Soler, L., S. Zwart, M. Lynch & V. Israel-Jost (eds). 2014. *Science After the Practice Turn in the Philosophy, History, and Social Studies of Science.* London: Routledge.

Solli, B. 1996. *Narratives of Veøy: An Investigation into the Poetics and Scientifics of Archaeology.* Universitetets Oldsaksamlings Skrifter No. 19. Oslo: Universitetets Oldsaksamlings.

Sørensen, T.F. 2015. More than a feeling: Towards an archaeology of atmosphere. *Emotion, Space and Society* 15: 64–73.

Sørensen, T.F. 2016. In Praise of Vagueness: Uncertainty, Ambiguity and Archaeological Methodology. *Journal of Archaeological Method and Theory* 23(2): 1–23.

Sosnoski, J. 1999. Hyper-Readings and Their Reading Engines. In G.E. Hawisher & C.L. Selfe (eds) *Passions, Pedagogies, and Twenty-First Century Technologies.* Urbana, IL: Utah State University Press, pp. 161–177.

Spalding, A.C. 1953. Statistical Techniques for the Discovery of Artifact Types. *American Antiquity* 18: 305–313.

Spalding, A.C. 1962. Comment. *Current Anthropology* 3: 508.

Spalding, A.C. 1968. Explanation in Archaeology. In S.R. Binford & L.R. Binford (eds) *New Perspectives in Archaeology.* Chicago: Aldine Publishing Co., pp. 33–39.

Spector, J. 1991. What this awl means: Toward a feminist archaeology. In J. Gero & M. Conkey (eds) *Engendering Archaeology: Women and Prehistory.* Oxford: Basil Blackwell, pp. 388–406.

Spector, J. 1993. *What this Awl Means: Feminist Archaeology at a Wahpeton Dakota Village.* St. Paul: Minnesota Historical Society Press.

Spencer-Wood, S. (ed.). 1987. *Consumer Choice in Historical Archaeology.* New York: Plenum Press.

Sperber, D., F. Clérmont, C. Heintz, O. Mascaro, H. Mercier, G. Origgi & D. Wilson. 2010. Epistemic vigilance. *Mind and Language* 25(4): 359–393.

Spriggs, M. 2008. Ethnographic parallels and the denial of history. *World Archaeology* 40(4): 538–552.

Squair, R. 1994. Time and the Privilege of Retrospect. In I.M. Mackenzie (ed.) *Archaeological Theory: Progress or Posture?* Aldershot: Avebury.

Stebbing, S. 1939. *Thinking to Some Purpose.* Harmondsworth: Penguin.

Stengers, I. 2000. *The Invention of Modern Science.* Minneapolis: University of Minnesota Press.

Steward, J. & F. Setzler. 1938. Function and Configuration in Archaeology. *American Antiquity* 4: 4–10.

Steward, J. 1949. Cultural Causality and Law: A Trial Formulation of the Development of Early Civilizations. *American Anthropologist* 51(1): 1–27.

Steward, J. 1955. *Theory of Culture Change.* Urbana: University of Illinois Press.

Stewart, K. 2008. Weak Theory in an Unfinished World. *Journal of Folklore Research* 45(1): 71–82.

Stickel, E.G. 1979. More on Theory Building in Archaeology. *Current Anthropology* 20(3): 621–624.

Strathern, M. 1988. *The Gender of the Gift.* Berkeley: University of California Press.

Strawson, G. 2004. Against Narrativity. *Ratio* 17(4): 428–452.

Strong, W.D. 1936. Anthropological Theory and Archeological Fact. In R.H. Lowie (ed.) *Essays in Anthropology.* Berkeley: University of California Press, pp. 359–369.

Stuiver, M., P.J. Reimer, E. Bard, J.W. Beck, G.S. Burr, K.A. Hughen, B. Kromer, G. McCormac, J. van der Plicht & M. Spurk. 1998. Radiocarbon age calibration, 24,000–0 cal BP. *Radiocarbon* 40(3): 1041–1083.

Stukeley, W. 1740. *Stonehenge, A Temple Restor'd to the British Druids.* London: W. Innys & R. Manby.

Stutt, A. & S. Shennan. 1990. The nature of archaeological arguments. *Antiquity* 64: 766–777.

Sullivan, A.P. 1978. Inference and Evidence in Archaeology: A Discussion of the Conceptual Problems. *Advances in Archaeological Method and Theory* 1: 183–221.

Taylor, W. 1948. *A Study of Archaeology*, Memoir Series of the American Anthropological Association No. 69 (Vol. 50).

Terrell, J. 1990. Storytelling and prehistory. *Archaeological Method and Theory* 2: 1–29.

Thomas, J. 1993. Discourse, Totalization and "The Neolithic". In C. Tilley (ed.) *Interpretative Archaeology*. Oxford: Berg, pp. 357–394.

Thomas, J. 2004a. The Great Dark Book: Archaeology, Experience and Interpretation. In J. Bintliff (ed.) *A Companion to Archaeology*. Oxford: Blackwell Publishing.

Thomas, J. 2004b. *Archaeology and Modernity*. London: Routledge.

Thomas, J. 2013. *The Birth of Neolithic Britain: An Interpretive Account*. Oxford: Oxford University Press.

Thomas, N. 1997. Anthropological epistemologies. *International Social Science Journal* 153: 333–343.

Thomas, R. 2015. Evidence, Archaeology and the Law: An Initial Exploration. In R. Chapman & A. Wylie (eds) *Material Evidence: Learning from Archaeological Practice*. London: Routledge, pp. 255–270.

Thompson, R.H. 1956. The subjective element in archaeological inference. *Southwestern Journal of Anthropology* 12: 327–332.

Thomson, W. 1867. Inaugural Address to the Annual Meeting of the Royal Archaeological Institute. *Archaeological Journal* 24: 83–91.

Tilley, C. 1989. Discourse and power: The genre of the Cambridge inaugural lecture. In D. Miller, M. Rowlands & C. Tilley (eds) *Domination and Resistance*. London: Unwin Hyman, pp. 41–62.

Tilley, C. 1990. On modernity and archaeological discourse. In I. Bapty and T. Yates (eds) *Archaeology after Structuralism*. London: Routledge, pp. 128–152.

Tilley, C. 1991. *Material Culture and Text: The Art of Ambiguity*. London: Routledge.

Tilley, C. (ed.). 1993. *Interpretative Archaeology*. Oxford: Berg.

Tilley, C. 1994. *The Phenomenology of Landscape*. Oxford: Berg.

Todorov, T. 1976. The Origin of Genres. *New Literary History* 8(1): 159–170.

Toulmin, S. 1958. *The Uses of Argument*. Cambridge: Cambridge University Press.

Toulmin, S. 2003. *The Uses of Argument* (2nd edition). Cambridge: Cambridge University Press.

Toulmin, S., R. Rieke & A. Janik. 1984. *An Introduction to Reasoning* (2nd edition). New York: Macmillan Publishing Co.

Trigger, B. 1970. Aims in Prehistoric Archaeology. *Antiquity* 44: 26–36.

Trigger, B. 1980. Archaeology and the Image of the American Indian. *American Antiquity* 45: 662–676.

Trigger, B. 1984. Alternative Archaeologies: Nationalist, Colonialist, Imperialist. *Man* 19: 355–370.

Trigger, B. 1989. Hyperrelativism, Responsibility, and the Social Sciences. *Canadian Review of Sociology and Anthropology* 26: 776–797.

Tringham, R. 2015. Creating Narratives of the Past as Recombinant Histories. In R.M. Van Dyke & R. Bernbeck (eds) *Subjects and Narratives in Archaeology*. Boulder: University Press of Colorado, pp. 27–54.

Trosberg, A. 1997. Text Typology: Register, Genre and Text Type. In A. Trosberg (ed.) *Text Typology and Translation*. Amsterdam/Philadelphia: Benjamins, pp. 3–23.

Tsipilako, S. & G. Floris. 2013. Never mind the text types, here's textual force: Towards a pragmatic reconceptualization of text type. *Journal of Pragmatics* 45: 119–130.

Tuggle, H.D., A.H. Townsend & T. Riley. 1972. Laws, Systems and Research Designs. *American Antiquity* 37: 3–12.

Turnbull, D. 2000. *Masons, Tricksters and Cartographers*. London: Routledge.

Twining, W., P. Dawid & D. Vasilaki (eds). 2012. *Evidence, Inference and Enquiry*. Oxford: Oxford University Press.

Van Deemter, K. 2010. *Not Exactly: In Praise of Vagueness*. Oxford: Oxford University Press.

Van Dyke, R.M. & R. Bernbeck (eds). 2015. *Subjects and Narratives in Archaeology*. Boulder: University Press of Colorado.

VanPool, C.S. & T.L. VanPool. 1999. The Scientific Nature of Postprocessualism. *American Antiquity* 64(1): 33–53.

VanPool, T.L. & C.S. VanPool. 2003. *Essential Tensions in Archaeological Method and Theory*. Foundations of Archaeological Inquiry. Salt Lake City: University of Utah.

Varzi, A.C. 2003. Vagueness. In L. Nadel (ed.) *Encyclopedia of Cognitive Science*. London: Macmillan, pp. 459–464.

Verbeek, P.-P. 2006. Materializing Morality: Design Ethics and Technological Mediation. *Science, Technology and Human Values* 31(3): 361–380.

Virbel, J. 2015. Speech Act Theory and Instructional Texts. In K. Chemla & J. Virbel (eds) *Texts, Textual Acts and the History of Science* (Archimedes 42. New Studies in the History and Philosophy of Science and Technology). New York: Springer, pp. 49–86.

Virtanen, T. 1992. Issues of text typology: Narrative – A 'basic' type of text? *Text* 12(2): 293–310.

Virtanen, T. 2010. Variation across texts and discourses: theoretical and methodological perspectives on text type and genre. In H. Dorgeloh & A. Wanner (eds) *Syntactic Variation and Genre*. Berlin/New York: Mouton de Gruyter, pp. 53–84.

Wagner, R. 1991. The Fractal Person. In M. Godelier & M. Strathern (eds) *Big Men and Great Men: Personifications of Power in Melanesia*. Cambridge: Cambridge University Press, pp. 159–173.

Wallace, S. 2011. *Contradictions of Archaeological Theory: Engaging Critical Realism and Archaeological Theory*. London: Routledge.

Walters, K. (ed.). 1994a. *Re-Thinking Reason: New Perspectives in Critical Thinking*. Albany: State University of New York Press.

Walters, K. 1994b. Introduction: Beyond Logicism in Critical Thinking. In K. Walters (ed.) *Re-Thinking Reason: New Perspectives in Critical Thinking*. Albany: State University of New York Press, pp. 1–22.

Walton, D. 2006. *Fundamentals of Critical Argumentation*. Cambridge: Cambridge University Press.

Watkins, J. 2000. *Indigenous Archaeology: American Indian Values and Scientific Practice*. Walnut Creek: AltaMira Press.

Watkins, J. 2005. Through Wary Eyes: Indigenous Perspectives on Archaeology. *Annual Review of Anthropology* 34: 429–449.

Watson, P.J. 1973. The Future of Archaeology in Anthropology: Culture History and Social Science. In C.L. Redman (ed.) *Research and Theory in Current Archaeology*. New York: John Wiley & Sons, pp. 113–124.

Watson, P.J. 1986. Archaeological Interpretation in 1985. In D.J. Meltzer, D.D. Fowler & J.A. Sabloff (eds) *American Archaeology Past and Future*. Washington: Smithsonian Institution Press, pp. 439–458.

Watson, P.J. & M. Fotiadis. 1990. The Razor's Edge: Symbolic-Structuralist Archeology and the Expansion of Archeological Inference. *American Anthropologist* 92(3): 613–629.

Watson, P.J., S. LeBlanc & C. Redman. 1971. *Explanation in Archaeology: An Explicitly Scientific Approach*. New York: Columbia University Press.

Watson, P.J., S. LeBlanc & C.L. Redman. 1974. The covering law model in archaeology: Practical uses and formal interpretations. *World Archaeology* 6: 125–132.

Watson, P.J., S.A. LeBlanc & C.L. Redman. 1984. *Archeological Explanation: The Scientific Method in Archeology*. New York: Columbia University Press.

Watson, R.A. 1976. Inference in Archaeology. *American Antiquity* 41(1): 58–66.

Weber, M. 1949. "Objectivity" in Social Science and Social Policy. In M. Weber, *The Methodology of the Social Sciences*. Glencoe: Free Press, pp. 50–112.

Webmoor, T. 2008. From Silicon Valley to the Valley of Teotihuacan: The "Yahho!s" of New Media and Digital Heritage. *Visual Anthropology* 24(2): 183–200.

Webster, G. 1963. *Practical Archaeology*. London: A&C Black.

Weiner, A. 1992. *Inalienable Possessions: The Paradox of Keeping-While-Giving*. Berkeley: University of California Press.

Weller, T. 2013. *History in the Digital Age*. London: Routledge.

Werlich, E. 1975. *Typologie der Texte: Entwurf eines textlinguistischen Modells zur Grundlegung einer Textgrammatik*. Heidelberg: Quelle and Meyer.

Weston, A. 2000. *Rulebook for Arguments*. Indianapolis: Hackett Publishing Company.

Wheeler, G. 2017. Machine Epistemology and Big Data. In L. McIntyre & A. Rosenberg (eds) *The Routledge Companion to the Philosophy of Social Science*. London: Routledge, pp. 321–329.

Wheeler, M. 1954. *Archaeology from the Earth*. Harmondsworth: Penguin Books.

Whewell, W. 1984 [1847]. The Philosophy of the Inductive Sciences. In *Selected Writings on the History of Science*, ed. Y. Elkana. Chicago: University of Chicago Press, pp. 121–260.

White, H. 1973. *Metahistory: The Historical Imagination in Nineteenth-Century Europe*. Baltimore: Johns Hopkins University Press.

White, H. 1980. The Value of Narrativity in the Representation of Reality. *Critical Inquiry* 7(1): 5–27.

White, L. 1945. History, Evolutionism and Functionalism: Three Types of Interpretation of Culture. *Southwestern Journal of Anthropology* 1: 221–248.

White, L. 1949. *The Science of Culture: A Study of Man and Civilization*. New York: Grove Press.

White, L. 1959. *The Evolution of Culture: The Development of Civilization to the Fall of Rome*. New York: McGraw-Hill.

Wickstead, H. 2013. Between the Lines: Drawing Archaeology. In P. Graves-Brown, R. Harrison & A. Piccini (eds) *The Oxford Handbook of the Archaeology of the Contemporary World*. Oxford: Oxford University Press, pp. 549–564.

Wilkie, L. 2003. *The Archaeology of Mothering: An African-American Midwife's Tale*. London: Routledge.

Wilkie, L. & K. Bartoy. 2000. A Critical Archaeology Revisited. *Current Anthropology* 41(5): 747–777.

Willey, G. 1953. Archaeological Theories and Interpretation: New World. In A.L. Kroeber (ed.) *Anthropology Today*. Chicago: Chicago University Press, pp. 361–385.

Willey, G. & P. Phillips. 1955. Method and Theory in American Archeology II: Historical-Developmental Interpretation. *American Anthropologist* 57(4): 723–819.

Willey, G.R. & P. Phillips. 1958. *Method and Theory in American Archaeology*. Chicago: University of Chicago Press.

Winch, P. 1958. *The Idea of a Social Science and Its Relation to Philosophy*. London: Routledge & Kegan Paul.

Winner, L. 1980. Do Artifacts Have Politics? *Daedalus* 109: 121–136.

Witmore, C. 2014. Archaeology and the New Materialisms. *Journal of Contemporary Archaeology* 1(2): 203–224.

Witmore, C. 2015. Archaeology and the Second Empiricism. In J. Siapkas & C. Hillerdal (eds) *Debating Archaeological Empiricism: The Ambiguity of Material Evidence*. London: Routledge, pp. 37–61.

Wright, T. 1861. *The Celt, the Roman and the Saxon: A History of the Early Inhabitants of Britain.* London: Arthur Hall, Virtue & Co.

Wright, T. 1866. On the Progress and Present Condition of Archaeological Science. *Journal of the British Archaeological Association* 22, 64–84.

Wylie, A. 1985. The Reaction against Analogy. *Advances in Archaeological Method and Theory* 8: 63–111.

Wylie, A. 1989a. The Interpretive Dilemma. In V. Pinsky & A. Wylie (eds) *Critical Traditions in Contemporary Archaeology: Essays in the Philosophy, History and Socio-Politics of Archaeology.* Cambridge: Cambridge University Press, pp. 18–27.

Wylie, A. 1989b. Archaeological Cables and Tacking: The Implications of Practice for Bernstein's' "Options beyond Objectivism and Relativism". *Philosophy of the Social Sciences* 19: 1–18.

Wylie, A. 1992a. The Interplay of Evidential Constraints and Political Interests: Recent Archaeological Research on Gender. *American Antiquity* 57: 15–34.

Wylie, A. 1992b. "On Heavily Decomposing Red Herrings": Scientific Method in Archaeology and the Ladening of Evidence with Theory. In L. Embree (ed.) *Metaarchaeology: Reflections by Archaeologists and Philosophers.* Boston: Kluwer, pp. 269–288.

Wylie, A. 1996. The constitution of archaeological evidence: Gender politics and science. In P. Galison & D. Stump (eds) *The Disunity of Science.* Stanford: Stanford University Press, pp. 311–343.

Wylie, A. 2000. Questions of Evidence, Legitimacy, and the (Dis)Unity of Science. *American Antiquity* 65(2): 227–237.

Wylie, A. 2002. *Thinking from Things: Essays in the Philosophy of Archaeology.* Berkeley: University of California Press.

Wylie, A. 2003. Why Standpoint Matters. In R. Figueroa & S. Harding (eds) *Science and Other Cultures: Issues in Philosophies of Science and Technology.* London: Routledge, pp. 26–48.

Wylie, A. 2007. Philosophy of Archaeology; Philosophy in Archaeology. In S. Turner & M. Risjord (eds) *Philosophy of Anthropology and Sociology (Handbook of the Philosophy of Science).* Amsterdam: Elsevier, pp. 517–549.

Wylie, A. 2008a. The Integrity of Narratives: Deliberative Practice, Pluralism, and Multivocality. In J. Habu, C. Fawcett & J.M. Matsunaga (eds) *Evaluating Multiple Narratives: Beyond Nationalist, Colonialist, and Imperialist Archaeologies.* New York: Springer, pp. 201–212.

Wylie, A. 2008b. Mapping Ignorance in Archaeology: The Advantages of Historical Hindsight. In R. Proctor & L. Schiebinger (eds) *Agnotology: The Making and Unmaking of Ignorance.* Stanford: Stanford University Press, pp. 183–207.

Wylie, A. 2014. Community-Based Collaborative Archaeology. In N. Cartwright & E. Montuschi (eds) *Philosophy of Social Science: A New Introduction.* Oxford: Oxford University Press, pp. 68–82.

Wylie, A. 2017. Representation and Experimental Modelling in Archaeology. In L. Magnani & T. Bertolotti (eds) *Springer Handbook of Model-Based Science.* New York: Springer, pp. 989–1002.

Zimmerman, L. 2005. First be humble: Working with Indigenous peoples and other descendent communities. In C. Smith & M. Wobst (eds) *Indigenous Archaeologies: Decolonizing Theory and Practice.* London: Routledge, pp. 301–314.

Zimmerman, L. 2008. Unusual or "Extreme" Beliefs about the Past, Community Identity, and Dealing with the Fringe. In C. Colwell-Chanthaphonh & T.J. Ferguson (eds) *Collaboration in Archaeological Practice: Engaging Descendant Communities.* Walnut Creek: AltaMira Press, pp. 55–86.

Zubrow, E. 1973. Environment, Subsistence and Society: The Changing Archaeological Perspective. *Annual Review of Anthropology* 1: 179–206.

# INDEX

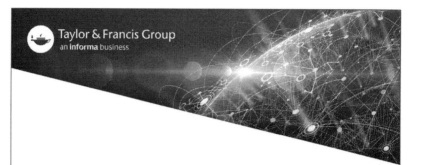

Made in the USA
Middletown, DE
16 January 2023